HUMAN BEHAVIOUR IN GEOGRAPHICAL SPACE

This book is one of a series of studies in Spatial Economic Analysis stimulated by theoretical and applied research conducted within the Netherlands Economic Institute, Rotterdam, and published by Gower. Titles in the series are:

J.H.P. Paelinck (ed.), *La Structure Urbaine en Europe Occidentale/ Urban Structure in Western Europe*

J.H.P. Paelinck and P. Nijkamp, *Operational Theory and Method in Regional Economics*

L.H. Klaassen, J.H.P. Paelinck and Sj. Wagenaar, *Spatial Systems: A General Introduction*

J.H.P. Paelinck and L.H. Klaassen (with J.P. Ancot, A.C.P. Verster and Sj. Wagenaar), *Spatial Econometrics*

W. Molle (with B. van Holst and H. Smit), *Regional Disparity and Economic Development in the European Community*

N. Vanhove and L.H. Klaassen, *Regional Policy: A European Approach*

L.H. Klaassen, J. Bourdrez and J. Volmuller, *Transport and Reurbanisation*

L.H. Klaassen, W. Molle and J.H.P. Paelinck (eds), *Dynamics of Urban Development*

J.H.P. Paelinck (with J-P. Ancot and H. Kuiper), *Formal Spatial Economic Analysis*

W. Molle and L.H. Klaassen (eds), *Industrial Mobility and Migration in the European Community*

W. Molle, *Industrial Location and Regional Development in the European Community: the FLEUR model*

W. Molle and E. Wever, *Oil Refineries and Petrochemical Industries in Western Europe*

J.H.P. Paelinck (ed.), *Human Behaviour in Geographical Space*

"Ce n'est rien d'entreprendre une chose dangereuse, mais d'échapper au péril en la menant à bien."
Pierre-Augustin Caron de Beaumarchais,
Le Mariage de Figaro

Human Behaviour in Geographical Space

Essays in Honour of Leo H. Klaassen

Edited by
J. H. P. PAELINCK

Gower

Published by
Gower Publishing Company Limited
Gower House
Croft Road
Aldershot
Hants GU11 3HR
England

Gower Publishing Company
Old Post Road
Brookfield
Vermont 05036
U.S.A.

British Library Cataloguing in Publication Data

Human behaviour in geographical space: essays in honour of Leo. H. Klaassen.––(Studies in spatial analysis)
1. Anthropo-geography
I. Paelinck, Jean H.P. II. Klaassen, Leo. H.
III. Series
304.2 GF95

ISBN 0-566-00807-6

Library of Congress Cataloging in Publication Data

Main entry under title:

Human behavior in geographical space.

Includes index.
1. Regional economics––Addresses, essays, lectures. 2. Space in economics––Addresses, essays, lectures. 3. Klaassen, Leo H. (Leo Hendrik), 1920– . I. Paelinck, Jean H.P.
HT391.H785 1985 338.9 85–5528
ISBN 0-566-00807-6

Printed and bound in Great Britain by Biddles Ltd, Guildford and King's Lynn

Contents

Preface: Jean H.P. Paelinck ix

1 Introduction: Leo Hendrik Klaassen, an entrepreneurial scholar 1
H.W. Lambers, Rotterdam

2 The central theme: from research methodology to the element of space 11
J. Tinbergen, Rotterdam

PART I: ELEMENTS OF REGIONAL DEVELOPMENT

3 Regional research and development revisited 27
W. Isard and B. Burton, Ithaca

4 Location quotients, export industries and shift-share analysis 45
N. Sakashita, Tsukuba

5 Land prices, negotiators' behaviour and game theory 63
A.L. Sallez, Paris

6 Regional impact of welfare policies in the European Community 77
W. Molle, Rotterdam

7 A consistent model for regional-sectoral dynamics 91
J.H.P. Paelinck, Rotterdam

PART II: LOCATION THEORY, GENERAL AND PARTIAL

8 On the timing of investment to maximise spatial diffusion 111
L.S. Burns, UCLA

9 Self-organisation: the foundation of spatial order of economy and society 123
R. Domański, Poznań

10 The role of political bodies in the allocation of produced locational qualities 133
D. Bökemann, Vienna

11 Locational decisions and regional structure 149
J.G. Lambooy, Amsterdam

PART III: URBAN TRENDS

12 Processes of urban development 165
R.H. Funck and U. Blum, Karlsruhe

13 An analysis of recent urban development trends in Japan 187
H. Yamada, Kyoto

14 Australian urban dynamics 211
J. Conner, Sydney

PART IV: TOURISM AND TRANSPORTATION

15 Recreation and regional development 267
A.J. Hendriks, Rotterdam

16 Tourism and regional economic development 281
N. Vanhove, Bruges

17 Transportation facilities and dispersion 299
E.H. van de Poll, Delft

18 Tele-information, demand for transport services
and vehicle traffic 309
J. Volmuller, Delft

Index 323

Preface

J. H. P. PAELINCK

Many splendid things have been said about Leo Klaassen by Henk Lambers and Jan Tinbergen in their contributions to this book; to this I add my own wholehearted praise.

This celebration volume tackles some – not all – of the topics Leo has delved into in a twenty-five year teaching and research career with the Netherlands School of Economics, now the Faculty of Economics, Erasmus University Rotterdam, and the Netherlands Economic Institute. Multiregional growth (chapters 3–7 by Walter Isard, Bruce Burton, Noboru Sakashita, Alain Sallez, Willem Molle and myself), locational analysis (chapters 8–11 in Part II by Lea Burns, Ryszard Domański, Dieter Bökemann and Jan Lambooy), urban trends (chapters 12–14 in Part III by Rolf Funck and Ulrich Blum, Hiroyuki Yamada, and Jim Conner), finally two special features in regional development (tourism: chapters 15 and 16 by Ad Hendriks and Norbert Vanhove, and transportation problems: chapters 17 and 18 by Erik van de Poll and Jacques Volmuller), such are the themes presented in this volume, organised in logical subsets. Any student of regional problems can start from there, complete the analysis by using parts of Leo's work, and quickly get to the point.

I want to express my gratitude to my colleagues who have contributed part of their recent work to this volume, but also to Messrs R. Iwema and E.H. Mulder, who supported Leo during his PhD, and suggested the idea of this book. The volume would not have the literary elegance it has attained without the permanent devoted efforts of Mrs A. Elderson, who carefully checked the quality of the English language used, and translated some contributions originally not drafted in English; our heartfelt thanks are expressed to her and also to William Cristofoletti (also of the Netherlands Economic Institute), who has drawn some graphs and figures.

Just some Latin to complete this preface: ad multos annos, Leo!

Jean H.P. Paelinck
March 1985

1 Introduction: Leo Hendrik Klaassen, an entrepreneurial scholar

H. W. LAMBERS

The beginning

The first time I heard Leo Klaassen's name mentioned, he must have been about eighteen years of age. My brother and his friends used to speak with grudging awe about one of their schoolfellows at the Hogere Burgerschool (Senior Highschool) in Rotterdam-South as a very able soccer player, and a tough one. That was Leo Klaassen, that still is Leo Klaassen, a highly competent man of inexhaustible stamina but there is more to him than that as I hope to show in this short biographical sketch.

The location of the school in Rotterdam-South deserves some further comment. Rotterdam, the town where he was born in 1920, now spreads along both banks of the river Nieuwe Maas. For centuries the city had developed on the North or right bank; the left bank being still a rural area. During the last quarter of the nineteenth century Rotterdam expanded fast. Factors like the new straight direct waterway to the North Sea, the rise in economic activity of the newly formed German Empire, and the decisive emergence of steam transport in world trade, worked together to give an uplift to the centuries-old network of nautical and commercial activities.

Room for the new activities could only be found on the left bank. New docks, new wharves, new living quarters were developed in rapid succession. When Leo (and I) were growing up there in the 1920s it had become one large built-up area, peopled by those who lived by the port or for the port, with a sprinkling of those who found their work in the infrastructure of administration, education, medical care. The left bank was labour and Labour. Some people living on the old right bank commiserated those of their number who were appointed to a position on the left bank. To a boy, however, all the activities going on in and around the docks were a constant appeal to inventiveness. Rotterdam South was of course hit hard by the long depression of the 1930s. Unemployment was all around us; at school, at sports, there was always a friend whose father was out of work.

It is curious how those left-bank roots seem to evolve in Leo's later life. His inventiveness in creating jobs and his unwillingness to lay people off. His urge to know about the forces behind urbanisation and regional economics, and his constant readiness to look outwards for international contacts. As a mere economist I can but point out the apparent coincidence; a mature human being of great gifts is not explained that easily.

Having finished his secondary schooling in 1939, Leo enrolled as a student of the Netherlands ('Rotterdam') School of Economics. This school, founded in 1913 as the first Dutch specialist academic institution in economics, by the late 1930s had achieved international standing. It possessed an impressive pioneering staff which Jan Tinbergen had already come to join earlier in the decade.

The curriculum as it then stood, consisted of two parts: a 'candidaats' (BA) programme of two or three years, to be followed by a 'doctoraal' (MA) programme of the same duration.

The German occupation of the Netherlands in May 1940 spelled the end of freedom. Leo still managed to take his BA. Then, a victim of certain measures against students, he was transported to Germany. But he succeeded in escaping and finding his way back to Rotterdam. In need of an income and administrative protection, he found employment as a research economist with the Economic-Technological Institute for South-Holland. Under the direction of A.G. van der Veen, alumnus of the Netherlands School of Economics and the South-Bank Senior Highschool, it had been founded – under trusted Dutch management – to prepare for the reconstruction of Rotterdam and its adjoining regions after the liberation. It gave Leo his first, somewhat troubled experience with regional economics, a discipline that had not been part of his study programme. And it inspired, in the same year, his first published article: 'The straw-board industry in the Netherlands'.

This was the first of around three hundred articles which were to follow through the years, not to mention thirty books and eighty contributions to books. In those numbers are not counted his contributions to various research papers and the series issued by the Netherlands Economic Institute. Figures that are amazing and a little disheartening to a man of a more common mould. Nevertheless, Leo Klaassen is not at all the kind of prolific writer who just throws words at any passing target. The steady stream of his writings and publishings is the outcome of an equally steady stream of observations, research and methodological reasoning on a succession of subjects with one factor in common: some application should be possible. The title of his PhD thesis (1959) is straight to the point: 'Directives for applied economic research'. Professor Dr L.H. Klaassen likes direct writing if it leads to fruit-bearing.

In the dark winter of 1944 all that was but a gleam in the eye, but some clever men spotted it. Conversations were opened to the effect that Mr Klaassen should join the Netherlands Economic Institute (NEI) as soon as the Netherlands were free. So, one day in May 1945 Leo Klaassen and I, then newly appointed as the executive secretary of the NEI, had our first formal conversation. I have never forgotten it.

Leo opened with the offhand remark that he had been offered a very attractive contract if he was willing to join the American forces as a pianist. I lamely answered that what we had to offer could hardly be called gainful employment compared with the other offer, but that I had to compliment the Americans on their quick ear and good taste. Leo then said he would not think of accepting: he wanted a career as an economist and a research worker, not a flash in the pan. I must confess with regret that I had nothing to do with that decision which later was to prove momentous. He was already his own man, a man who had worked out his route.

In management development, exogenous factors – often called coincidence – are rife, as anyone knows who works in it. But with an intelligent, efficient and orderly man like Leo Klaassen, the lines of activities are interdependent, and coincidence becomes the rational consequence of prior action. Thus his threefold career – academic, international economic advisor, President of the NEI – is actually one continuous lifelong movement. Here that movement is split up only for reasons of description. As we are honouring a silver professor, the academic comes first.

Lecturer and leader of research

Working for the NEI since May 1945, Leo simultaneously completed his interrupted doctoral study in economics. He took his degree in 1947. Then he had what some saw as a piece of luck. Professor J.G. Koopmans – of 'neutral money' fame – needed an assistant professor.

Out of the promising postwar group Leo Klaassen was chosen. Professor Koopmans, analytically highly gifted, with a background of humanities but strong mathematical interests, worked hand-in-glove with his young mathematically trained assistant. It was the first of the many teams that were to become typical of Klaassen; his professional life had taken shape.

The Netherlands Economic Institute had been founded in 1929 as an independent foundation to be connected with the Netherlands School of Economics by personal unions of directors-professors. It was intended to become a research laboratory in economics for professors and graduate students. Under the direction of Professor P. Lieftinck and Professor J. Tinbergen, among others, it had become internationally known by the end of the 1930s. The German occupation shut it off from its main international contacts and research projects. At the same time part of the income from abroad fell away. The decision was made to keep together and protect the group of young researchers by offering contract research to trusted Dutch groups. Somehow the NEI came through the war, ready for immediate expansion thereafter. We have already mentioned that Leo Klaassen was one of those asked to participate in the group.

In the Dutch academic hierarchy of the period, the stepping stone to a professorate was a 'lectoraat' (lecturership). Thus it happened with Leo Klaassen. In 1951 he was offered a position as lecturer in economic statistics. I remember some other teachers complaining that Mr Klaassen put too much mathematics in his statistics. That, they said, claimed too much of the students' time; time, that is, which ought to be available for those other gentlemen's subjects. Leo Klaassen's programme was completely successful, however, in showing the students how mathematical statistics, applied economic research and economic policy are related. Economic research was the key concept to be explained.

Following Tinbergen's dictum, dating from 1945, that applied research should show its usefulness by fetching an income at market prices, the NEI took up economic research on behalf of urban and regional postwar reconstruction. An early and intellectually very co-operative territory was the town of Amersfoort. As a member of the team Leo went to live there. He learnt the art of combining economic thought and policy advice from the bottom upwards, collecting and constructing his data, consulting officials from the lower and higher echelons, meeting the townspeople and eliciting their opinion. He polished his gift to write a theoretically sound report that could be easily understood by the layman. That clearness of purpose, that willingness to explain but not to retreat, has always remained one of his strong points as a designer of research projects. The NEI-team consisted of three men much of an age; their names are on the book on methods and results in Amersfoort, published in 1949. The book marked two beginnings. It was the first of the long series of books (a list of which is appended to this chapter) and articles which Leo would publish 'in co-operation with', gladly giving from the first every young man his due. And it was the start of a new and very strong team: Dr L.M. Koyck as a professor of economics and director of the NEI, and Leo as a lecturer and leader of research, two academic researchers working together as equals and as friends.

In the 1950s their publications on methods – and results – in mathematical economics, statistics and research earned them international fame. They also took the NEI into the international market for contract research. They both abhorred routine, and entered and sometimes stumbled upon new fields of analysis and applied research. It was a most fertile decade for the NEI, but also for the potential of academic teaching.

Professor and director

Obviously at the Netherlands School of Economics we needed Leo Klaassen as a professor of methods of economic research. In the meantime he had written a large number of scientific texts, but he had never found time to fulfil the formalities of a doctor's thesis. Somehow, time was made. With Professor J. Tinbergen as his PhD director he took his PhD in economics (1959). The appointments as a professor of regional and socio-economic research and as a director of the NEI followed that same year.

The decade of the 1960s began, a most productive one, though marred for all of us by the early death of Professor L.M. Koyck in 1962.

From the beginning Professor Klaassen was convinced that Dutch economists and geographers were lagging behind in regional and spatial economics, which was becoming progressively important on two levels. Nationally, as income growth showed up the differences among regions and called for corrective policies. Internationally, especially in Western Europe, as the implications of the European Economic Community had to be analysed and responded to by policy measures. In world terms, there was the problem of the developing countries; on that score at least, the NEI and the Rotterdam School, with its division 'Balanced International Growth' under the direction of Professor J. Tinbergen, could be considered on a par with the best abroad.

To those who have experience with academic administrations, the next development will not come as a surprise. The official history of the Netherlands School of Economics 1963–72 (in 1972 the School became part of the newly created Erasmus University Rotterdam) first mentions the appointment of Professor L.H. Klaassen (1959), then continues with an accurate and trustworthy account of moves and countermoves, to conclude with the information that with the academic year 1969/70 a specialised graduate programme of spatial and regional economics was introduced. A simpler and not even inaccurate vision of history would have been given by just the name 'Professor L.H. Klaassen' on that page, and nothing else. Of course, all other teachers thought that the new outlook was wonderful and should be given ample room, as long as their own areas were left alone.

A specialised postgraduate programme is more than a programme of teaching. It mirrors the old idea of a unit of teachers and students, a centre of intellectual activity with a sense of direction. In that respect the structure drawn up by Klaassen and his team, among whom I wish to mention Professor J.H.P. Paelinck, has been successful. Separately and with their academic staff – often at the same time their co-workers at the NEI – they have written textbooks on various subjects that have received international recognition. They have put students in contact with examples of socially meaningful current research, straight after discussions about the methods to be used. They have made the study come alive. Response has come from a number of students who – as I know from my own seminars – possessed well above average intellectual gifts and application.

The academic record is clear. Since 1961 Professor Klaassen has acted eighteen times as a director of a PhD thesis. A performance which is the more impressive as many candidates from abroad came to take their doctor's degree in Rotterdam.

There is reason to congratulate the University on this professional team's staying in Rotterdam. Not that they stayed put all the time, for to successful professors of spatial economics and regional research travelling is part of the job.

International economic advisor and President

That takes us to the third wave, the international activities. Not being raised in the fields which Leo teaches and publishes about, I have so far given the backgrounds as they are remembered in the waning memories of a small group of men. The discussion of Leo's scholarly work I have to leave to competent authors. As to his international work, this biographer is even more at a loss. Belonging to the other kind of Rotterdammers – those who have never been able to leave their town – I have never joined Leo in his travels. I was always one of those who were waiting for his return, a bit nervous sometimes because of the intricacy of his travel schemes. Leo Klaassen is a born traveller, with enduring physical and mental stamina, an adventurous soul and a searching mind, and to cap all that, boundless optimism. That whole army of forces was set in motion at the beginning of the 1960s, when he became convinced that there should be a complementary approach to development programming. A combination of analytical thinking, practical insight and character brought Leo Klaassen to the conviction that a project approach to development programmes would be worthwhile. While the subject surpasses a sketch, I have to stress its importance. The team Koyck-Klaassen had taken the NEI well into international work; the expansion of the 1960s makes the list of missions an illustration of the device of the Rotterdam-based Dutch marines: 'qua patet orbis', as far as the world reaches. It all began with Niger and Dahomey (1961) . . . or so it seems.

Actually, the foundations lie deeper. As far back as 1945 Leo Klaassen was convinced that a scholar should be willing to share his knowledge with everyone asking for it, with or without payment. He was among the first academics to accept German demands for rehabilitation of their academic programmes. In the 1950s he roamed all the countries of Central Europe to find out where they stood on urban problems, and to give advice. His relations with Poland are deep and of long standing. On the other hand he has always encouraged research fellows from abroad to come to the NEI, to learn as well as to teach. To him the only yardstick for a small country has always been the international standard, as international personal contacts to him are the only way of life for a humanitarian scholar.

To his personal and moral conviction was added the duty of keeping the NEI alive. With the death of Koyck, the whole burden of final responsibility came to fall on his shoulders. The curriculum of missions just cited, shows how he responded: Niger, Dahomey, Syria, Zambia, Turkey, Curaçao, Finland, Korea, Brazil. That takes us only up to 1965; when one is of a historian's turn of mind, the list makes one think of the regiments of proven virtue who were allowed to show on their banner where they had done battle.

The work went on with the help of rather a small group of hand-picked men and women, who were willing to take responsibility and initiatives before running to the telex. The NEI grew in manpower and volume of contracts. In 1968 the other directors of the NEI proposed to the Board of Governors to appoint Leo Klaassen President of the NEI. The decision to put central responsibility where it had naturally gravitated, was the right one.

An entrepreneurial scholar

Leo Klaassen is a scientist first and foremost. He delights in a beautiful piece of analysis, all the more as it occurs to him that it may be used in some part of current research. He has been constantly on the move to convince his pupils and co-workers that in research only quality counts. In that way he has made a small institution, depending on a few big names, into an institute whose name is great by itself. He is so deeply the economist, however, that substitution coefficients are always on his mind. In that respect he is a Schumpeterian entrepreneur, who knows that to find continuity one needs the courage to forego past results.

A man who has achieved so much knows, of course, how to organise himself and others. But his main organisational principle is that of the entrepreneurial breakthrough into new fields of research promising to become markets. Those who are somewhat slower he carries along on the momentum of his thought and optimism. And when they see the light, he is quick to delegate that line of development to those who have shown aptness for the work.

Born administrators may find him a bit difficult. They may have a profession too, perhaps even a vocation, but Leo Klaassen is unable to accept that organisation charts and job qualifications should supersede life's force. Because he is a most amiable man, he will stay reasonable for quite a time, perhaps even for ten minutes!

It may all sound quite simple and self-propelling. It has not, of course, been that simple. The NEI, with between 90 and 100 qualified people on its payroll, has lived through years when pipelines full of acquisition did not ripen into contracts owing to restrictive policies of governments and international institutions. Or the additional manpower needed to man a very large research project left the NEI overcommitted when the follow-up was delayed. In such cases, Leo Klaassen has proved that his optimism was backed by an untiring urge to see his people through. And they, perhaps kibitzing as academics do, found that he had done it again. In those situations the soccer-player of long ago returned: an inventive driving force set on scoring, and hard to get past.

He has been showered with honours, at home and abroad. He has fully deserved them, having proved his mettle.

In a life with so many and manifold interests and obligations, an anchorage is needed if one is to survive personally. There is no doubt that he has found such an anchorage in his marriage with Annemarie Ablinger. Through the years she has gladly taken on all the tasks of a near permanent hostess, travelling companion and sharer of good and bad times. To her, there is only one man in the world.

In this year of his silver professorate, Leo stands in his full vigour and intellectual force. The many friends he has made all over the world certainly wish that his wife, his work, and his train de vie may remain with him for many, many years.

List of books (co)authored by Leo Klaassen

1949, with D.H. van Dongen Torman and L.M. Koyck (1949), *The Development of the City of Amersfoort 1900–1970*, Leiden (Dutch).
1956, with E.H. Mulder and J. Tinbergen (1956), *Observations on the Planned Provision of Nitrogen Fertilizers for the World*, Leiden (English).
1959, with A. de Klerk (1959), *Heating of Low-Rent Houses*, H.E. Stenfert Kroese, Leiden (Dutch).
1959, with W.C. Kroft and W.M. van Liefland (1959), *Deventer, City of 250,000*, Deventer-Antwerpen (Dutch).
1959, *Principles of Economic Research*, Leiden (Dutch).
1965, *Area Economic and Social Redevelopment*, OECD, Paris (English, French and Japanese).
1966, with R. Iwema, A. de Klerk and J.W. Meijer, *Energy in Perspective*, Steenkolen Handelsvereniging, Utrecht (Dutch).
1966, *Short-term Social Solutions and Long-run Regional Policy*, Hamburg-Berlin (German).
1967, *Selecting Industries for Location in Depressed Areas*, OECD, Paris (English and French), reprint.
1968, *Social Amenities in Area Economic Growth*, Paris (English and French).
1968, with E.H. van de Poll, *Economic Policy in the Netherlands*, Rome (Italian).
1969, with E. Bloembergen, E.D. Kruijtbosch and M.C. Verburg, The Hague (Dutch).
1972, *Regional Economics* (editor and co-author), Groningen (Dutch).
1972, with P. Drewe, *Migration Policy in Europa*, with special reference to Great Britain, France, Sweden and the Netherlands, Saxon House/ Lexington Books, Farnborough and Massachusetts (English).
1974, with G. Rehn and A. Bernfeld, *Manpower Policy in Germany*, OECD, Paris (English and French).
1974, with A.C.P. Verster, *Cost Benefit Analysis in Regional Perspective*, Groningen (Dutch).
1974, with J.H.P. Paelinck, *Integration of Socio-Economic and Physical Planning*, Rotterdam (English).
1975, with J.A.M. Heijke and J.C. Offereins, *Towards a Labour Market*

Model, Groningen (Dutch).

1976, with J.A. Bourdrez and G. Billet, *Transport Policy in Western Europe*, Madrid (Spanish).

1977, *Integrated Planning Systems in Western Europe*, Wroclaw-Warszawa-Kraków-Gdańsk (Polish).

1979, with J.H.P. Paelinck and Sj. Wagenaar, *Spatial Systems*, Saxon House (English); Polish edition (1982), Warsaw; Reprint Gower 1982.

1979, with J.H.P. Paelinck, *Spatial Econometrics*, Saxon House (English); Polish edition (1983), Warsaw.

1980, with N. Vanhove, *Regional Policy, (A European View)*, Saxon House, Farnborough (English); reprint (1983), Gower, Aldershot; Greek edition forthcoming.

1981, with J.A. Bourdrez and J. Volmuller, *Transport and Reurbanisation*, Gower, Aldershot (English).

1981, *Dynamics of Urban Development* (co-editor and co-author), Gower, Aldershot (English).

1981, The Dynamics of Dutch Urban Development (co-editor and co-author), *Olijfreeks* 1981/1, NEI, Rotterdam (Dutch).

1982, with others, *Urban Europe, A Study of Growth and Decline*, Pergamon Press, Oxford (English).

1982, *Markets and Institutions* (co-editor and co-author), NEI, Rotterdam (Dutch).

1983, with A.C.P. Verster and Sj. Wagenaar, Spatial Interaction, *Olijfreeks*, NEI, Rotterdam (Dutch).

1983, *Industrial Mobility and Migration in the European Community* (co-editor and co-author), Gower, Aldershot (English).

2 The central theme: from research methodology to the element of space

J. TINBERGEN

General research methodology

In a way a scientist's dissertation marks his entry into a scientific career; to a majority of students it is the final stage of their 'schooling'. There are exceptions, even important ones, where a dissertation is the fruit of lessons from experience. Leo Klaassen had already taught statistics since 1951 when in 1959 he completed his doctor's thesis (Klaassen, 1952, 1959). A good deal of research experience was reflected in nine concrete examples of research projects, scattered in a text that set out systematically and carefully the methodology of research. The nine examples had been taken from actual research done at the Netherlands Economic Institute, one of the large research institutes in our discipline (and other disciplines), which paid its own way to an impressive percentage of its total budget. The examples refer to such diverse subjects as the taxi business in Amsterdam, the influence of the cyclical position on reinvestment activity, the competition between railways and lorries in Western Germany, the competition between coal and diesel oil, the propensity to go to college, the interpretation of questionnaire answers, the number of accounts at the postal banking service, and an estimate of the stock of whales.

Klaassen's doctoral thesis systematically discussed the stages a good research project has to pass through, preceded by an analysis of its logical structure, its objectives and identification problems. Among the stages he stresses the importance of a proper setting of the problem to be investigated, indicating how a preparatory stage can help to attain it. The execution of a project requires first a *theoretical* analysis; the author emphasises the importance of a *quantitative* method and the use of clear-cut concepts. He subsequently deals with the economics of (economic) research: the financial means available *set limits* to the degree of refinement to be introduced, and a cost-benefit comparison has to be applied to find out what details are worthwhile. Finally, he also enumerates some personality traits required for a good research leader.

The final sub-section of Klaassen's dissertation deals with what was to become his most important specialisation: the introduction and elaboration of the *element of space* into economic science and research. A large part of quantitative economic research or econometrics is *time-series research*, and several of its checks (for instance the Durbin-Watson test) and methods (using first, second, etc. differences of variables) apply to time-series data only. Besides time-series research we have *cross-section research*, referring to observations at one point or period of time; cross-section data may refer to different individuals or firms, in which case they make relevant conclusions with respect to many problems possible. Often, though not always, such observations made at one point in time show differences in location, and that introduces the element of *space*. Recent economic investigations have given increasing attention to that element, and Klaassen has been among the productive contributors to economics-with-space.

In this chapter the role of space will be the main subject. Our elaboration will illustrate the part played by Leo Klaassen in the twenty-five years of teaching he has now completed – teaching that has always been closely connected with and inspired by the practical research carried out under his leadership.

Expansion of space-oriented economic research

About two decades after his inaugural address as a lecturer of statistics (Klaassen, 1952), and some fifteen years after his doctor's thesis (Klaassen, 1959), Klaassen and Paelinck (1974, with the co-operation of Loet B.M. Mennes and Ep H. Mulder) report to the United Nations Centre for Housing, Building and Planning on the integration of socio-economic and physical planning. The report covers a first-order practical problem encountered in many countries where socio-economic and physical planning are the tasks of two different organisations, using different methods, and with largely differently trained staff. Socio-economic planning is done mainly by institutions of economists, whereas most physical planning is the job of engineering consultants. To be sure, some technical experts are included in the former and some economists in the latter, and there is some co-ordinating contact between the agencies concerned. But the authors rightly argue that a higher degree of *integration* is needed; such integration requires integrated models of research, and has to be implemented at a variety of *levels* by appropriate institutions.

Since the publication of this report another decade has elapsed and the relative importance of the element of space has continued to increase. The process may be compared to the integration of a few subjects in elementary and secondary schooling: geography, history and economics, but apart from subjects, and perhaps more importantly, scientific methods have to be integrated. Later in this chapter we shall see that still more aspects of human life have to be integrated too.

The enrichment of economic science by the element of space

With a facet of space added to it, economics becomes considerably more complicated. The *number of variables* increases enormously. The variable of, say, production of bread is now replaced with production of bread in each of a number of locations, which may be quite large. For some commodities there may be fewer locations as the (optimum) production units are larger: there are fewer locations of steel production than there are of bakeries; on the other hand agricultural production may be spread almost continuously across a large area.

Alongside production and consumption, the element of space affects activities not bound to one location, but establishing *connections* between locations: transportation and communication. On the simplifying assumption of a fixed number of 'n' locations (towns, for instance), the number of connections tends to increase more than n-fold: a unit connection being characterised by two locations, the number of possible connections is $\frac{1}{2}\, n(n-1)$. While in transportation not all these connections will be needed, in the field of communication (telephone conversations, for example) they may indeed be relevant.

The element of connections carries with it the aspect of the number of *dimensions* of the space considered. Because a large part of economic activity occurs close to the earth surface on which we live, a two-dimensional description may often suffice; for some problems even one dimension may do, for instance for a country like Chile, or for the problems of a narrow valley. For problems of mining or air transportation, on the other hand, three dimensions are needed; the section 'Some complications caused by geographical and historical elements' will go into some details of that aspect.

For a systematic treatment of the phenomenon of space, the measurement of spaces has to be introduced. As a rule there is little sense in following strict geometrical methods, sub-dividing, for instance, a country into parts of one square kilometre. Historically grown sub-divisions into provinces (Canada, the Netherlands), Länder (Federal Republic of Germany), départements (France), etc., and a further sub-division into municipalities, are more likely to be useful. In a few cases (USA, Australia) frontiers have been established along straight lines.

A disturbing aspect of using existing divisions such as nations is the enormous variety in size. An attempt made in Mennes et al. (1969) to avoid the confusion by using the terms mega, macro, major, minor and micro space, has not found support so far.

Simplifying assumptions may sometimes help to avoid the enormous complications described. Instead of classifying commodities by their transportation costs over a given distance, crude sub-divisions have been made by assuming transportation costs to be zero below one limit, and to be infinitely large (prohibitive) above another. Such divisions entail the classification of goods into local (freely transportable within a municipality), regional (freely transportable within a province), national, and international goods, a classification introduced by Leontieff (cf. also the next section).

The introduction of *hierarchies of spaces* entails the introduction of hierarchies of authorities resulting in levels of decision making. For socio-economic policies and their planning, a central problem is on what level to make various types of decisions to ensure maximum welfare.

Some contributions to economics with a space aspect

A number of economists have felt challenged to contribute to the solution of economic problems with a space element. Such contributions have been made by some of the 'founding fathers' and some of the great economists of the nineteenth century, but the more specialised studies tend to quote Cristaller (1933) and Lösch (1944) as the initiators of intensive research into space problems in economics; in that worldwide process some Rotterdam-based scholars have participated. In his dissertation, H.C. Bos (1964) sets out to explain the occurrence of centres (that is to say, cities, towns and villages) of various size and composition (number of firms, branches of activity), and to investigate what an optimum dispersion of centres amounts to. In 1969 L.B.M. Mennes, J. Tinbergen and J.G. Waardenburg made an attempt at improving the definition of space categories already mentioned, and experimented with various ways to simplify costs of transportation (*mobility*) and differences of production costs in various locations (*shiftability*). They introduced the concept of levels of decision making corresponding to a hierarchy of spaces, already mentioned in the previous section.

Also working in Rotterdam for some time, the Norwegian economist Jan Serck-Hansen made a series of contributions to the element of space in economics (Serck-Hansen, 1961, 1969). The same element is a major aspect in the work of Hans Linnemann (1966) and his pupils. The volume of trade between pairs of countries very clearly tends to be larger as the distance is smaller, but the measurement of distance poses many problems, for distance in this context must not be interpreted geometrically only. Linnemann carefully analyses the problem and finds cultural and political aspects to play a considerable role, such as the fact of belonging to a colonial and hence linguistic system; much later Bakker (1982) was able to study how the impact of such factors changes.

From 1973 on, Klaassen and Paelinck take the lead in the publication referred to above, which had been preceded by two others: Klaassen (1973) and Paelinck (1973), and was followed by Paelinck (1979). The works mentioned are only a sample from a much larger number of studies actually carried out.

The contributions made by the sub-group of 'space economists' (not usually involved in what has become known as 'outer space') referred to at least two elements. First, a series of new concepts had to be introduced, several of which have been mentioned before. Second, the complexity of the subject called for adequate simplifications, and here creativity is a helpful tool of scientific work. In the remainder of this section a brief survey of the relevant contributions will be given.

Defining space units

One simplification is to reduce space to one dimension, which is possible in a country like Chile (but not for all problems, of course) or in a deep valley.

Another is the sub-division of a plane into regular parts; if these are interpreted as regular polygons, it is possible only for triangles, squares and hexagons. Bos (1964) shows that for an estimate of total transportation costs of the products of one company, all markets of such shapes can (with an error of less than 5 per cent) be approximated by circular markets.

Transportation networks

Transportation is organised in the simplest way in a linear space. For a two-dimensional space (that is, a plane) a very simple assumption is that transportation between any two points is along a straight line. More realistic is the assumption of a road system along the sides of squares of equal size (two sets of equidistant parallel straight roads at right angles, the streets of most American and some European cities).

Transportation costs

Transportation costs can be assumed to be proportional to the transportation distance; a fixed element can be added. Costs also depend on whether or not (or the extent to which) there is return freight.

Differences in transportation costs can also be limited, as observed, by neglecting them within a certain area and considering them prohibitive outside a certain area; for a wider interpretation of transportation costs (including import duties) that may even be fairly realistic. Various areas can be distinguished, and that leads to Leontief's distinction, mentioned in the last section, among local, regional, national and world-trade goods. Local goods cannot move out of the locality of production, regional goods not out of the region, and so on.

Hierarchy of areas

The world can be divided into continents, continents (usually) into nations, nations into provinces (or similar parts), down to municipalities. The sub-division of nations is hierarchical in two senses: (a) geographically, smaller areas adding up to a larger one, and (b) politically, their authorities being governed by the larger ones to which they belong. Nations are included in the type (a) hierarchy, and to a very low extent in type (b) through treaties.

Distribution of industries across areas

Distribution of industries is the subject dealt with by L.H. Klaassen's attraction models (Klaassen and Van Wickeren, 1969; Van Wickeren, 1971). A strategic concept is that of an industry's 'relevant area', that is the smallest area for which the production equals the consumption of the industry's product; for that area the product considered is called 'non tradable' by other authors, who add the assumption of negligible transportation costs within the relevant area. Attraction models treat transportation costs in another way: an industry will be attracted by its consumers (if the cost of transportation to them is relatively high), or by one or more of its suppliers of raw materials or intermediate products.

Industries with negligible transportation costs from suppliers and to consumers are called 'footloose'; they can locate anywhere or wherever other factors dictate location.

Distribution of centres across an area

Activities requiring equipment of an indivisible nature have to be carried on in units larger than some minimum, and hence at locations at more than some minimum distance from one another. Under the simplifying assumption of a constant density level of activities with very small production units (usually agricultural activities, which moreover 'consume' a lot of land for production), such activities should be spread in a regular pattern, for instance at the corners of regular hexagons. The corners of equal squares are a second choice, possibly preferred because they correspond with the road network. Finally, the corners of regular triangles are a third and last choice (Cristaller, 1933; Lösch, 1944; Bos, 1964). Because demand cumulates in them, centres offer optimum welfare. Any combination of production units may be called a centre, but centres of special combinations reduce the transportation costs most. Simplifying assumptions include equal size of production units in the same branch, and combinations of an integer number of units. Another simplifying assumption sometimes used is that of vertical integration of successive processes (spinning, weaving, finishing, tailoring). Admitting only centres of a hierarchical type (Tinbergen, 1964; Bos, 1964) may contribute to optimality under some of the other simplifying assumptions listed. Industries are ranked, 1 being assigned to the industry needing the maximum number of units to comply with the demand for their products, N to that requiring the minimum. Centres are also ranked, being given the rank n of the highest ranking industry. A centre of rank n contains all industries from the rank of n downwards but none of a higher rank; industries of rank n − 1 do not export their products, but that of rank n does.

The system of centres just described is optimum only if more conditions than those listed are satisfied; in other words, many systems are not optimum. With increasing N, the complications accumulate, and to my knowledge we are still close to the frontier of the 'state of the art', meaning that only cases with low values of N can be solved completely.

Some complications caused by geographical and historical elements

Certain geographical and historical elements *limit* the extent to which problems of space in economics can be solved with the aid of clear models. As the pure science of space is geometry, theorists are inclined to combine purely (that is, non-spatial) economic relations with purely geometrical propositions. Natural though the inclination may be, it is severely handicapped by geographic reality: models can only be kept relatively simple if the object studied resembles as closely as possible a plain of homogeneous soil. A mountainous landscape spells complications: slopes and irregular hill shapes set narrow limits to transportation facilities; the shortest and therefore cheapest way of transportation between two points is no longer the straight line. If the landscape is extremely mountainous, with deep valleys as the only possible trajectory for roads, railways and waterways, some problems become geometrically one-dimensional and almost independent of the curvilinearities of the valley, which is at least one simplification.

The Zuiderzee case is famous: to estimate the probable effects of the dyke planned to start its reclamation, the physicist H.A. Lorentz successfully approximated the submarine landscape of the Dutch Zuiderzee with the help of a set of planes with different slopes and lines of intersection with the water level. On later occasions – for the so-called *Delta Project* for the province of Zeeland following the great flood of 1953 – two other models were used. One was a physical replica of the set of islands and sea arms of Zeeland, reduced at different scales vertically and horizontally; in this model in the Delft Hydraulic Laboratory all the water movements caused by different combinations of dams and dykes could be produced and observed. The other was an electrical analogue, in which each sea arm was represented by a metal thread with a resistance corresponding to the friction which the water flows in the sea arm experienced. Not for the first time, economists had to learn from engineers; especially in France economics was created largely by engineers.

So much for geographical 'handicaps'; but as we said, there are also handicaps produced by history. They are perhaps identified most objectively by the hypothesis that the costs of transportation and production have changed through time, and that the optimum use of space in previous periods is not necessarily the same as today's. Buildings and highways have a long life, and as a consequence a large portion of our infrastructure is not optimum; the location of steel mills is a well-known macro-example. Past activities can probably also be explained in a less objective manner: part of our inherited infrastructure may not be explicable in economic terms. To the extent that economic considerations were at the base, changes in economic thinking may be responsible, but political thinking carries at least some of the responsibility.

Short history makes for less historical handicaps. As pointed out already, the sub-division of the USA and Australia into states shows geometrically simpler shapes than the sub-division of Europe into nations, provinces, and so on; Manhattan's plan is simpler than that of Amsterdam. Nevertheless, there are examples of a sub-division into square blocks also in the older towns of Europe (Elburg in Gelderland, the Netherlands, Friedrichstadt in Schleswig-Holstein, Germany).

New aspects added since 1970

In their 1974 report to the United Nations, Klaassen and Paelinck dealt mainly with the desirability of ultimately integrating economic and social planning with physical planning. No doubt that integration was the most urgent and remained so for quite some time: half a century ago a highway system could not be planned without a view of the long-term growth of traffic, and it still cannot. New aspects of physical planning recently developed indeed strengthen the need for integrating socio-economic and physical planning. The impact of demographic and economic growth on the environment was already mentioned in the 1974 report; in particular the kinds of pollution caused by the fast growing chemical industries is now known to have harmed the quality of life even far from the polluting plant. The environmental aspect is interesting too because it stresses the need for decision making on higher than national levels. The phenomenon of 'acid rain' is our most recent environmental concern; to prevent it, integration across at least the area of Western Europe is imperative, integration covering the whole of Europe preferable. The issue might even become a *pilot project for East-West co-operation*, something which Leo Klaassen rightly considers important and to which he is actively contributing in other fields of activity.

Planning in the Netherlands gained a new dimension when the *Social and Cultural Planning Office* was established in 1973. Clearly, the aspects of the Dutch community covered by that institute's responsibility also need to be integrated with the aspects discussed so far, so that a common approach is called for. The increasing intensity of the present cultural crisis has made that integration even more urgent; by 'cultural crisis' I mean increasing vandalism and violence, and more generally the neglect of the human norms and values we once adhered to.

There is an outspoken need for research in at least two major directions: can we find the *causes* of and a *cure* for the cultural crisis? In other words, how can we *motivate* people to stop vandalism, to stop violence against innocent victims, perpetrated even as a form of amusement? A purely economic analysis may show already that considerable financial means can be spent on this type of research, given the amount of annual destruction by vandalism, including the medical services needed to cure, as far as possible, the persons injured.

Another, less serious but still important, component of cultural changes can probably be found in education. An increasing number of complaints are heard about the lack of motivation among high-school students in the underprivileged quarters of large cities. Lack of motivation may be one, not necessarily the only cause of the low quality of school leavers; recent experiences suggest that the average quality of teachers may also play a role. The tendencies described seem to be in accordance with the general trend to take less seriously the values and norms western society was believed to be built on.

The time has come to leave the aspects 'already added' to the types of planning to be integrated, and deal with some aspects yet to be added in view of more recent developments.

Aspects to be integrated because of recent developments

In this final section we will discuss some further aspects of integrating space in planning. The space to be considered in planning should include the Third World, for one thing because economic interdependence has increased considerably, as the share of the Third World in international trade testifies, and for another because to accelerate consumption growth for the poorest groups in the Third World (or the 'South'), the co-operation of western countries is indispensable. An important example of such planning was carried out by W. Leontief et al. (1977); an essential feature of his study is that it contains several alternatives. Its 'Scenario C' results in a less unequal distribution in the year 2000 than 'Scenario I', which is based on the extrapolation of the development in previous decades. While in the latter the income ratio between developed and developing regions (measured by gross national product per capita) remains about the same as it was in 1970 (12 : 1), in Scenario C it becomes 7 : 1. Not only for humanitarian reasons – in the South many people are underfed if not starving – but also for political stability the outcome of Scenario C is preferable; indeed, the existing inequality (already worse now than it was in 1970) will not be accepted for ever. Already the results of poverty are visible in the progressive illegal immigration into the more prosperous parts of the world: in the USA there are as many Mexicans working illegally as legally (their number being estimated at 7 million each). To Europe and some rich oil countries, comparable illegal migration from the Mediterranean has taken place. Better information about and understanding of these migration flows is in the interest of the countries of origin as well as that of the receiving countries.

Next to the problem of the South, which has occupied us since the beginning of decolonisation, other problems have come up in western societies which also need to be integrated in our planning, such as environmental quality.

Central to the newer developments is the stagnation of production and employment combined with inflation, a combination often called *stagflation*. How to get out of stagflation is a problem that must be given top priority; the novelty of the situation has led to extensive discussions on its causes, and several 'schools' have offered differing theories, which have not yet been sufficiently tested. Similarly, opinions differ on what instruments of economic policy had best be used to further a recovery from stagnation with a minimum of inflation. One important question, presumably under-represented in the planning models used so far, is how the expectations from strategic variables are formed. Another is whether international co-operation has been adequate to tackle a worldwide lack of productive activity. A third question to be considered in an anti-stagflation policy is how to further innovations, both technological and socio-political. The research done on all these problems is considerable in volume but still insufficient on many counts.

What degree of international co-operation is needed, may partly be assessed by comparing the decision making structures of two important economic areas, the USA and the European Community. They happen to have about the same total production, amounting to some $2500 billion (in the American sense of 1000 million); but while the American federal budget (without defence expenditures) amounts to some $300 billion, that of the European Community is less than $30 billion. Presumably, then, considerable tasks, now duplicated or otherwise wasted, should be transferred from national governments to the European Community.

A related problem is that of dividing tasks between the public and private sectors, in other words the question whether or not the reprivatisation of some public activities makes sense, that is, contributes to general welfare. The answer depends on several phenomena about which we do not have sufficient information. Figures are needed on the relative productivity of a given activity when carried out by a private or public agency, the differences being explained. Explanatory factors will be the competence given to the agencies concerned, the quality of the services offered, and several others. Some historical examples are interesting and enlightening: the Dutch State Mines (DSM) were created in 1902 because insufficient private capital could be interested in the venture; farms on newly reclaimed land are temporarily run by the government because on previous occasions (reclamation of the Haarlemmermeer) large initial risks were experienced which had not been known beforehand.

The shock-wise innovation of research into the public sector achieved by Van Winden (1981) may contribute to the solution of the problems in hand.

One consequence of stagflation has been the fast growth of the so-called illegal or black sector in developed countries (Dallago, 1983), a sector that until a short time ago used to be far more characteristic of under-developed countries, evidently not under-developed on that score. The development of the black sector illustrates that there is a limit to government intervention or to the welfare state, and is related to the discussion 'reprivatisation versus socialisation'.

All this also illustrates that the over-simplified prototypes of social orders – complete *laissez-faire* and perfect central planning –, so often used in laymen's and political discussions, are not feasible, and that the real choice is quantitative rather than qualitative. Whether the advocates of the over-simplified prototypes, polarising the political discussion, are serving mankind is highly doubtful; there is a close connection between their polarisation and the mutual distrust of the two superpowers – US and SU – and the senseless and threatening over-armament.

That statement takes us to the last and most important aspect to be integrated in world planning and world policy; we may call it the *military* or the *security* aspect. So far, the International Institute for Comparative Social Research, part of the Wissenschaftszentrum Berlin headed by Karl W. Deutsch, has been leading in attempts at integrating this aspect in political modelling; let us quote Sontag (1981) as one example out of many. This branch of modelling tries to explain the frequency and size of interstate conflicts and the level of armament. An impressive amount of research has been carried out, and for good reasons. The greatest potential threat to world welfare is no doubt the policy instrument which the two superpowers and their satellites have been wielding so far: the armament deterrent; not only is this instrument excessively expensive, but the equilibrium it has wrought is endangered by destabilising developments, both quantitative and qualitative. The only instruments that can possibly achieve stable security are a tolerant instead of a polarising attitude, and the willingness to use scientific arguments rather than military means to change social orders. Such a change in attitude requires time, possibly more time than is left to us.

References

Bikker, J.A. (1982), *Vraag-aanbodmodellen voor stelsels van geografisch gespreide markten* (Demand-and-supply models for systems of geographically dispersed markets), VU-boekhandel-uitgeverij, Amsterdam.

Bos, H.C. (1964), *Spatial Dispersion of Economic Activity*, Universitaire Pers Rotterdam.

Cristaller, W. (1933), *Die zentralen Orte in Süddeutschland*, Gustav Fischer, Jena.

Dallago, B. (1983), Aspetti e interpretazioni dell'economia sommersa in Italia, *Economia, Banca e Congiuntura*, pp.246 and 265.

Klaassen, L.H. (1952), *Statistische conjunctuurdocumentatie* (Statistical documentation on business cycles), De Erven Bohn N.V., Haarlem.

Klaassen, L.H. (1959), *Richtlijnen voor het toegepast economisch onderzoek* (Guidelines for applied economic research), H.E. Stenfert Kroese N.B., Leiden.

Klaassen, L.H. (1973), *SPAMO II, A Spatial Model*, Netherlands Economic Institute, Rotterdam, mimeographed.

Klaassen, L.H. and Paelinck, J.H.P. (1974), *Integration of socio-economic and physical planning*, Rotterdam University Press, Rotterdam.

Leontieff, W. et al. (1977), *The Future of the World Economy, A United Nations Study*, Oxford University Press, New York.

Lösch, A. (1944), *Die räumliche Ordnung der Wirtschaft*, Gustav Fischer, Jena.

Mennes, L.B.M., Tinbergen, J. and Waardenburg, G. (1969), *The Element of Space in Development Planning*, Netherlands Economic Institute, North Holland Publishing Company, Amsterdam/London.

Paelinck, J.H.P. (1973), *Hoe doelmatig kan regionaal en sectoraal beleid zijn?* (How efficient can regional and sectoral policy be?), H.E. Stenfert Kroese, Leiden.

Paelinck, J.H.P. (1979), *Een raadselachtige wereldkaart vol beweeglijke stippen en vlekken . . .* (An enigmatic world map full of moving points and spots . . .), Diesrede (Anniversary Address), Erasmus University, Rotterdam.

Serck-Hansen, J. (1961), *Some mathematical models on the spatial dispersion of industry*, Netherlands Economic Institute, Rotterdam, mimeographed.

Serck-Hansen (1969), The optimal number of factories in a spatial market, in H.C. Bos (ed.), *Towards Balanced International Growth*, North-Holland Publishing Company, Amsterdam-London, pp. 269–81.

Sontag, Ph. (1981), *Ein Planet verteidigt sich – politometrische Untersuchung der globalen Aufrüstung*, IIVG/dp 81–115, Wissenschaftszentrum Berlin, Berlin.

Tinbergen, J. (1964), Sur un modèle de la dispersion géographique de l'activité économique, *Revue d'économie politique*, Numéro spécial, janv.-févr., pp.30–44.

Wickeren, A.C. van (1971), *Interindustry relations: some attraction models*, M.J. van der Loeff, Enschede.

Winden, F. van and Praag, B. van (1981), A dynamic model of the interaction between the state and the private sector, *Journal of Public Economics*, 16, pp.53–86.

PART I
ELEMENTS OF REGIONAL DEVELOPMENT

3 Regional research and development revisited

W. ISARD AND B. BURTON

Introduction

The purpose of this chapter is to develop a way to pull together in a systematic framework some of the many hypotheses and relationships on regional research and development policy that have been found to be valid. It does not attempt to present any new hypotheses. In fact this chapter repeats in very large part the materials to be presented in a future book (Isard, 1986) related to the invention of new conflict management procedures. We reproduce with some improvements the efficient framework and discussion developed there so that we can address more effectively the very important problem of research and development for regions. In our presentation, we draw heavily upon the work of Torsten Hagerstrand (who has pioneered the area of spatial diffusion processes) and his many followers in the fields of geography and regional science; we also draw upon economics: the findings of the Schumpeter (1939), Usher (1954) and other schools of economic thought; and we utilise ideas from the natural sciences on the development of physical systems over space and time to help provide scaffolding for our framework.

There exist many definitions of invention and innovation; it does not matter which set we use. However, if we are to be precise in what we present we must adopt one set of clear definitions. Following Kennedy and Thirwell (1972), we formally define invention as *devising new ways of attaining given ends*; as such, invention embraces both the creation of things previously non-existent, using either new or

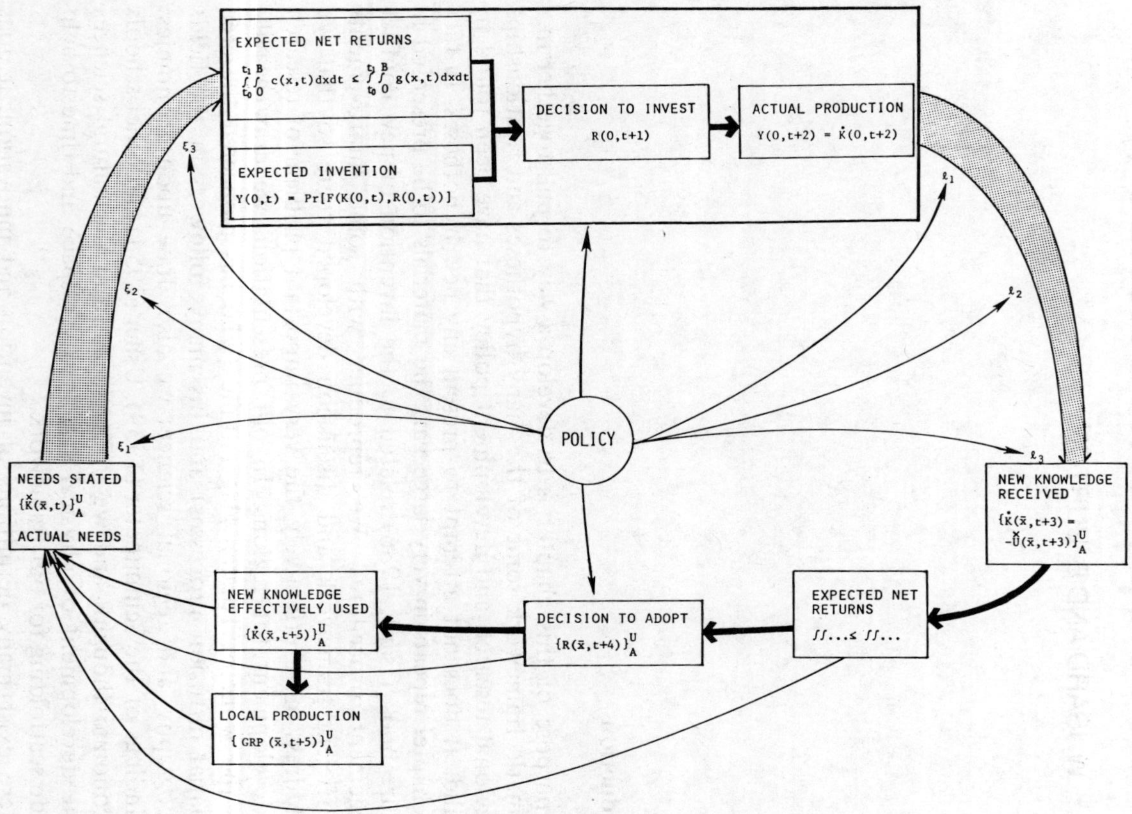

Figure 3.1 The process of invention and research and development

existing knowledge, and the creation of things by discovery which have existed all the time (e.g. penicillin). We define innovation *as the commercial application of inventions in a locality or firm for the first time*; innovation typically raises the level of technology to the best practice technique (state of the art) for the locality of firm.

Five categories of factors define the process of invention and innovation for regional and sectoral development:

1 Needs and demands (the $\overset{x}{K}$ factor; this factor is actually an indirect factor of which the meaning will become apparent later on in the text.)
2 Communication (presentation) of need or demand (the ξ factor);
3 Invention, the production of scientific knowledge (basic research) and know-how (applied research or potential innovation) (the $\dot{K}$ factor);
4 Communication (transmission and diffusion) of invention (scientific knowledge and potential innovation to locations of possible use);
5 Adoption and implementation.

Categories 4 and 5 are contained in the ℓ factor.

The discussion of these factors follows a physical system framework that is illustrated in Figure 3.1. We consider that such an approach insures that the resulting analysis will have greater consistency and balance than would otherwise be the case. In the following section we put the argument in mathematical form, and in the next section we develop the argument in verbal form.

The mathematical formulation

Basic variables and parameters in a two equation (laws of change) model

In developing our mathematical framework we draw analogies with physical systems which, discussed elsewhere (Isard and Liossatos, 1975; and 1979, pp.150–85), have been found to be appealing for defining optimal space-time development. A one commodity model is constructed having the production relation:

$$Y(x,t) = F[K(x,t),R(x,t)] \tag{2.1}$$

where we take the one commodity to be knowledge (information, know-how); and where:

$Y(x,t)$	=	the amount of knowledge produced at location x at time t per unit of distance;
$K(x,t)$	=	the stock of the knowledge at location x at time t, the stock being a density (a magnitude per unit distance); and
$R(x,t)$	=	the amount of resources (labour, capital and others) applied at location x at time t per unit of time per unit of distance;

and the two equations of motion:

$$\dot{K}(x,t) = F[K(x,t), R(x,t)] - C(x,t) - \overset{x}{U}(x,t) \qquad (2.2)$$

$$\ell\dot{U}(x,t) = -\xi\overset{x}{K}(x,t) - \nu U(x,t) \qquad (2.3)$$

where:

$\dot{K}(x,t)$	=	the addition to stock at (x,t) per unit of time, a time rate of change,
$C(x,t)$	=	consumption at location x at time t per unit of time per unit of distance,
$U(x,t)$	=	amount of flow through x at time t per unit of time per unit of distance,
$\dot{U}(x,t)$	=	the addition to flow at (x,t) per unit of time, or time rate of change,
$\overset{x}{U}(x,t)$	=	spatial rate of change of U(x,t), and
$\overset{x}{K}(x,t)$	=	spatial rate of change of K(x,t),

ℓ, ξ, ν are parameters to be discussed below.

It should be noted that equation (2.2) is derived from the production relation (2.1) and the conservation equation:

$$\dot{K}(x,t) = Y(x,t) - C(x,t) - \overset{x}{U}(x,t) \qquad (2.4)$$

We now adapt this model to the problem at hand.

Discussion of the model

1 To avoid complicating mathematical statements, we do not include in equation (2.2) a term $-\sigma K(x,t)$ which would correspond to the depreciation of a stock per unit of time, σ being a rate. Such would correspond to the term $-\frac{G}{C}\rho(x,t)$ in the physical system for an electric transmission line discussed in Isard and Liossatos (1979, pp.153); this latter term corresponds to a loss of charge density, $\frac{G}{C}$ being the loss coefficient. The reader, however, can refer to Isard and Liossatos (1979, pp.72–84) for discussion pertaining to depreciation.

2 Although at times information, as a commodity, may be physically consumable, by and large it is not. We therefore treat it as a public good whose use (consumption) by one unit does not diminish the stock that is available for use (consumption) by any other unit; by this convention, C(x,t) in equation (2.2) is always zero.

3 For simplicity we assume that all production of information takes place at a single location which, for convenience, we designate $x = 0$. It may be a single basic research centre, consisting of many or as few as one inventor; the many may be working in teams or individually. The location $x = 0$ may also be viewed as an aggregate of all locations at which inventive research is being conducted. Thus from equation (2.1):

$$Y(0,t) = F[K(0,t), R(0,t)] \geqslant 0,$$

and (2.5)

$$Y(\bar{x},t) = F(K(\bar{x},t), R(\bar{x},t)) = 0$$

for all $\bar{x} \neq 0$

4 The distance between $x = 0$ and any using location $\bar{x}$, $\bar{x} = x_1, x_2, x_3, \ldots$, is defined by the number of behaving units (agencies and the like including those at other using locations) through which messages and information must flow. To ease exposition we assume that no two behaving units are situated at the same location, and that the distance between any two neighbouring units is always Δx; thus the distance between $x = 0$ and $\bar{x} = x$ is $(n+1)\Delta x$ where n is the number of intervening units. For any using location $\bar{x}$, the locations of intervening units in order are $x_1, x_2, \ldots x_n$, all to the right of $x = 0$ in the positive x-direction. Distance may consist of not only physical distance, but also economic, psychological, political, social, ideological and other kinds of distances.

5 From the standpoint of any using location $\bar{x}$, all information $U(x',t)$ arriving at an intervening location x' passes through it, subject to the normal delays and losses defined by the parameters of the system. However, from the standpoint of x' all information received is available for use and becomes an addition to its capital stock, none being lost through export, and likewise for $\bar{x}$. Thus, by statements 2 and 3 above, equation (2.2) becomes

$$K(\bar{x},t) = -\overset{x}{U}(\bar{x},t) \qquad (2.6)$$

for all $\bar{x} \neq 0$

where $\overset{x}{U}(\bar{x},t)$ is gross imports. This convention, characteristic of many public goods and of information in particular, violates the law of conservation so often employed in physics, economics and regional science.

6 Since all information is taken to flow in the positive x-direction, location $x = 0$ receives no inflow (all locations are at or to the right of $x = 0$ by convention). This follows also from our assumption that all locations of invention are assumed to be aggregated at the location $x = 0$. This assumption can be weakened if we assume that any using location $\bar{x}$ is connected, institutionally or otherwise, to one and only one source of new information; we shall discuss other relaxations of this assumption later. Hence, $\overset{x}{U}(0,t) = 0$, and so by this convention and statement 2, equation (2.2) becomes for $x = 0$:

$$\dot{K}(0,t) = F[K(0,t), R(0,t)] \tag{2.7}$$

7 We now consider the $-\xi\overset{x}{K}(x,t)$ term in equation (2.3), the second equation of motion. Let $D(\bar{x},t)$ be the demand (need) for new information at time t at location $\bar{x}$, which represents the difference between a desired (aspired for) stock of knowledge $K(\theta,t)$ and an existing stock $K(\bar{x},t)$ that is:

$$D(\bar{x},t) = K(\theta,t) - K(\bar{x},t) \tag{2.8}$$

8 Suppose the desired level of information is attained at $x = 0$, that is, suppose after sufficient resources are applied to production, $K(0,t) = K(\theta,t)$. Then, using the calculus formulation to ease exposition, we assume for convenience that the number n of intervening units (one at each unit of distance) is infinitely large; hence we may set $\frac{\max \bar{x}}{n} = dx$, so that

$$\frac{D(\bar{x},t)}{n} = \frac{K(0,t) - K(\bar{x},t)}{n} = \overset{x}{K}(x,t) \quad \text{for } x = 0, x_1, x_2, \ldots, \bar{x} \tag{2.9}$$

that is, the $K(x,t)$ function over x as we have defined the x-dimension in non-physical space is a straight line with negative slope $-\frac{D(\bar{x},t)}{n}$. Alternatively, we may imagine the line connecting $x = 0$ to $x = \bar{x}$ to be an elastic band, so that when convenient any location at distance x from the zero point may be contracted to the distance Δx or dx when we use the notion of a spatial rate of change.

9 Take the parameter ξ to represent a velocity. In some physical systems, it corresponds to an elasticity coefficient; in our model it is the speed at which the message on the local demand (need) at $\bar{x}$ reaches $x = 0$, the location of invention (production of new information). When there are n intervening points between $x = 0$ and $x = \bar{x}$, ξ may be

viewed as the average speed at which the message passes through these points, that is through the units of distance corresponding to these n points (1/2 Δx being to the left and 1/2 Δx to the right of each point). The transmission speed in some cases may be retarded and in others accelerated.

10 In equation (2.3) we take $\dot{U}$ to represent the production of new information, that is $\dot{U}(0,t) = \dot{K}(0,t)$. We may consider for a problem on hand that the existing flow of relevant information $U(0,t)$ is zero; or if some actually exists, we may arbitrarily set the level at zero.

11 Accordingly, the ℓ parameter may be viewed as an inertial coefficient, the inverse of a velocity, or the time it takes for a flow to cover a unit of distance; or equation (2.3) may be rewritten as:

$$\dot{U}(x,t) = -\frac{\xi}{\ell}\overset{x}{K}(x,t) - \frac{\nu}{\ell}\,U(x,t) \tag{2.10}$$

Then the $1/\ell$ parameter may be viewed as a velocity, giving the average speed at which new information produced at $x = 0$ is transmitted to the using location $x = \bar{x}$. Were the ν factor zero, the ratio ξ/ℓ might be interpreted as measuring the rate of progress in the adoption of an inventive idea or procedure, as it is made applicable, that is embodied in a potential innovation; the larger it is, the greater the rate of progress. This follows since at any receiving location $\bar{x}$, $\dot{K}(\bar{x},t) = -\overset{x}{U}(\bar{x},t)$, that is the realised increase in know-how (which we take to be know-how implementable in terms of a realisable innovation) is equal to the realised 'flow in'. But such a 'flow in' ($-\overset{x}{U}(\bar{x},t)$) is also dependent on (1) the 'flow out' ($\xi\overset{x}{K}(\bar{x},t)$) of the demand message, from $\bar{x}$ to its neighbour on the way to the location of inventive action ($x = 0$), and hence is directly proportional to the ξ coefficient; and (2) the resulting 'flow out' $\ell\dot{U}$ of requested (needed) new information (invention) from $x = 0$, and hence is inversely proportional to the ℓ coefficient.

12 In equation (2.3) the term $-\nu U(x,t)$ corresponds to a loss of newly produced information in passing through location x (the unit of distance centring around x) due to resistance. It is a frictional force which may be said to reduce the force associated with the term $-\xi\overset{x}{K}(x,t)$. Or, if $\dot{U}(x,t)$ is the information that must be received at $\bar{x}$ for the realisation of a new effective development action, then $-\frac{\nu}{\ell}(U(x,t))$ must be added to $\dot{U}(x,t)$ to give the total information that must be produced at $x = 0$, or transmitted when x is an intervening location, so that the demand $\overset{x}{K}(\bar{x},t)$ is met.

The verbal formulation

Need and demand for invention (new technology and know-how): the $\overset{x}{K}$ *factor*

Start with the 'Needs Stated' box at the upper left of Figure 3.1. The need and demand for invention arises from several factors:

1. Looked at nationally, a population is never satiated with goods and services and always wants more. Hence, present is the driving force to increase real Gross National Product and real income per capita through increasing the productivity of different sectors of the economy.
2. Nations whose economies are export-oriented are presently facing intense competition on the world market. They need invention to increase the competitiveness of their basic export sectors and to explore the possibilities for new ones. Hence, the second force present is to upgrade technology in export sectors.
3. Given the unequal real income per capita among the regions of a nation, there is the need and demand to raise the general productivity and real per capita income levels of lagging regions. Hence, the third force present is to raise as far as is possible the productivity of those sectors in those regions which can be most competitive with respect to national and international markets.

There is, however, one exceedingly difficult issue in considering that type of problem region which is low income. While an inadequate income (spending power) results in deficiencies in meeting a region's needs and demands, the question of what exactly these deficiencies are cannot easily be identified in practice. Given that different regions have different resources (energy, ore, traditional skills and so forth), the specification of such deficiencies must take into account resource constraints on production possibilities and their implications for requirements of labour inputs. It is no easy task to specify these deficiencies (and this is not unrelated to the aspirations of the people), and thus the need for new knowledge and know-how to increase the productivity of those sectors that can be most competitive in national and international markets.

From the standpoint of low-income problem regions, technology needs vary depending upon whether reliance is primarily placed on growth of locally based small and medium sized independent (or subcontracting) firms or upon the location of externally controlled branch plants. Further, for older regions the major problem may be not so much the current but rather the *prospect* of a deficiency of real income per capita; they must confront the inevitable decline of old industries such as ship building and steel fabricating activities. For them, the question is how to shift from old to new operations such as in the high technology sector; once again there is need for invention and new know-how to be incorporated into existing and new sectors to effect sound economic transition.

Often a region's needs for invention and innovation are covered up (never stated) and policy makers are not aware of them. This can be attributed to the different abilities regions have to perceive needs, ranging from the poverty stricken community that is almost completely isolated from society, with a primitive educational system, and thus knowing little about what is possible, to the advanced old urbanised community which fails to perceive the impending decline in its old basic industries (like traditional open-hearth steel) since currently and in the past they have been stable and strong bulwarks of the local community. There are also differences among regions in their access to the locations of new invention – differences in face-to-face contacts, institutional ties, receptivity and culture resistances, and so forth – which can delay the identification and statement of needs. The time factor can also play an important role in the statement of needs or demands. In the case of a natural disaster (earthquake, an energy crisis, a war or other major disruption affecting a region), an immediate statement of needs is often required; consequently, the issues may be incorrectly perceived and an incorrect needs statement formalised.

Communication (presentation) of need or demands: the ξ factor

Once actual needs and demands are identified, estimated, or otherwise specified, there exist the problems of making them known at the location(s) where policy decisions on the support of invention and research and development are made, or at which the desired new knowledge can be produced (the point of supply of new knowledge). This is indicated by the arrow in the upper left of Figure 3.1 going from the 'Needs Stated' box to the 'Expected Net Return' box.[1]

One aspect of this problem is apathy, the lack of motivation to take the effort to transmit information on needs and demands: the affected party may consider it not worth the effort, especially if in the past they have had their voice stifled. A second aspect of the problem is translation: people in any given location (problem region) need to put their demands and needs into the language of the receiver. Difficulties may be involved even when the sender and the receiver speak the same language due, for example, to the sender not having the proper vocabulary and/or grammar to express accurately their needs and demands.

A third aspect occurs when political representatives (leaders) of that region must transmit the needs and demands. All too often a representative fails to do so, perhaps because he is not a 100 per cent true representative (for example, he may feel compelled to state the needs and demands of the majority only), or he fails to perceive these needs and demands accurately, or is interested to some degree or entirely in his own welfare and that of his party. His statements thus distort these needs and demands.

These and other aspects constitute the problem of initiating the transmission of the message at a location (region $\bar{x}$). Once the message is initiated, it must be transmitted to the point of decision making ($x = 0$) for the creation of new knowledge or some other policy response. It may need to flow through a network of channels, spatial or nonspatial, or a series of nodes, such as a policymaker, an administrator and an assistant; all of which may slow or distort the message. Even in the case of direct transmission, as when only the policymaker is involved and he assumes the role of inventor, there is still intervening distance present (psychological, social, ideological), due to the different roles of the participants. Moreover, a channel for transmission may not exist or be blocked, as is frequently the case for minority groups. Society may judge that the cost of providing channel infrastructure may not be warranted by potential gains to society. Further, at each of the bureaucratic agencies, firm divisions, levels of a religious hierarchy and so forth to which the message must go, there may be problems of both reception (recognition) and retranslation for further transmission. This problem of reception is again one of language understanding, while the problem of retransmission is again one of apathy and ability to retranslate the message for receipt at the next node along the channel. Moreover, congestion from the information overload at a point in the transmission network may impede the transmission of the message or cause part of it to be lost.

In short, the message, however adequately stated at the initial point of propagation, may be subject to a series of distortions, losses and other alterations before it is finally received and digested at the location $x = 0$ where production of new knowledge takes place.

Invention, the production of scientific knowledge (basic research) and know-how (applied research or potential innovation): the $\dot{K}$ *factor*

Following economics we conceive of a production function for scientific knowledge as involving all kinds of inputs – labour, capital, energy, materials – and the existing stock of knowledge K at the points of production (see the boxes at the top of Figure 3.1). For the purposes of this chapter, we assume the stock is never diminished when services from it are employed in production, and does not become obsolete over time; such loss, however, may be associated with a resistance parameter ρ (or a set of such factors $\rho_1, \rho_2, \ldots$) which does not appear explicitly in the equations of the previous section. However it can be considered analogous to the ν resistance factor, and may be viewed as decreasing the speed and increasing the time it takes to pass on the full message.

The decision to produce new information is an investment decision since once the new information is produced it is added to the stock of knowledge K. Hence, like any investment decision, the volume of investment whether by private enterprise (profit-motivated) or by a public body (social welfare-motivated) or a consortium of both is determined by an appropriate benefit-cost relation over an appropriate period of time. Ignoring discounting over time, and taking the planning horizon to extend from time t_1 to t_0, we may in an oversimplified fashion state the relation as

$$\int_{t_0}^{t_1} \int_{O}^{B} c(x,t)dxdt \leqslant \int_{t_0}^{t_1} \int_{O}^{B} g(x,t)dxdt \qquad (3.1)$$

In estimating any such relation, opportunity costs must be explicitly considered where $c(x,t)$ = costs at location x at time t, and $g(x,t)$ = gains (benefits) at location x at time t. (Clearly marginal (first-order) conditions should also be stated as well as others; and in addition, numerous constraints imposed.) Moreover, unlike most production functions, there exists a highly stochastic element in invention, namely that the creation of a new idea or synthesis is unpredictable; hence the above relations should be restated in terms of expectations.

The production of scientific knowledge for policy purposes can often be disaggregated into two main parts: (1) production of basic scientific knowledge; and that of (2) applied knowledge. Following the US National Science Foundation, we may define *basic research* to consist of original investigations for the advancement of scientific knowledge, and *applied research* to consist of investigations that are directed to the discovery of new scientific knowledge that have specific commercial objectives with regard to products and processes. Our notion of the combination of diffusion, adoption and implementation corresponds to the Foundation's notion of *development* as consisting of technical activities of a non-routine nature concerned with translating research findings or other scientific knowledge into products and processes. While for this chapter we take the production of both basic and applied research to occur at and only at the aggregated location $x = 0$, there is often reason for decentralising the production of applied knowledge. One reason is a need for some ongoing applied research at any $\bar{x}$ to have available locally skills and know-how to implement an innovation when such needs to be done, or to adapt a particular innovation to local conditions. Ongoing applied research may also contribute to diversification of the economic base of a local area, a factor frequently considered desirable (Goddard, 1980). Put another way, the question for each region is: should it import all new technology or should it produce some locally? Theoretically, this question involves the 'equilibrium price-transport cost' relation governing interregional trade. If any location were to engage in applied research, the price (set equal to total average cost) would depend upon its stock of knowledge, the cost of labour (PhD, etc.) and other inputs. Further, one must consider the agglomeration economies which might be associated with local basic or applied research, and its effect on the local price. Note, again, that while from an R and D policy standpoint this benefit-cost (economic) approach is appropriate for 'motivating' invention (a supply of new knowledge), in actuality much invention takes place autonomously by the creative and curious minds concerned with 'pure understanding' only.

Disaggregating scientific knowledge into basic and applied confronts the problem of how much to allocate to basic and how much to applied. The appropriate statement of benefit-cost conditions for this trade-off problem is difficult because of the stochastic nature of the outcome of basic research. It is also difficult because there is a need for at least a modest amount of continuing basic research, for otherwise new opportunities for applied research may cease to come about. Also, continuing basic research is of great value for training personnel for research, whether basic or applied. (Ruttan, 1959, pp.202–4). Further it complicates the more aggregate resource allocation problem between production of knowledge and its diffusion.

Still finer trade-off problems exist. In encouraging invention, to what extent should there be a bias towards the saving of labour (labour-saving), capital or any factor that is expected to be progressively more expensive? Moreover, should there be allocations by sector and, if so, how should one determine them?[2]

Once expected net returns calculations are made, a decision to invest resources may be made and an actual output yielded at some point in time.

Communication (transmission and diffusion) of scientific knowledge and potential innovation to locations of possible use: the ℓ factor

Once an invention has been created and worked over so that it corresponds to a potential innovation, we reach the problem of communication (transmission and diffusion). See the shaded arrow at the right in Figure 3.1. Drawing heavily upon the work of Hägerstrand (1953) and his followers, the problem is broken down into several parts.

The first sub-problem is the actual statement of the invention and advance in scientific knowledge. Inertia may result from excessive conservatism (risk-avoidance) by those who have achieved the invention and advance. A report on an advance may be delayed until there is 100 per cent certainty about it. Or the inventor (or scientist) may lack concern with putting the advance to use or may fail to translate the advance into a form which is understandable by a potential user or a necessary intermediary.

Another sub-problem is associated with the hierarchical structure of communication (Pred, 1977a). Frequently a message must proceed from the point of invention to a primary node (for example, a capital city), then to a second-order node, a third-order node, and so forth – or through other sets of formal and informal transmission channels. The diffusion network may be exceedingly complex, involving diverse communication modes and spatial-temporal overlaps of many diffusion sub-processes (face-to-face contacts, firm-to-firm ties, agency-to-agency links, agency to individual or to firm or to other behavioural unit connections, etc.). There are usually one or more bureaucratic or organisational divisions through which the report must go, each involving a retranslation or restatement. Further delays and obstacles may appear at one or more stages, such as when making refinements to the advance or in the writing of the report in an appropriate language for future receivers. Moreover, it takes time to demonstrate an innovation successfully, and where distance intervenes, for the message to be passed on by word of mouth from one person to another. Hence, further increases occur in the length of time that it takes the invention to reach the ultimate firm or region of application.

Another sub-problem relates to the disembodiment hypothesis. As noted by Arrow (1962) who emphasises learning by doing, invention and potential innovations cannot be automatically incorporated into the existing capital stock (plant and equipment). By and large, new technology can be embodied in only new or replacement investment. However, at times some technical advance can be incorporated into existing plant and equipment, but probably at a decreasing rate of effectiveness as the vintage of capital stock gets older and older. In this context, where the higher educational level of younger labourers is found to be significant, learning and education of the labour force should be viewed as embodied progress.

Adoption and implementation

Possession of information about a potential innovation at the location of need does not insure that the potential innovation will in fact be adopted and implemented (see the boxes at the lower part of Figure 3.1). An obstacle is the inertia about doing anything, even if one has knowledge; particularly in the established sectors, such as shipbuilding, there may be the attitude: 'things have worked well (or satisfactorily enough) in the past'. Further, the knowledge of potential innovation may result only in stimulating an existing firm to make its current plant and equipment more productive to meet the competition of the new innovation, particularly if in accord with standard accounting practices the existing plant and equipment have not been fully depreciated.

Then, there are the problems associated with: obtaining the necessary financial resources; the costs of screening knowledge and making appropriate changes to existing practices (part of the problem of establishing local outlets (diffusing agencies) through which information about innovation should be distributed to local populations); royalties to pay for patents; cultural resistances to overcome; training (educating) the labour force; achieving the necessary scale of production operations to make them economic; developing new markets and the necessary marketing expertise and control; providing infrastructure (roads, power and educational facilities); furnishing other complementary (private or public) activities; halting a drain of best minds from a community (although some of the best minds in other regions may see opportunities in depressed and lagging regions); resolving basic conflicts among the many different interest groups at the local level with different objectives [or reaching a compromise through the use of a conflict management procedure (see Isard and Smith, 1983)], hedging against uncertainties; and finally providing subsidies (lower interest rates, tax rebates, guaranteed mortgages, taxfree bonds) if such are required in order that expected returns over the planning horizon equal or exceed net costs.

A la Schumpeter (1939) a major part of the problem is the provision of adequate and cheap slack resources to entrepreneurs. A la Kaniss (1977), this is akin to the problem of taking power away from the élite and transferring it to the exiles and making a community more receptive to the new ideas of exiles. Note that à la Pred (1977b) the problems of achieving an economic scale of operation and of developing new and adequate markets are threshold-type problems. Thus when innovation is primarily within market-oriented activities, it leads to a hierarchical diffusion pattern. The first level node tends to be the earliest innovator; then second level nodes when appropriate thresholds are reached; and then third level nodes, etc. Such a pattern reinforces tendencies for a hierarchical threshold-oriented structure in communication channels.

The possibility for subsidisation (the provision of infrastructure facilities, the training of the labour force in the requisite skills etc.) may provide some incentive for implementation; however, operations may still be judged to be uneconomical when not only the costs of factor inputs but also cultural and other resistances are considered. There may be other grounds for implementation, for example, an 'infant industry' argument that states that a particular innovation may yield such significant positive multiplier effects for society at large over time that it may be justified, or grounds that an economic development or economic history approach might suggest. If there are not, then implementation must be foregone.

Finally, note that if the information does not conform to what is expected as defined by the goals and aspirations of one or more key individuals, or of the community, it is often discarded or ignored. Hence, adoption of new applicable technology requires learning and the changing of perceptions as part of the communication (diffusion) process (Hägerstrand, 1953). The factors treated in the relatively new field of cognitive psychology are often of critical importance here and elsewhere in this chapter (see Isard, 1983a, 1983b and the literature cited there). In addition, we should keep in mind that many institutional innovations must be effected if the potential innovation in production is to be implemented. Here is where knowledge in the social sciences and related professions such as law can be essential, and so research may be required to obtain this knowledge.

The role of policy

In the centre of Figure 3.1 we have constructed a policy circle. At every point in the process discussed in this chapter policy may and often does enter. Policy exists at the start of the process through encouraging and helping regions to state their needs. Through the provision of monitoring of communication channels it affects the speed and ease by which the message is communicated. The very decision whether or not to invest in the production of invention is a policy issue. The dissemination (diffusion) of new basic knowledge and its transformation into applied knowledge ready for innovation is a function of policies in force. Adoption and implementation are, as already suggested, affected by numerous types of policies. Full discussion of the role of policy will be presented in later chapters.

Conclusion

We have attempted to collect together, in a systematic way, various insights and relationships (tested or only hypothesised) on the process of research and development and its impact on the problem region.

The physical system suggested a five-fold set of factors, namely:

1 Needs and demands (the $\overset{x}{K}$ factor);
2 Communication of demands (the ξ factor);
3 Invention (basic and applied research, the $\dot{K}$ factor);
4 Communication of invention;
5 Adoption and implementation (together with communication, the ℓ factor).

While we found this set useful for our analysis it should not be considered the only fruitful one. Furthermore, our mathematical statement should not be viewed too seriously since it should be restated as a set of difference equations with time lags, and also since it violates the law of conservation. Despite these and other deficiencies, we found the framework helpful and look forward to drastic improvements of it. Finally, we have tried but cannot claim to have covered all the significant factors relating to research and development for the problem region.

Notes

1 This problem exists, however, not only at the point of time chosen to represent the beginning point for analysis in policy formulation. It also exists at any subsequent point of time when it is desirable to have feedback of information on difficulties in implementation and on changes in the spatial distribution of knowledge or other elements resulting from a policy.

2 We note that Kennedy and Thirwell (1972, pp.45–53) observe that only a small amount of private R and D is on basic research; that probably a good amount of R and D generates no new knowledge at all, but sometimes its results are spectacular; that most studies indicate that there is underinvestment in R and D (especially when externalities

are considered); that most R and D is devoted to new and improved products rather than to new processes; that evidence is inconclusive on scale economies in inventive activity; that findings are inconclusive re: the hypothesis that R and D activity is an increasing function of size of firm, or of the degree of concentration within an industry, or of the product diversification of a firm presumably because of a lower probability that additional R and D will yield worthwhile results.

References

The references include a selection of works that were consulted but which have not been specifically cited.

Arrow, K. (1962), The Economic Implications of Learning by Doing, *Review of Economic Studies*, June 1962.

Brown, L.A. (1980), *Innovation Diffusion: A New Perspective*, Methuen, London and New York.

Burswanger, H.P., Ruttan, V.W., et al. (1978), *Induced Innovation*, Johns Hopkins, Baltimore, Md.

Domanski, R. (1977), The Diffusion of Technology and Innovation on the International Level, *Peace and the Sciences*, International Institute, Vienna.

Ewers, H.J. and Wettmann, R.W. (1980), Innovation-Oriented Regional Policy, *Regional Studies*, vol. 14, pp.161–79.

Goddard, J.B. (1980), *Industrial Innovation and Regional Economic Development in Britain*, Discussion Paper No. 32, Centre for Urban and Regional Development Studies, University of Newcastle-upon-Tyne.

Hägerstrand, T. (1953), *Innovationsforloppet ur Korologisk Synpunkt*, Gleerup, and translated by A. Pred as *Innovation Diffusion as a Spatial Process*, University of Chicago Press, 1967.

Isard, W. (1983a), Social System Framework and Causal History: Part I, Learning Processes, *Conflict Management and Peace Science*, vol. 6, no. 1.

Isard, W. (1983b), Social System Framework and Causal History: Part II, Behaviour Under Stress and Cognition, *Conflict Management and Peace Science*, vol. 6, no. 2.

Isard, W. and Liossatos, P. (1975), Parallels from Physics for Space-Time Development Models: Part I, *Regional Science and Urban Economics*, vol. V, no. 1.

Isard, W. and Liossatos, P. (1979), *Spatial Dynamics and Optimal Space-Time Development*, North Holland, New York.

Isard, W. and Smith, C. (1983), *Conflict Analysis and Practical Conflict Management Procedures*, Ballinger Publishing Co., Cambridge, Mass.
Kaniss, P. (1977), *Evolutionary Change in Hierarchical Systems: A General Theory*, Regional Science Studies Series, Cornell University.
Kennedy, C. and Thirwell, A.P. (1972), Surveys in Applied Economics: Technical Progress, *The Economic Journal*, vol. 82, no. 325, pp. 11–72.
Pred, A.R. (1977a), The Location of Economic Activity since the Early Nineteenth Century: A City-systems Perspective, in Ohlin, B., Hesselborn, P.O. and Wijkman, P.M. (eds), *The International Allocation of Economic Activity*, 1977, pp.127–47, Macmillan Press Ltd., Great Britain.
Pred, A.R. (1977b), *City Systems in Advanced Economies: Past Growth, Present Processes and Future Development Options*, Halstead, New York.
Ruttan, V.W. (1959), Usher and Schumpeter on Invention, Innovation and Technological Change, *Quarterly Journal of Economics*, vol. 73, November, pp.596–606.
Schumpeter, J.A. (1939), *Business Cycles*, McGraw-Hill, New York.
Usher, A.P. (1954), *A History of Mechanical Inventions*, 2nd edition, Harvard University Press, Cambridge, Mass.

4 Location quotients, export industries and shift-share analysis

N. SAKASHITA

1. Introduction

Identification of export industries and forecasting growth potentials of those industries for a specific region are the most important procedures in the empirical analysis of a regional economy. If we have sufficient data of input-output relations as in the case of quite a number of regions (states) in Japan, the identification of export industries is not a formidable task at all. However if we turn to the smaller units of regions, e.g. cities or towns, such data become out of our reach even for the data-conscious municipalities in Japan.

As a more intuitive indicator of exportability, regional economists favoured the concept of location quotients especially because they are easily calculated with a modest degree of data requirement. Let the share of the employment of industry i in region j in the total employment of the same region be λ_i^j, and the national counterpart of the share be λ_i^o, then the location quotient of industry i in region j, q_i^j, is simply defined by

$$q_i^j = \lambda_i^j / \lambda_i^o \tag{1.1}$$

If the value of q_i^j is larger than unity, it may indicate that region j is more or less specialised in industry i so that we can safely conjecture that industry i may be an export industry for region j. So far so simple and so clear.

The above statement is, however, totally dependent on an intuitive conjecture and is not based on any rigorous economic theory. Regional economists were well aware of this weakness of the concept of location quotients, but they carefully avoided the discussion of the theoretical foundation of the concept, perhaps being afraid to lose this all-round convenient tool of empirical analysis under certain conditions where it is not justifiable to use the concept.

In 1975, Mayer and Pleeter bravely broke the silence and examined the conditions under which a more-than-unity value of the location quotient for an industry actually meant that the industry was an export-oriented one, using a neoclassical two-region model with three industries. In their analysis one of the industries was supposed to be producing a non-tradable commodity. Their problem consciousness and their method of approach can be highly appreciated, but there is a methodological drawback in their analysis: they applied a mathematical technique of total differentiation in analysing cross-sectional differences among regions, but that method is only justifiable for an extreme case in which an almost infinite number of regions are scattered as a continuous spectrum of regional characteristics, but this is certainly not applicable to the case of the discrete two-region economy which they formulated.

In this chapter we adopt a simpler two-region two-industry model to analyse the relations among the exogenous conditions, the exporting or importing property of particular industry in a particular region, and the relevant value of the location quotient without methodological difficulties. Our two-industry assumption can be justified in an advanced economy where almost all commodities (even services) are tradable given the high technologies of transportation and communication.

In addition we discuss the relation between location quotient analysis and shift-share analysis by a somewhat more specific mode in a dynamic setting. Shift-share analysis is another intuitive tool used in dynamic regional economics. Some efforts to establish a theoretical background to the shift-share analysis have already been made (e.g. Sakashita, 1973), but so far were not so successful. The present chapter could be a first step to its further theoretical elaboration.

2. Assumptions and symbols

We postulate the following eight assumptions regarding our theoretical model.

1 The national economy consists of two regions, and two factors of production, capital and labour, are immobile between regions at least in the short run.
2 Both regions produce two types of final commodities by the same technologies (i.e. by a common production function for each of the final commodities) and consume them. The interregional movement of final commodities and the intraregional interindustry movement of factors of production are completely free.
3 The national economy itself is a closed one so that there is no international import or export.
4 Labour employment as a factor of production and the size of population are proportional to each other by a fixed and interregionally common ratio so that they can be treated as a single variable.
5 Each region has a specific factor endowment in the short run so that regional ratios of factor endowment are exogenously fixed at least in that short run.
6 As for the mobile commodities or factors, perfect competition prevails interregionally and intraregionally so that there is a full employment or full utilisation of factors.
7 The production function of each industry is linear homogeneous, twice continuously differentiable, and strictly quasi-concave; in addition there will be no reversal of factor intensities between two industries.
8 The per capita demand function for each final commodity is the same among regions except for a shift parameter, and the arguments of the per capita demand function are the relative price of two commodities and per capita income.

The above assumptions are of course restrictive in their nature but none of them are particularly purposeful, and altogether they describe an ordinary world of neoclassical economy.

Symbols in our model, except for the already defined λ_i^j, λ_i^o and q_i^j, are defined as follows using *a* and *b* as regional superfixes and 1 and 2 as industrial suffixes:

k_i = capital – labour ratio of industry i (no regional difference), i = 1, 2;

$f_i(k_i)$ = average labour productivity function of industry i;

p_i = price of the final commodity produced by industry i ($p_1 = 1$ as the numeraire);

$\bar{k}^j$ = factor endowment (regional capital – labour) ratio of region j, j = *a, b*;

x_i^j = per capita output of final commodity i in region j;

y^j = per capita income in region j in terms of the first final commodity;

d_i^j = per capita demand for final commodity i in region j;

$e_i^j = x_i^j - d_i^j$ = per capita export of final commodity i from region j;

$\bar{n}^j$ = proportion of the national population in region j; $(\bar{n}^a + \bar{n}^b \equiv 1)$;

$f_i' = \dfrac{df_i}{dk_i}$

α^j = a shift parameter in the demand function of region j.

Henceforth we shall call final commodities simply commodities, and factors of production simply factors.

3. Interregional general equilibrium

Under the set of assumptions given in the previous section, we can formulate an interregional general equilibrium by the following equations. First of all, we have the marginal productivity relations between two industries which are common for the two regions by assumptions 2, 6 and 7.

$$f_1' = p_2 f_2' \qquad \text{: determination of rent} \qquad (3.1)$$

$$f_1 - k_1 f_1' = p_2 (f_2 - k_2 f_2') \qquad \text{: determination of wage} \qquad (3.2)$$

When p_2 is given as a common relative price for both regions, equations (3.1) and (3.2) determine k_1 and k_2 which are also common to both regions. This is the simplest case of the well-known factor-price-equalisation theorem in international economics. The uniqueness of the values of k_1 and k_2 for any specific value of p_2 is assured by the non-reversibility of factor intensities in assumption 7.

Next, we have the following two equations by the definition of λ_i^j $(i = 1, 2; j = a, b)$:

$$\lambda_1^j + \lambda_2^j \equiv 1, \; j = a, b \qquad (3.3)$$

$$\lambda_1^j k_1 + \lambda_2^j k_2 = \bar{k}^j, j = a, b \tag{3.4}$$

Since k_1 and k_2 are predetermined in the sense that they are given functions of given p_2, equations (3.3) and (3.4) suffice to determine λ_1^j and λ_2^j in each region ($j = a, b$) as functions of p_2 too.

As a third step, the x_i^j ($i = 1, 2;\ j = a, b$) are determined by the following (four) equations again as functions of p_2:

$$x_i^j = \lambda_i^j f_i(k_i), \quad i = 1, 2; j = a, b \tag{3.5}$$

These equations also determine the supply side of commodities.

Per capita income of each region in terms of the first commodity is defined by:

$$y^j = x_1^j + p_2 x_2^j, \quad j = a, b \tag{3.6}$$

and finally per capita demand for each commodity in each region is determined by the following equation owing to assumption 8:

$$d_i^j = d_i\ (p_2, y^j; \alpha^j), \ i = 1, 2; j = a, b \tag{3.7}$$

In this and the next sections, it will be assumed that $\alpha^a = \alpha^b = \alpha$, so that provisionally we have completely identical per capita demand functions for the two regions.

By equations (3.1) to (3.7), all endogenous variables except p_2 itself are determined as functions of p_2, so that our final step is to determine p_2 by either of the following two equations of supply–demand balance:

$$\bar{n}^a x_i^a + \bar{n}^b x_i^b = \bar{n}^a d_i^a + \bar{n}^b d_i^b, \quad i = 1, 2 \tag{3.8}$$

Actually since one of the two equations in (3.8) is derived from the other by using equation (3.6) and an implicit relation:

$$y^j = d_1^j + p_2 d_2^j, \quad j = a, b \tag{3.9}$$

behind equations (3.7), there is no equation redundancy (an example of the Walrasian Law).

The determination of p_2 by one of the equations in (3.8) completes our system of interregional general equilibrium in which the regional equilibrium for either of the regions *a* and *b* is determined separately to a certain extent by taking p_2, k_1, and k_2 as 'quasi-exogenous' variables for the region.

Now let us fix j for a particular region and consider the seven equations of (3.3) to (3.7) simultaneously. They form a system of simultaneous equations for seven regional endogenous variables, λ_1^j, λ_2^j, x_1^j, x_2^j, y^j, d_1^j, and d_2^j, and the latter variables are determined as functions of exogenous and quasi-exogenous variables, $\bar{k}^j$, p_2, k_1, and k_2. However, all functions in that system are common to both regions on the additional assumption of $\alpha^a = \alpha^b$ so that if $\bar{k}^a = \bar{k}^b$, by coincidence we have the same set of solutions to the seven regional endogenous variables.

Under this circumstance of *twin* regions, we have the following two consequences. First, since $\lambda_i^a = \lambda_i^b = \lambda_i$ (i = 1, 2), by the definition of equation (1.1) all four location quotients become unity, i.e.

$$q_i^j = \frac{\lambda_i^j}{\bar{n}^a \lambda_i^a + \bar{n}^b \lambda_i^b} = \frac{\lambda_i}{(\bar{n}^a + \bar{n}^b)\lambda_i} = 1, \quad i = 1, 2; j = a, b \tag{3.10}$$

Secondly, by equations (3.8) it is obvious that

$$x_i^a = x_i^b = x_i = d_i^a = d_i^b = d_i, \quad i = 1, 2 \tag{3.11}$$

so that by the definition of e_i^j we will have

$$e_i^j = 0, \qquad i = 1, 2; j = a, b \tag{3.12}$$

Equation (3.12) tell us that there will be no interregional trade of commodities (more exactly no need for it) under the circumstance of twin regions. These conclusions are by no means of much interest to us, but they form a starting point of our analysis in the following sections.

Before going on, we now define symbols for the values of variables *after* the change:

$$\tilde{q}_1^a = q_1^a(\bar{k}^a) + \Delta q_1^a(\Delta\bar{k}^a) \tag{3.13}$$

$$\tilde{q}_1^b = \tilde{q}_1^b(\bar{k}^a) + \Delta q_1^b(\Delta\bar{k}^a) \tag{3.14}$$

$$\tilde{e}_1^a = e_1^a(\bar{k}^a) + \Delta e_1^a(\Delta\bar{k}^a) \tag{3.15}$$

$$\tilde{e}_1^b = \tilde{e}_1^b(\bar{k}^a) + \Delta_1^b(\Delta\bar{k}^a), \text{etc.} \tag{3.16}$$

$$\tilde{y}^a = y^a(\bar{k}^a) + \Delta y^a(\Delta\bar{k}^a) \tag{3.17}$$

$$\tilde{y}^b = y^b(\bar{k}^a) + \Delta y^a(\Delta\bar{k}^a) \tag{3.18}$$

$$\approx{e}_1^a = e_1^a(\alpha^a) + \Delta e_1^a(\Delta\alpha^a) \tag{3.19}$$

$$\tilde{\tilde{e}}_1^b = e_1^b(\alpha^a) + \Delta e_1^b(\Delta\alpha^b), \text{ etc.} \tag{3.20}$$

4. Effect of a change in factor endowment

Starting from the initial state of twin regions, now let us assume that only $\bar{k}^a$ increases marginally; by differentiation of both sides of equations (3.3) and (3.4), we have

$$(k_1 - k_2)\frac{d\lambda_1^a}{d\bar{k}^a} = 1 - \lambda_1^a \frac{dk_1}{d\bar{k}^a} - (1 - \lambda_1^a)\frac{dk_2}{d\bar{k}^a} \tag{4.1}$$

$$(k_1 - k_2)\frac{d\lambda_1^b}{d\bar{k}^a} = \quad - \lambda_1^b \frac{dk_1}{d\bar{k}^a} - (1 - \lambda_1^b)\frac{dk_2}{d\bar{k}^a} \tag{4.2}$$

Since $\lambda_1^a = \lambda_1^b$ at the initial state, we can derive

$$\frac{d_1\ (\lambda_1^a - \lambda_1^b)}{d\bar{k}^a} = \frac{1}{k_1 - k_2} \tag{4.3}$$

from equations (4.1) and (4.2).

If we assume that always $k_1 > k_2$ on assumption 7 and without loss of generality, equation (4.3) implies that

$$\frac{d(\lambda_1^a - \lambda_1^b)}{d\bar{k}^a} > 0 \tag{4.4}$$

By the definition of location quotients, it is obvious that sign $(q_1^a - q_1^b)$ = sign $(\lambda_1^a - \lambda_1^b)$ and that it is impossible to have $(1 - q_1^a)(1 - q_1^b) > 0$ so that relations (3.10) and (4.4) mean that

$$\tilde{q}_1^a > 1 > \tilde{q}_1^b \tag{4.5}$$

after the change in $\bar{k}^a$. It is also clear that we have $\tilde{q}_2^a < 1 < \tilde{q}_2^b$. In words this means that if region *a* becomes relatively more capital-abundant than region *b*, region *a* will be more or less specialised in more capital-intensive industry 1 and it will have a more-than-unity location quotient for industry 1 and a less-than-unity location quotient for industry 2 under this specific circumstance.

On the other hand, the effect of a change in $\bar{k}^a$ on e_1^j is derived as follows; from equations (3.3) and (3.5) to (3.7) e_1^j is expressed as:

$$e_1^j = \lambda_1^j f_1(k_1) - d_1 \{p_2, \lambda_1^j f_1(k_1) + p_2(1-\lambda_1^j) f_2(k_2), \alpha\} \tag{4.6}$$

$$j = a, b$$

By total differentiation of both sides of equation (4.6) with respect to $\bar{k}^a$, we have:

$$\frac{de_1^j}{d\bar{k}^a} = \frac{d\lambda_1^j}{d\bar{k}^a} f_1 + \lambda_1^j f_1' \frac{dk_1}{d\bar{k}^a} - \left(\frac{\partial d_1}{\partial p_2}\right)^j \frac{dp_2}{d\bar{k}^a}$$

$$- \frac{\partial d_1}{\partial y^j} \left\{ \frac{d\lambda_1^j}{d\bar{k}^a} f_1 + \lambda_1^j f_1' \frac{dk_1}{d\bar{k}^a} + \frac{dp_2}{d\bar{k}^a}(1-\lambda_1^j) f_2 \right.$$

$$\left. - p_2 \frac{d\lambda_1^j}{d\bar{k}^a} f_2 - p_2(1-\lambda_1^j) f_2' \frac{dk_2}{d\bar{k}^a} \right\}, \quad j = a, b \tag{4.7}$$

At the initial state of $\bar{k}^a = \bar{k}^b$, we know that $\lambda_1^a = \lambda_1^b$, $\left(\frac{\partial d_1}{\partial p_2}\right)^a = \left(\frac{\partial d_1}{\partial p_2}\right)^b$ and $\left(\frac{\partial d_1}{\partial y^a}\right) = \left(\frac{\partial d_1}{\partial y_1^b}\right)$ therefore, the deduction of equation (4.7) for b from the same equation for a gives us:

$$\frac{d(e_1^a - e_1^b)}{d\bar{k}^a} = \left\{ f_1\left(1 - \frac{\partial d_1}{\partial y}\right) + p_2 f_2 \frac{\partial d_1}{\partial y} \right\} \frac{d(\lambda_1^a - \lambda_1^b)}{d\bar{k}^a} \tag{4.8}$$

We can safely assume that neither of two commodities is an inferior commodity in consumption so that $0 < \frac{\partial d_1}{\partial y} < 1$. With this additional assumption and relation (4.4), it is obvious that:

$$\text{sign}\left\{\frac{d(e_1^a - e_1^b)}{d\bar{k}^a}\right\} = \text{sign}\left\{\frac{d(\lambda_1^a - \lambda_1^b)}{d\bar{k}^a}\right\} = \text{positive} \tag{4.9}$$

By a similar discussion as in the case of q_1^a and q_1^b, we can say that:

$$\tilde{e}_1^a > 0 > \tilde{e}_1^b \tag{4.10}$$

as well as $\tilde{e}_2^a < 0 < \tilde{e}_2^b$ after the change. In words, capital-abundant region *a* exports capital-intensive commodity 1 and this exactly corresponds to the more-than-unity location quotient for industry 1 in region *a* under this specific circumstance; the opposite situation emerges in labour-abundant region *b* and the situation in that region is easy to spell out.

It is important to notice that we have the following equation concomitantly in the process of deduction concerning equation (4.7):

$$\begin{aligned}\frac{d(y^a - y^b)}{d\bar{k}^a} &= (f_1 - p_2 f_2)\frac{d(\lambda_1^a - \lambda_1^b)}{d\bar{k}^a} \\ &= (k_1 - k_2) f_1' \frac{d(\lambda_1^a - \lambda_1^b)}{d\bar{k}^a} > 0\end{aligned} \tag{4.11}$$

using equations (3.1) and (3.2). Apparently, therefore, $\tilde{y}^a > \tilde{y}^b$ after the change in $\bar{k}^a$, i.e. capital-abundant region *a* will now have a larger amount of per capita (per unit of labour) income than labour-abundant region *b*.

In this section we have seen that, in a setting of twin regions as the starting point, if the export of commodity 1 from region *a* is initiated by a change of the factor-endowment ratio in the same region, this 'exportability' exactly corresponds to a more-than-unity location quotient of industry 1 in region *a*, as the 'exportability' of commodity 2 from region *b* does to more-than-unity location quotient of industry 2 in region *b*. By our analysis (particularly by relation (4.9)), it has been clarified that the value of the location quotient for an industry in a region and the exportability of the commodity produced by that industry for the same region do not have any *direct causal* relationship, but they are simultaneous outcomes of changes in the common exogenous factors which determine the interregional equilibrium. We will see, therefore, a different set of outcomes for a change in different causes.

5. Effect of a change in taste

Returning to the initial state of twin regions, we analyse the effect of a marginal change in α^a from its common value α with α^b. First of all we should recall that:

$$\frac{\partial d_1}{\partial \alpha^a} = - p_2 \frac{\partial d_2}{\partial \alpha^a} \tag{5.1}$$

as an outcome of consistent consumer behaviour because of an implicit relation of (3.9), and in addition we assume that $\frac{\partial d_1}{\partial \alpha^a} < 0$.

By a similar discussion as in the beginning of the previous section we have this time:

$$\frac{d(\lambda_1^a - \lambda_1^b)}{d\alpha^a} = 0 \tag{5.2}$$

i.e. λ_1^a and λ_1^b change in the same direction and in the same amount so that all location quotients will not change from the value of unity.

On the other hand, the effects of a change in α^a on e_1^j can be analysed in a similar manner as done in the previous section and the result will be:

$$\frac{d(e_1^a - e_1^b)}{d\alpha^a} = \left\{ f_1 \left(1 - \frac{\partial d_1}{\partial y}\right) + p_2 f_2 \frac{\partial d_1}{\partial y} \right\} \frac{d(\lambda_1^a - \lambda_1^b)}{d\alpha^a}$$

$$- \frac{\partial d_1}{\partial d^a} = - \frac{\partial d_1}{\partial \alpha^a} > 0 \tag{5.3}$$

Therefore we shall have $\tilde{\tilde{e}}_1^a > 0 > \tilde{\tilde{e}}_1^b$ as well as $\tilde{\tilde{e}}_2^a < 0 < \tilde{\tilde{e}}_2^b$ after the change, and there is no correspondence between the value of the location quotient and the exportability of a particular industry in a particular region. In addition y^a and y^b remain equal in this case although both of them may change in the same direction and to the same amount (since commodity 1 loses some of the demand for it by assumption, p_2 may rise and y^a and y^b in terms of commodity 1 may increase).

6. Interregional general equilibrium for specific functions

Our analysis in the previous three sections was heavily dependent on the initial setting of twin regions; if instead we have different values of $\bar{k}^a$ and $\bar{k}^b$ the comparative-statics calculation becomes formidable even if we assume completely identical per capita demand functions in the two regions. Because of this difficulty, we introduce specific functional forms regarding production functions and demand functions to analyse a more general case of non-twin regions.

As for the production side, we introduce fixed input coefficients instead of the flexible production functions in assumption 7; m_i is the capital input coefficient and n_i is the labour input coefficient for industry i. The capital–labour ratio of each industry becomes a fixed coefficient in this case, i.e.:

$$k_i = \frac{m_i}{n_i}, \quad i = 1, 2 \tag{6.1}$$

and we again assume that:

$$k_1 > k_2 \tag{6.2}$$

without loss of generality.

As for the demand functions, we basically assume a log-linear utility function with allocation coefficients α and $(1 - \alpha)$ for commodities 1 and 2.

Now instead of equations (3.1) and (3.2), we have:

$$rm_1 + wn_1 = 1 \tag{6.3}$$

$$rm_2 + wn_2 = p_2 \tag{6.4}$$

in which r and w are rent and wage in terms of commodity 1 respectively. Solutions for r and w are:

$$r = s(n_2 - n_1 p_2) \tag{6.5}$$

$$w = s(m_1 p_2 - m_2) \tag{6.6}$$

in which $s = (m_1 n_2 - m_2 n_1)^{-1} > 0$. We need special conditions regarding k_1 and k_2, and the national factor endowment ratio, $\bar{k}$, to assure non-negativity of r and w. We shall come back to this point later.

By equations (3.3) and (3.4), we have the following solutions for λ_i^j which are independent from p_2 in this case:

$$\lambda_1^j = \frac{\bar{k}^j - k_2}{k_1 - k_2} \quad , \quad j = a\ ,\ b \tag{6.7}$$

$$\lambda_2^j = \frac{k_1 - \bar{k}^j}{k_1 - k_2} \quad , \quad j = a\ ,\ b \tag{6.8}$$

Here we assume $k_1 > \bar{k}^j > k_2$ for both regions. Solutions to x_i^j, y^j, and d_i^j are straightforwardly calculated by equations (3.5), (3.6) and (3.7) with the additional assumption of this section.

$$x_1^j = \frac{1}{n_1}\left(\frac{\bar{k}^j - k_2}{k_1 - k_2}\right) \ , \quad j = a\ ,\ b \tag{6.9}$$

$$x_2^j = \frac{1}{n_2}\left(\frac{k_1 - \bar{k}^j}{k_1 - k_2}\right) \ , \quad j = a\ ,\ b \tag{6.10}$$

$$y^j = \frac{1}{k_1 - k_2}\left\{\frac{1}{n_1}(\bar{k}^j - k_2) + \frac{1}{n_2}(k_1 - \bar{k}^j)\ p_2\right\} \ , \ j = a\ ,\ b \tag{6.11}$$

$$d_1^j = \alpha\, y^j, \qquad j = a\ ,\ b \tag{6.12}$$

$$d_2^j = \frac{(1-\alpha)\, y^j}{p_2}, \qquad j = a\ ,\ b \tag{6.13}$$

We are now in a position to carry out the calculation of equation (3.8) to obtain an explicit solution for p_2; the solution becomes surprisingly simple as:

$$p_2 = \frac{1-\alpha}{\alpha}\ \frac{n_2}{n_1}\ \frac{\bar{k} - k_2}{k_1 - \bar{k}} \tag{6.14}$$

in which $\bar{k}$ is the national factor endowment ratio defined by

$$\bar{k} = \bar{n}^a\, \bar{k}^a + \bar{n}^b\, \bar{k}^b \tag{6.15}$$

Equation (6.14) implies that the relative price of commodities is independent from the interregional allocation of factors in this model. $\bar{k}$ is also defined as a doubly weighted average of k_1 and k_2 so that we can safely say that $k_1 - \bar{k} > 0$ and $\bar{k} - k_2 > 0$.[1]

Coming back to (6.5) and (6.6), we need:

$$\alpha k_1 + (1 - \alpha) k_2 > \bar{k} \tag{6.16}$$

for the non-negativity of r, and:

$$\frac{\alpha}{k_1} + \frac{1-\alpha}{k_2} > \frac{1}{\bar{k}} \tag{6.17}$$

for that of w. These rather delicate conditions are met, for the set $k_1 = 5, k_2 = 2, \bar{k} = 4$, and $\alpha = 0.8$.

Substituting equation (6.14) into equations (6.11) and (6.12), we finally obtain:

$$e_1^a = x_1^a - d_1^a = \frac{1-\alpha}{n_1} \quad \frac{\bar{k}^a - \bar{k}}{k_1 - \bar{k}} \tag{6.18}$$

which is comparable with

$$\lambda_1^a - \lambda_1^b = \frac{\bar{k}^a - \bar{k}^b}{k_1 - k_2} \tag{6.19}$$

Considering equations (6.18) and (6.19) under the condition of $\bar{k}^a > \bar{k}^b$ for instance, we reach a conclusion that exportability of commodity 1 in region *a* exactly corresponds to the more than unity value of the location quotient for industry 1 in the same region for the model of this section. We can say, almost in general, that location quotients may be taken as the indicators of exportability if the latter reflects the difference in factor endowment ratios between two regions.

As an additional proposition, we have

$$y^a - y^b = \frac{\bar{k}^a - \bar{k}^b}{\alpha n_1 \ (k_1 - k_2)(k_1 - \bar{k})} \ [\{\alpha k_1 + (1 - \alpha) k_2\} - \bar{k}] > 0 \tag{6.20}$$

if $\bar{k}^a > \bar{k}^b$ and condition (6.16) is met; again we find that the difference in per capita incomes between the two regions corresponds to the difference in factor endowment ratios.

7. Shift-share analysis

So far we have assumed that $\bar{n}^j$ and $\bar{k}^j$ are fixed exogenous variables (or parameters). The labour force, however, has an incentive to move interregionally in the long run because the levels of per capita income are not equal among regions. Of course we are assuming here that all of the produced income in a region is distributed *within* the same region and therefore there is no transfer of incomes between the two regions. If there is an interregional movement of labour force, it implies changes in the amounts of employment of the respective industries in the respective regions, and that is certainly a situation which shift-share analysis is eager to deal with.

In this section we attempt to formulate a shift-share analysis on the basis of the non-twin-regions model developed in the previous section. For that purpose, we first introduce some absolute-level variables with related assumptions:

1 $\bar{K}^j$ = capital endowment in region j which is fixed, j = *a,b*

2 N_i^j = employment in industry i in region j which is changeable in the long run, i = 1, 2; j = *a, b*

3 $N = \sum_i \sum_j N_i^j$ = total amount of employment in the nation (fixed)

4 $N_i = \sum_j N_i^j$ = total employment in industry i, i = 1, 2

5 $N^j = \sum_i N_i^j$ = total employment in region j, j = *a, b*

We also define a general symbol for the instantaneous growth rate of a variable X as:

6 $X^* = \dfrac{dX}{dt} / X$

Now let us assume that at a short run equilibrium described in the previous section we observe $\bar{n}^{a*} > 0$ up to the next short run equilibrium, because $y^a > y^b$ owing to $\bar{k}^a > \bar{k}^b$. According to the new assumptions 1 and 3 (actually capital has no incentive to move because there is no interregional difference in rents), $\bar{k}^a$ and $\bar{n}^a$ are in a reciprocal relation so that we can show that:

$$\bar{k}^a{}_* = -\,\bar{n}^a{}_* \tag{7.1}$$

On the other hand, by equations (3.3) and (3.4) which were also used for the model in the previous section we have:

$$\lambda_1^{a*} = \left(\frac{\bar{k}^a}{\bar{k}^a - k_2}\right) \bar{k}^{a*} \tag{7.2}$$

$$\lambda_2^{a*} = \left(-\frac{\bar{k}^a}{k_1 - \bar{k}^a}\right) \bar{k}^{a*} \tag{7.3}$$

Since $N_1^a = \lambda_1^a \bar{n}^a N$, using (7.1), (7.2) and (7.3) with the new assumption 3, we finally have the following growth (or decline) formula:

$$N_1^{a*} = -\frac{k_2}{\bar{k}^a - k_2} \bar{n}^{a*} \tag{7.4}$$

$$N_2^{a*} = \frac{k_1}{k_1 - \bar{k}^a} \bar{n}^{a*} \tag{7.5}$$

Symmetrically we have

$$N_1^{b*} = \left(\frac{k_2}{\bar{k}^b - k_2}\right) \frac{\bar{n}^a}{\bar{n}^b} \bar{n}^{a*} \tag{7.6}$$

$$N_2^{b*} = -\left(\frac{k_1}{k_1 - \bar{k}^b}\right) \frac{\bar{n}^a}{\bar{n}^b} \bar{n}^{a*} \tag{7.7}$$

for region *b*, and from these four equations finally we see that:

$$N_i^* = 0, \qquad i = 1, 2 \tag{7.8}$$

implying that there will be no change in employment in each industry as a whole; there will be just an across-the-border-type movement of labour from industry 2 in region *b* to the same industry in region *a* and some inter-industry reshuffle of employment within each region.

A shift-share decomposition of regional employment growth is something like:

– shift factor –

$$N^{j*} = \left\{ \sum_i \lambda_i^j (N_i^{j*} - N_i^*) \right\}$$

– share factor –

$$+ \left\{ \sum_i \lambda_i^j N_i^* \right\}, \qquad j = a, b \tag{7.9}$$

In our case equation (7.9) takes a very special form of:

$$N^{a*} = \left\{ \frac{\bar{k}^a - k_2}{k_1 - k_2} \left(- \frac{k_2}{\bar{k}^a - k_2} \bar{n}^{a*} \right) + \frac{k_1 - \bar{k}^a}{k_1 - k_2} \left(\frac{k_1}{k_1 - \bar{k}^a} \bar{n}^{a*} \right) \right\} \tag{7.10}$$

$$+ \left\{ 0 + 0 \right\} = \bar{n}^{a*}$$

for region *a*. Apparently the share factor is zero and the shift factor is composed of a negative and a positive element which together produce positive growth of total employment in region *a*.

In this section we have examined consequences of the labour force movement from region *b* to region *a* caused by the difference in per capita income between the two regions, and we have achieved a shift-share expression of interrelated changes. It is important to see that there are specific internal relationships among the different industrial elements that construct the shift factor. By the labour-force movement which initiates the shift-share changes, the factor-endowment ratios of the two regions, $\bar{k}^a$ and $\bar{k}^b$, will ultimately be converged to a common value $\bar{k}$ and the twin-region model emerges again.

8. Conclusion

In this chapter, we first examined the relationship between the exportability of a specific industry in a region and the value of the location quotient of an industry in a given region using a two-region, two-industry neoclassical model in a special setting of initially twin regions. We have found that the existence or non-existence of exact correspondence between the two characteristics (exportability and location quotient) depends on what causes initiated interregional trade.

In the section 'Interregional general equilibrium for specific functions' we formulated an operational general equilibrium model with specific forms of production and demand functions but in a more general setting of non-twin regions. For this model we have established unambiguous relationships among exportability, location quotients, regional factor endowment ratios, and interregional differentials in per capita incomes. Finally in the previous section we explored a relation between our preceding analysis and so-called shift-share analysis and established a theoretically informative expression of the latter.

In the light of our analysis in the earlier sections the conclusions which were reached by Mayer and Pleeter in 1975 can be considered generally correct for their three-industry two-region model in spite of a conceptual difficulty in their analysis. This means that the mathematical operations in their paper must be interpreted differently from their own interpretation with some additional mathematical rigour. Reformulation of a three-industry two-region model in that direction and some further study of comparative statics (concerning the behaviour of the relative price, for example) on our own model may be our next task.

Note

1 For a general case where region ^{b} has allocation coefficients β and $(1-\beta)$ distinct from region ^{a}, however, (6.14) changes into

$$p_2 = \frac{n_2}{n_1}\left\{\frac{(1-\alpha)(\bar{k}-k_2)+(\alpha-\beta)\bar{n}^b(\bar{k}^b-k_2)}{\alpha(k_1-\bar{k})+(\beta-\alpha)\bar{n}^b(k_1-\bar{k}^b)}\right\} \qquad (6.14)$$

which is dependent on the interregional allocation of factors.

References

Mayer, Wolfgang and Pleeter, Saul (1975), A Theoretical Justification for the Use of Location Quotients, *Regional Science and Urban Economics*, vol. 5, pp.343–55.

Sakashita, N. (1973), An Axiomatic Approach to Shift-and-Share Analysis, *Regional and Urban Economics*, vol. 3, no. 3, pp.263–72.

5 Land prices, negotiators' behaviour and game theory

A. L. SALLEZ*

Introduction

Experience shows that land market prices undergo violent shifts in value when land use changes, especially from agricultural to urban use; for instance, in the urban periphery the price of an agricultural field intended for residential building may increase from 10 French francs to 150. The reason for such a change may lie in the owner's attitude, but most of the time it is brought about by an intervention of the municipality, either through zoning modification or through investments in infra- or superstructures.

Various authors have tried to deal with this phenomenon using rent theories. Regnault and Sallez (1983) in that spirit built a model of land-price formation, selecting for sectors claiming land the indicators capital intensity, profit rates, and the cost of access to financial resources. That model, like those derived from other theories, implies that surplus value is created when a field switches from function 1 to function 2, the price difference per square metre ($p_2 - p_1$) exceeding the public or private investment (again per square metre) that make the transformation possible.

* The author would like to thank J. Paelinck, who developed some mathematical parts of this contribution.

Very often three actors are seen to compete for a share in the surplus value $(p_2 - p_1) \times s$, s representing the area of land:

1 the owner;
2 the buyer ('developer');
3 the state.

The state may decide to take back the surplus value through a tax levied on the field, the construction, or the increase in value observed at the moment of transaction. A local council may try to collect part of the surplus value either by negotiating a participation of future builders in a ZAC,[1] or, as in Switzerland, by making owners participate in financing the infrastructural works supposed to modify the use of their land.

As far as owner and seller are concerned, their relative power and the information they have on market prices and buyers' targets is observed to determine the effective transaction price (p_t) on which they will settle.

In what follows, we will consider two aspects of the social stakes involved in the sale of a field that is bound to change use, in particular an agricultural field being converted into residential land. The first aspect is how the increase in land value will be shared between the buyer and the seller; that problem will be tackled with static and dynamic game theory. The second aspect refers to the state taking back a portion of the surplus value; this will not be examined in the present article but a few tracks for future research, implementing coalition strategies, will be proposed.

Land-price determination through non co-operative static equilibrium between a seller and a buyer

Observing land transactions in urban or sub-urban areas, some authors have been led to reduce the market to the confrontation of two actors in a situation of bilateral monopoly in a local market. Such a situation is not unique, and other modes of imperfect competition may exist as we shall see below; a situation of bilateral monopoly frequently occurs, however, as far as land transactions are concerned. Game theory is perfectly adapted to its analysis; in the static version of a non co-operative equilibrium we are going to develop now, the following hypotheses are introduced:

H1: we consider a zero sum game, the value of which, to be shared between a buyer and a seller of land, being defined by two extreme figures corresponding to a zero profit result for one or the other protagonist;

H2: each player must avail himself of different strategies to which are associated different expectations of financial benefits;

H3: each player knows the possible strategies and profit expectations of his challenger as well as his own;

H4: the two players simultaneously choose the strategies that will be their final choice.

Players' strategies

In the case we are considering, the buyer is a developer who selects one from three strategies: to offer a high, medium or low price. The 'low-price' proposal, which constitutes the lower limit of the game, corresponds to the market price for the present agricultural use of the field; if the owner accepts this proposal he will make no profit, for he could claim the same amount from any agricultural buyer (we suppose the agricultural land market to be competitive and active).

The owner can choose from three strategies: accept, make a counter-proposal, negotiate. The highest counter-proposal constitutes the upper limit of the game; it corresponds to a zero profit for the buyer (developer).

If we suppose that the buyer contemplates building immediately after acquiring the piece of land, his future financial gain can be represented in Figure 5.1.[2]

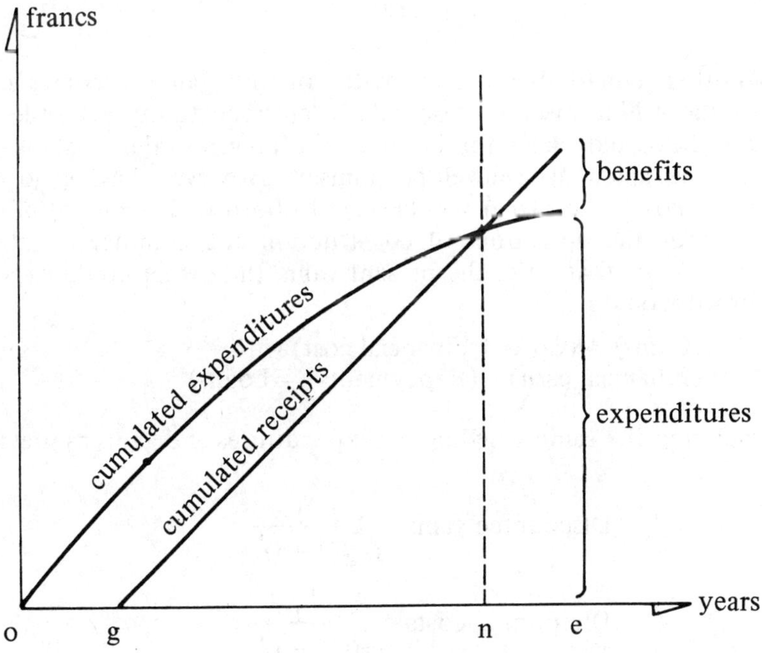

Figure 5.1

In Figure 5.1 the following definitions apply:

- o: date of the sale of the field;
- g: beginning of the sale (of apartments, flats, etc.);
- n: break-even point;
- e: end of the process.

Defining furthermore:

- v_j: sales in year j;
- k_j: expenditures in year j;
- i: interest rate on the financial market;
- p: price of the field;

we obtain a profit b_1:

$$b_1 = \sum_{j=0}^{e} \frac{v_j - k_j}{(1+i)^j} - p \tag{2.1}$$

If the profit for the developer is b = 0, the maximum price for the field will obviously be:

$$p_{max} = \sum_{j=0}^{e} \frac{v_j - k_j}{(1+i)^j} \tag{2.2}$$

Another remarkable characteristic of the game becomes evident when the selling price corresponds to an opportunity available to the owner; he could claim for his field the present value that he would earn if he acted as a developer himself. However, having no capital at his disposal, the owner would have to borrow the amount of capital needed for the operations of construction and commercialisation, at the rate i. In that case, the present value the owner could expect for his profit would be:

(Gains) – (Costs + Financial cost) with
(Financial cash) = (Repayments) – Loans)

Considering the same schedule for expenditures and gains as previously, we have:

$$\text{Discounted gains} = \sum_{j=g}^{e} \frac{v_j}{(1+i)^j} \tag{2.3}$$

$$\text{Discounted costs} = \sum_{j=0}^{e} \frac{k_j}{(1+i)^j} \tag{2.4}$$

$$\text{Discounted repayments} = (1 + i)^{-n} \sum_{j=0}^{n-1} (k_j - v_j)(1 + i^*)^{n-j} \qquad (2.5)$$

$$\text{Discounted loans} = \sum_{j=0}^{n-1} \frac{k_j - v_j}{(1 + i)^j} \qquad (2.6)$$

The opportunity cost b_2 for the owner will thus be equal to (2.3) – (2.4) – (2.5) + (2.6), or, after reduction:

$$b_2 = \sum_{j=n-1}^{e} (v_j - k_j)\,(1 + i)^{-j} - (1 + i)^{-n} \sum_{j=0}^{n-1} (k_j - v_j)\,(1 + i^*)^{n-j} \qquad (2.7)$$

The static minimax solution

In the following matrix, (Table 5.1), arbitrary transaction values have been attributed to the respective strategies of the developer and the owner. The lowest value of the game (30) corresponds to p_1 (price of the agricultural land); the highest value (110) corresponds to p_{max} of equation (2.2); the opportunity cost b_2 i.e. equation (2.7), is likely to reach intermediary values between 70 and 90.

Table 5.1

Profit matrix

		Developer's strategies: proposals		
		High	Medium	Low
Owner's strategies	Accept	90	60	30
	Counter-proposal	110	90	100
	Negotiate	100	80	70

In this zero-sum game, the maxi-min criterion being applied to solution can be seen to be 90, which corresponds to a medium proposal for the developer and a strategy of counter-proposal for the owner.[3]

Of course, the above example is very simple, but, still within the framework of a bilateral monopoly, the strategies could be diversified and the case of mixed strategies examined. Because of its simplicity, the former example implies problems that may be difficult to solve, such as: is the information about his strategies really available to the actors? Could not the solution(s) to the game be found more easily by using the real-estate agents' flair than by formally solving a linear programme?

The main criticism of the proposed model should indeed be directed against the hypotheses of certainty (H3) and choice simultaneity (H4), both flagrantly unrealistic; to overcome them, a dynamic step-by-step negotiation procedure will now be presented.

Determining the price of a field by dynamic negotiation between a seller and a buyer

An interesting question would be whether the dynamic negotiation process can be modelled within the static game, and whether that process leads to the above static equilibrium. To answer it, let us examine some hypotheses of negotiation games,[4] and see whether they can be applied to land transactions. The current hypotheses are of two kinds as shown below.

Behavioural hypotheses

H5: the actors' choices are complete, reflexive, transitive and continuous;

H6: the actors optimise, are able to do so, and use all the information available;

H7: the actors have rational expectations, in the sense that they suppose other actors to be rational, and everyone to have complete information about all others.

Under these conditions, the existence of a solution to the exchange problem can be proved; it can be found on the Pareto-optimal contract-curve, and for a very large sample of situation is even unique.

Institutional hypotheses

To limit the extensive game – that is, in a temporal form – the following institutional hypotheses must be introduced:

H8: the actors maximise their monetary profit, the total amount of which is limited within each period;

H9: in any one period, only one actor makes a bid, and his offers are repeated periodically;

H10: a final solution is reached if the most recent offer stands up against the offer the other player has first made;

H11: the information on offers and results is complete.

Under such conditions, the game admits of at least one equilibrium point; the interest of the problem consists in checking whether these conditions are present in the case of land-transaction negotiations. Very likely, the rationality hypotheses (H5, H8) and the hypotheses of rational expectations (H7) can be considered verified in reality; the hypotheses concerning the game process (H9 and H10) are also, according to us, realistic. It is doubtful, however, that the information hypotheses are satisfied, for, especially when positive externalities are speculated on (for instance, creation of equipment), some actors might have more information at their disposal than others about some aspects of the game. In such a situation, an equilibrium could be achieved, but it will not necessarily be found on the paretian exchange track; the dynamic game thus might not lead to an equilibrium solution, which would mean in practice that the negotiations would be (artificially) hampered. That is what has happened in certain well-known cases, the transactions of which have been postponed *sine die*, because of the reticence of one (or more) of the parties who have (or think they have) no access to the available information, and therefore are not confident about the results of the proposals made by other actors. The problem of the transparency of the market is all the more important in a real-estate framework, as the appearance of (negative or positive) externalities creating differential rents is much more frequent there than in many other sectors.

The result of the previous analysis is that in the land-rent sector, transactions need to be open for protagonists to find themselves in a game as close as possible to a Pareto-optimal game; besides, the consultation of governments about the matter of urbanisation is important for guaranteeing sufficiently transparent negotiations. That the seller may obtain complete information about the buyer's intentions, is true, however.

In fact, the process described above can be analysed as a system of two systems of discrete dynamic equations:

$$p_1 = \mathrm{A}p_o \tag{3.1}$$

$$p_2 = \mathrm{B}p_1 \tag{3.2}$$

where

$p_o = \begin{bmatrix} p_{10} \\ p_{20} \end{bmatrix}$, the vector of prices at the beginning of the negotiation process;

p_1 = the corresponding vector after a first counter-proposal, and where:

$$A = \begin{bmatrix} 1-\alpha & \alpha \\ 0 & 1 \end{bmatrix} \tag{3.3}$$

$$B = \begin{bmatrix} 1 & 0 \\ \beta & 1-\beta \end{bmatrix} \tag{3.4}$$

α and β being the 'cession rates' or the players' 'speeds' of adaptation to the differences remaining between price p_1 (buyer) and p_2 (seller), with, for example, $p_2 > p_1$.

The system can be rewritten by redefining the periods to include a bid from each player:

$$p_t = BAp_{t-1} \tag{3.5}$$

where

$$BA = \begin{bmatrix} 1-\alpha & \alpha \\ \beta(1-\alpha) & \alpha\beta + (1-\beta) \end{bmatrix} \tag{3.6}$$

$$BAi = i \tag{3.7}$$

which characterises a Markovian process, from which it is easy to verify that:

$p_{1\infty} = p_{2\infty}$, starting from the system:

$$(I - BA)p_\infty = 0 \tag{3.8}$$

with

$$I - BA = \begin{bmatrix} \alpha & -\alpha \\ -\beta(1-\alpha) & \beta(1-\alpha) \end{bmatrix} \tag{3.9}$$

In fact, the final medium price, p_∞, will on the whole be a weighted mean of the initial prices through:

$$p_\infty i = (BA)^\infty p_o \tag{3.10}$$

the weighting:

$$p_\infty = \mu p_{10} + (1-\mu)p_{20} \tag{3.11}$$

being a function of the cession speeds α and β. It is easy to verify that if $\alpha = 0$, $p_\infty = p_{10}$, and if $\beta = 0$, $p_\infty = p_{20}$; hence both parties should be 'cautious' in the course of the process! This can be seen again from the explicit solution[5] of:

$$p_\infty = \frac{\alpha p_{20} + \beta(1-\alpha)p_{10}}{\alpha + \beta(1-\alpha)} \text{ [from (3.10)]} \qquad (3.12)$$

with

$$(BA)^\infty = \frac{1}{\alpha + \beta(1-\alpha)} \begin{bmatrix} \beta(1-\alpha) & \alpha \\ \beta(1-\alpha) & \alpha \end{bmatrix} \qquad (3.13)$$

From expression (3.12) one can see that the first player to make a proposal will finally be at a disadvantage; that fact does not hurt our common sense, by which one should never be the first to reveal one's plans!

We can also verify that:

$$\frac{\delta p_\infty}{\delta \alpha} > 0 \qquad (3.14)$$

which means that the final price will be all the more important as the buyer s rate of concession itself is important.

As an example, and by comparison with the static game, let us consider:

$p_{10} = 30$
$p_{20} = 110$
$\alpha = 0.3$, and $\beta = 0.15$;

the convergence to p_∞ then shows a final price of 89,258; Figure 5.2 shows the convergence process.

Finally returning to a negotiation process for Table 5.1, we can reproduce the case of the 'developer's' medium proposal as an Edgeworth box diagram as shown in Figure 5.3.

In this case, 60 represents the figure in the upper centre quarter of Table 5.1, 120 is an ideal figure which the owner keeps in mind, 90 the figure of his firm counter proposal (see again Table 5.1), and 80 the expected result of a negotiation by the process exposed above, with:

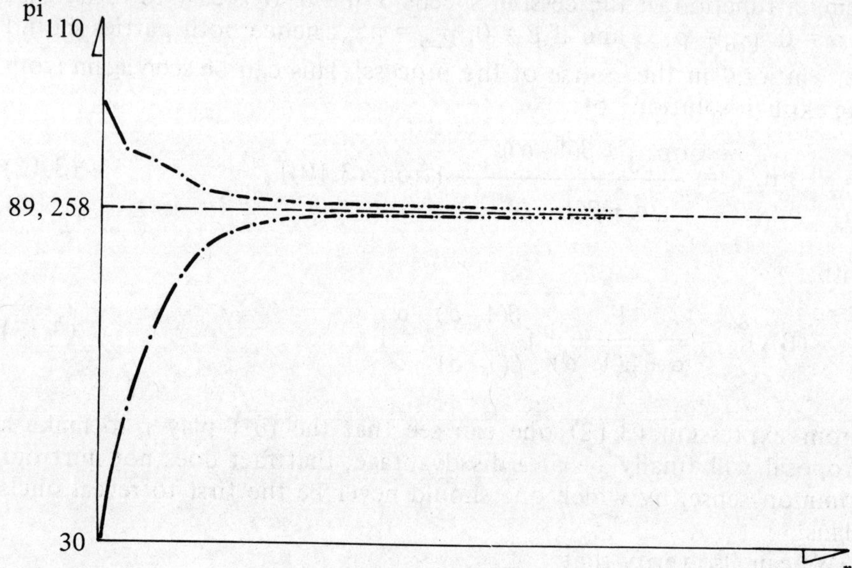

Figure 5.2

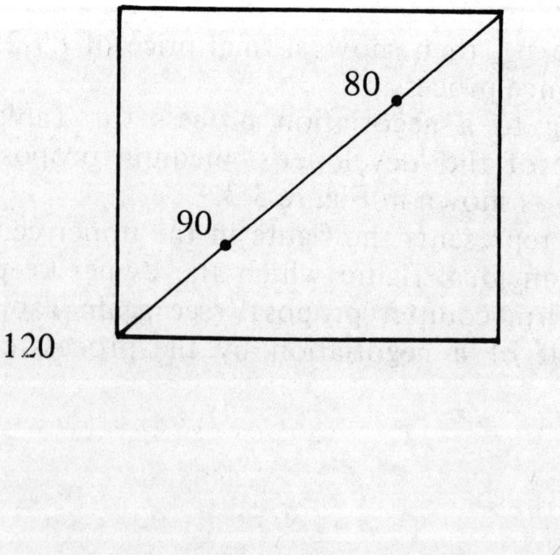

Figure 5.3

$$\frac{\alpha}{\alpha + \beta(1-\alpha)} = .33$$

$$\frac{\beta(1-\alpha)}{\alpha + \beta(1-\alpha)} = .66$$

or

$$\beta = 2\alpha(1-\alpha)^{-1}$$

which means that in terms of negotiation the buyer reacts faster than the developer, perhaps as a consequence of their different 'negotiation powers'.[6]

Concluding remarks on n-player games

A first remark refers to the case in which the state or local council intervenes in the transaction between seller and buyer. That adds one more dimension to the game (which becomes a three persons' game), and there is nothing to guarantee that this three-dimensional game will have a solution; that is a way of expressing the observation that in practice certain real-estate operations may be 'blocked' by a third party.

A local council exercising its rights of pre-emption within its zone of intervention in matters of land transactions may be a case in point. A possible solution might be that seller and buyer form a coalition to agree on a price higher than the one estimated by the public authorities, dissimulating it, however, by some sort of 'under-cover payment'.

Another form of coalition is that of a local council and a developer agreeing to the latter paying a fraction of the future excess land value to them in the framework of a ZAC convention. Next, the proprietor, or the proprietors, are expropriated, unless a voluntary agreement can be reached. Yet another way would be for the different actors to look for a perfect dynamic optimum with the help of a probabilised game tree.[7]

Let us finally, without presenting all the situations of imperfect competition that may intervene in the land market, look into the possibility of sharing excess values in a normative way in the framework of game theory. The point would be, then, to calculate certain characteristic valuators of games including coalitions. If information is available about the results that each actor can obtain by intervening marginally in a coalition (by all possible combinations), the Shapley value offers a model of fair distribution.[8] Such a system could be successfully applied to the distribution of profits among a set of proprietors choosing to associate themselves with a developer, or even to associate among themselves in the framework of an Association Foncière Urbaine (AFU, Urban Land Association) with a view to realising a land operation on their territories.

Those are just a few tentative reflections suggesting certain formalisations of game theory applies to the price formation for land on the way to urbanisation.

Notes

1 ZAC: 'Zone d'Aménagement Concerté' (Concerted development between local authorities and private or public developers).
2 See J.F. Dhuis, 1975.
3 In fact, the vector of minima for the owner is v_1 = (30, 90, 70) with max v_1 = 90, for the developer the max-vector is v_2 = (110, 90, 100) with min v_2 = 90; hence the game has a single solution in terms of pure strategies as expressed above.
4 See J. Staahl, 1977.
5 See W. Feller, 1957, pp.384–5.
6 An alternative path, via mathematical duel theory, has not been exploited; see G. Kimeldorf, 1983, especially p.55.
7 See J.P. Ponssard, 1977, pp.66–87.
8 See W. Rothengatter, 1983.

References

Dhuis, J.F. (1975), *Les Promoteurs*, Seuil, Paris.

Feller, W. (1957), *An Introduction to Probability Theory and its Applications*, vol. 1, second edition, Wiley, New York and London.

Kimeldorf, G. (1983), Duels: An Overview, in Shubik, M. (ed.), *Mathematics of Conflict*, North Holland Publishing Company, Amsterdam, pp.55–71.

Ponssard, J.P. (1977), *Logique de la négociation et théorie des jeux*, Les Editions d'Organisation, Paris.

Regnault, H. and Sallez, A. (1983), De la rente foncière au prix du sol urbain, in Paelinck, J.H.P. and Sallez, A. (eds), *Espace et Localisation*, Economica, Paris.

Rothengatter, W. (1983), Allocating common costs of public investments, paper presented at the ASRDLF – RSA conference 'Local and Micro-regional Development', Poitiers.
Staahl, J. (1977), A n-person bargaining game in the extensive form, in Henn, R. and Moeschlin, O. (eds), *Mathematical Economics and Game Theory*, Springer, Berlin, pp.155–72.

6 Regional impact of welfare policies in the European Community

W. MOLLE

Introduction

Since the war all the countries that are now members of the European Community have built up what is called the 'welfare state'. The principal motive for pursuing welfare state policies (such as full employment, income redistribution, and provision of social services) was the wish to reduce inequalities, notably economic and social ones. Indeed, serious inequalities are considered unjust or immoral and incompatible with true democracy, as well as economically inefficient (Bohm, 1973).

Regional policy, too, is generally justified by arguments of morality and 'equity', in other words, social arguments. Moreover, all EC countries justify their regional policy by economic or 'efficiency' arguments (Molle, 1983). Vanhove and Klaassen (1981, p.30) mention as major motives for regional policy: (1) full employment, (2) more equal income and welfare distribution.

Regional policies are easily associated with welfare state policies, in view of their kinship in justification and objectives. Some textbooks on welfare economics refer to regional problems (e.g. Bohm, 1973, p.79), and welfare considerations are among the foundations of the theory of regional economics (Lambooy, 1972). Nevertheless, the relation between the welfare state and regional development, is still unclear, as is, for that matter, that between the welfare state and development in general. Indeed, the OECD remarked recently (1981, p.16): 'How far the welfare state changed the pattern of advantage between classes, ethnic groups, regions, age groups and the sexes remains in dispute'.

In this chapter we will re-enter this dispute, focusing on the regions and trying to appraise the past contributions of the welfare state to regional equilibrium.

The expression 'welfare state' can be interpreted in many ways (Albeda, 1984), but in all conceptions four elements stand out which we consider essential to our study:

1 The pursuit of policies that aim at full employment;
2 Build-up of a fairly complete system of social security and a comprehensive system of income redistribution;
3 The provision of various kinds of social services;
4 The existence of a large bureaucratic apparatus to assist the government.

In line with these basic elements, we shall present the results of four types of analysis of the regional impact made by the welfare state. In the next section we shall go into the question of full employment. Following the line of fiscal and income redistribution policies, we shall next examine trends in regional income inequality. Social policies and in particular the differences in access to social services among regions, are the object of the third part of the analysis, which will also deal with the regional employment aspects of the bureaucracy. A more qualitative argument enters into the last part, dealing with the different perception of happiness or well-being among inhabitants of different regions in the EC.

Some conclusions and remarks on probable future developments will round off this contribution.

Full employment

In most European countries, unemployment was a major problem just after the war, but the situation improved rapidly as the economic recovery gained momentum. From 1950 onwards unemployment continued to decrease in most countries of the European Community; the national evolution of unemployment is given in Table 6.1.

In 1950, only in Germany and Italy were the unemployment rates high in respect of the EC average. By 1970, when EC average unemployment had reached a low of 2 per cent of total employment, there were only two countries where unemployment was relatively high namely, Italy and Ireland. The low level of unemployment attained in that year reflects the success of macro full employment policies pursued in practically all the countries of the European Community.

The regional pattern of unemployment in the period 1950–70 was very like the national one: in 1950 nearly all regions of Germany and

Table 6.1
Unemployment as a percentage of total employment by country of the EC (9), 1950–80

Year	BRD	UK	IT	FR	NL	B	DK	IR	LUX	EC
1950	8.8	1.5	9.2	0.8	1.6	5.3	3.0	4.7	0.0	4.9
1960	1.0	1.6	8.3	0.7	0.8	3.5	1.6	5.3	0.1	2.6
1970	0.6	2.6	4.9	1.3	1.0	2.5	1.1	6.3	0.0	2.1
1980	3.5	7.8	9.4	7.1	5.4	11.4	7.2	10.0	0.8	6.8

Source: Eurostat and NEI 1981.

Italy were much afflicted by unemployment, with those of Ireland and Belgium closely following. The picture changed considerably between 1950 and 1970; in line with national developments, we find that by 1970 the situation was relatively serious only for regions in Italy (unemployment rates in Mezzogiorno regions being, at 8 per cent, four times the low average of the European Community as a whole), and for the northern and north-western regions of the United Kingdom and for Ireland (where unemployment was twice to three times as high as the EC average). There was also much unemployment in certain restructuring regions, like Wallonia (NEI, 1980). One may say that in the period 1950–70 the objective of full employment had been realised in all but a few regions in the European Communities. In the 1970s that picture changed drastically.

Indeed, since 1972 unemployment has been on the increase in all countries of the European Community, attaining an average of seven per cent in 1980 (Table 6.1), and still increasing. Unemployment has become particularly serious in countries like the United Kingdom and Belgium. Mark that, although by 1980 unemployment had become an all-European affliction, the most stricken areas were still the regions of Ireland, the United Kingdom, Belgium and Southern Italy. Unemployment also rose sharply in the regions of the Netherlands. In many cases unemployment has grown most rapidly in regions where the unemployment was already quite substantial, thus leading to an increase in disparity (the standard deviation weighted by labour force rose from about 2 in 1970 to 4 in 1980, EC 1984).

The change in the unemployment level is the result of two developments: that of the labour force and that of employment. The former depends largely on demographic changes and on changes in the participation ratios; the latter hangs together with the development of total production and productivity. In many regions, especially those of the Netherlands, Ireland and Italy, the increase in unemployment was largely attributable to the rapid growth of the labour force, which the regional economy was unable to match by employment growth (EC, 1984).

Future population growth in the EC as a whole will be slow, but owing to increased participation the labour force will grow about twice as fast. Production is expected to grow at a moderate pace, while productivity will presumably rise consistently. Owing to the expected changes in employment and the labour force, unemployment will probably increase fast in the 1980s; from our prospective analysis with the LABEUR-model (Van Haselen c.s. 1983; Van Haselen and Molle, 1984) it is likely to rise to extreme levels in Ireland, the Netherlands and Belgium, affecting all the regions in these countries in more or less the same way, and putting even further out of reach both the general objective of regional full employment and the specific objective of less disparity in access to jobs.

Income distribution

Reducing income inequality among individuals is an important objective of welfare state policy in the countries of Europe. In much the same spirit, reducing regional income inequality is an important objective of regional policy in all European countries. While income inequality among persons is a widely studied topic internationally (for instance, Moroney, 1980; OECD, 1976), interregional income inequality is far less so. The reason is that unfortunately complete and consistent data of the evolution of regional incomes are not available on the level of the European Community. As a consequence, to study the development of the inequality in regional incomes one has to resort to approximations, either by analysing the components of income, or by applying to the fragmentary national statistics certain reasonings on the affects of national policies.

Let us first throw a glance at the development of the various components of household income in the EC (Table 6.2). By far the largest component of household income is wage income, its share being relatively stable at some 60 per cent. The share of entrepreneurial income, much smaller to begin with, has decreased a lot in the last two decades. Transfer incomes (comprising social security payments and a large set of welfare benefits) were still fairly small in 1960; the table shows clearly how much the share of transfers in total household income has increased, as the welfare state developed. In 1980, on the average transfer payment accounted for as much as profit income in Europe, even exceeding the latter in Germany, France and the Netherlands.

Table 6.2
Components of household income (EC) (10) in percentages, 1960–80

	Component	1960	1970	1980
1	Compensation of employee (+ social-security contribution)	57	59	59
2/4	Entrepreneurial, property income	29	25	20
5/8	Transfer income	14	16	20
9/10	Non-resident transfers	–	1	1
Total		100	100	100

Source: OECD, National Accounts of OECD countries, 1961–78 and 1964–81, vol. II, detailed tables (table 8), Paris 1983.

With a variant of the well-known shift-and-share method (Molle and Beumer, 1984), the above information on components can now be used to analyse the causes of different levels of average income among regions; to that end we distinguish:

1 *The structural effect:* categories of people who on the national level have different incomes are unequally represented in the regions. For example: experienced employees with a university degree tend to have higher incomes than persons out of work and drawing unemployment benefit; hence a region with a high proportion of unemployed will have a lower average income than a region with a flourishing economy.

2 *The residual effect:* individuals of the same type have different incomes in different regions. For example: qualified operators tend to earn more in a region with a tight labour market than in one with large pools of available labour.

Let us first take the wage component. Various national statistics on average wages by employee in the regions of the most important countries of the EC show a marked tendency to equalisation (NEI, 1980), which can be explained by economic as well as political factors. A mainly economic, structural factor is the tendency towards more equal industrial structures in all European regions (Molle c.s., 1980), that is, the tendency for high-wage and low-wage industries to be spread more equally across space. This tendency is due in part to the move of manufacturing industry to areas that used to be mainly agricultural (see Klaassen and Molle, 1982), and in part to the development of services in the same areas (see p.82).

A mainly political factor is the drive towards the equalisation of earnings among different sectors of the economy and among the various regions, in other words, the intersectoral co-ordination of nationwide wage bargaining, which attenuates both the structural and the residual effect.

One remaining source of interregional income differences may be intrasectoral specialisation in high quality work, for instance the concentration of the better paid management functions of a sector in larger cities and the low-wage production functions in rural areas. Specialisation seems largely responsible for the remaining regional income differentials in the EC (Camagni and Cappelin, 1983). However, on that score too, equalising tendencies are at work, national policies generally tending to decrease the pay differentials among professional groups with different qualifications. Molle and Beumer, 1984, have found these tendencies to explain much of the decrease in regional income differences in the Netherlands.

Hardly anything being known about the determinants of the regional distribution of profit income, we cannot elaborate on that category.

Transfer income per head is unlikely to vary much among the regions of a country, different shares of transfer income in total regional income mostly reflecting different proportions of transfer income drawers among all income receivers in the regions involved (a structural effect in our terminology). Efficient regional full employment policy tends to decrease the differences in average income due to the varying proportions of transfer income drawers. Moreover, the smaller the difference between transfer income per head and the average wage income, the smaller will be the differences in average regional income springing from different wage opportunities. With the very low transfer payments of the past, naturally differences in employment could cause large differences in regional income; their gradual improvement has contributed directly to a better equilibrium. Indirectly they have done so by maintaining in low opportunity regions a minimum level of purchasing power, which made it possible for many service industries to survive, thus providing a basis for new development.

From the fragmentary evidence available the conclusion is warranted that the decrease in regional income disparity observed in many studies (Molle and Beumer, 1984; CERC, 1980; Rossi, 1971; Van Rompuy a.o., 1979) is largely due to a combination of full employment policy and income redistribution policy (transfer incomes and wage equalisation).

Access to social services

Among the numerous writers who have tried to define the social services that are judged characteristic of the welfare state, there seems to be some consensus as to the following groups.

1 *Welfare:* the broadest category of services, covering different forms of help to almost everyone in need; this group is often merged with specific services for the disabled, injured, problem families, immigrants, etc.;
2 *Education:* essentially an investment in persons to form well educated, alert, intelligent citizens whose innate abilities have been developed and enhanced;
3 *Health:* this group of services comprises those that aim at the prevention and cure of sickness, and more generally now the obtainment of health at all stages of life for the whole nation;
4 *Art and leisure:* the expansion of state interest in this field is based on the belief that our culture is an essential part of our welfare; leisure occupations are favoured because they are felt to be beneficial to health, etc.;
5 *Other government services:* the general tasks of government, such as police, pollution control, country planning, are sometimes considered (for instance Robson, 1970) essential services of the welfare state, welfare being understood in a very general way.

These five categories of welfare services in the extended sense include many economic activities; together they seem to cover practically all non-market services including general government.

The regional dimensions of social service provisions can be measured in several ways. One line of thought is associated with the so-called social indicators. Physical indicators of availability could be the number of hospital beds, the number of books in libraries, the number of square metres of sports grounds. Another type of indicator could be the number of users of facilities, for instance the proportion of students among 1,000 inhabitants, or the number of telephone calls. For lack of consistent statistical data, analysing regional access to services either with the help of proxies of their output or by proxies of their (physical) input is difficult, however, and so it has become common practice to measure them by labour input or by the number of persons involved in providing the service. That is the approach we shall follow here.

The social services enumerated above have been grouped under five headings corresponding in outline with the industrial classification of the UN and the EC. For each category, we have established employment figures for all regions of the EC, with respect to the years 1950, 1960, 1970 and 1980. The figures in Table 6.3 give the EC totals for employment in each category. They show that in the period considered, employment in welfare state services increased from 9 to 21 million people, or by almost 3 per cent a year. In the same period, total employment grew from 82 million in 1950 to 99 million in 1980, an increase of only 0.4 per cent. As a result, the share of welfare services in total employment rose in that period from about 10 to more than 20 per cent. Increased employment in welfare activities has occurred in all member states, which indicates that the development shown here for the total EC represents indeed a highly general trend.

Table 6.3
Employment by sector of welfare state service (x 1000) in the European Community of 10, 1950–80

	Sector	1950	1960	1970	1980
91	General government	3532	4067	5289	7025
92	Education	1993	2977	4551	6188
93	Health	1796	2352	3407	4712
94	Welfare	967	985	1404	1780
95	Leisure	592	738	840	1051
9	Total	8881	11120	15592	20757

Source: NEI, FLEUR study; Eurostat, various statistics.

After this brief overall sketch, let us now turn to the regional aspects. Klaassen (1968) shows that the accessibility of social amenities largely determines the use made of them. If all citizens are to have equal opportunities to benefit from welfare services such as hospitals, cultural provisions, leisure facilities, schools etc., these services must be developed harmoniously in all regions. In the 1950s and 1960s, practically all member states had made efforts to provide welfare services for the whole population. A simple analysis of our employment data is enough to show that in the 1950s, welfare services were small and fairly concentrated in central regions. However, as they expanded, they spread to all other regions.

The regional dispersion of welfare services can be pictured more precisely by calculating disparity indexes. Quite a few statistical indicators are available for the purpose (Molle c.s., 1980), of which the index of Theil seems the best suited. It has the advantage that it allows a split-up into the effect due to differences among countries within the EC and the effect due to differences among the regions of each country. Applied to our data, the Theil index measures the difference between the regional distribution of employment in the total group of welfare services and the regional distribution of total employment. The results of the calculation are given in Table 6.4.

Table 6.4
Disparity in the regional distribution of welfare state services, (division 9), in the EC (9), 1950–80

	1950	1960	1970	1980
Regions versus EC	0.041	0.035	0.023	0.018
Countries versus EC	0.014	0.017	0.012	0.008
Regions versus FRG	0.023	0.018	0.013	0.013
Regions versus UK	0.020	0.013	0.008	0.006
Regions versus Italy	0.049	0.042	0.031	0.024
Regions versus France	0.037	0.016	0.007	0.006

Source: 1950–1960–1970: NEI, FLEUR study.
1980: Eurostat.

Table 6.4 shows that the regional disparity in access to welfare services has much decreased in the past decades (row 1) and that this was due first to a small decrease in disparity among countries but mostly to a decrease in disparity among the regions of individual member countries (rows 3–6). The disparity among countries (row 2) reflects some basic differences in the political and societal choices of the various member states of the Community.

The details of the five sectors we have distinguished earlier are also interesting. Without reproducing all the results, we present the following interesting features emerging from them. Three sectors appear to follow the general pattern very closely: general government, health, and leisure. For education and welfare services the picture is different: national differences determine to a large extent the differences among regions; the former having hardly decreased, the latter have been fairly stable too.

Welfare, solidarity and satisfaction

The conclusions reached in the previous sections resulted from the analysis of statistical data. But statistical data, objective as they may appear, can be used fallaciously. For one thing, what does income equalisation mean? Popular wisdom has it that more money does not make one happier. Moreover, some researchers say that more social help does not make people any happier either (Illich, 1971, 1977; Achterhuis, 1979). How to measure and compare the wealth and happiness of people is a problem that has been taken up by many economists, among them Easterlin (1974), Veenhoven (1984) and

Scitovsky (1976). On the whole, scientific literature tends to uphold the popular wisdom referred to above. Because the subject is too complicated for an in-depth discussion in this contribution, we will content ourselves with analysing it with the help of just two crude comparisons.

The first comparison is based on the results of a survey recently carried out by the Commission of the EC in the regions of the Community (EC, 1983), to find out how citizens appreciate the welfare position of their home region in relation to that of other regions.[1] Several criteria could be used to compare the subjective judgement of satisfaction with the equally subjective impression of regional prosperity. The situation with respect to employment opportunities appearing dominant, we have selected it as our principal indicator. The choice is justified, for the rankings of variables like the region's relative situation with respect to specific sectoral development (agriculture, industry), income levels, transport infrastructure, prospects for young people, culture, amenities, etc. are all highly correlated with the indicator 'good job opportunities'.

In Table 6.5 we have grouped the regions into seven categories, from A to G, of different levels of economic health, as perceived by the people living in each region. The upper row shows by the central indicator 'employment opportunities' that in regions of type A far more respondents than in the average EC region consider the situation of their region favourable (index 133), while in regions of type G there are far fewer (index 65).

Table 6.5

Claims for support and degree of satisfaction of citizens in regions of various degrees of economic health (index: percentage in region in respect of percentage in EC (9) as a whole)

	A	B	C	D	E	F	G
Good job opportunities	133	130	109	108	88	70	65
Needs support	17	33	83	60	113	193	273
Pays for others	230	170	96	74	52	43	35
Satisfaction	103	112	110	114	108	104	68

Figures based on data from EC 1980.

To investigate how far people's views of their own region's relative wealth influence their *solidarity,* we have summarised in rows 2 and 3 of Table 6.5 the replies to the first additional set of questions asked in the survey: do respondents consider their region to be in need of outside support, or do they think their region pays (too much) to help other regions? The responses appear to be fully consistent with the employment opportunities available in the regions: in regions of type A relatively few people think that their regions need support, while relatively many think they are paying for others; the ideas change gradually and consistently as we move from type A to type G regions.

Calls for solidarity seem indeed to be based on people's impression of their relative position on the scale of economic health. Apparently the principal instrument of the welfare state: transfer payments, is either claimed on behalf of regional equity or resented by those who think they are carrying the burden.

The survey has produced some interesting supplementary results with respect to interregional solidarity. The first concerns the support given to, respectively, the efficiency or economic, and the equity or social, arguments in regional policy. Apparently, a large majority favours the social argument rather than the economic one. Indeed in the whole EC, there are nearly twice as many supporters of aid to regions needing it most than supporters of aid to regions making the best use of it. Although there are wide variations among countries, the general picture applies to all member states.

The second interesting aspect is the European as compared to the national dimension of interregional solidarity. The survey shows that while four out of every five respondents accept to pay a fiscal contribution for aid to regions in their own country, only one in three feels the same way about aid to regions in other EC countries. That, too, applies to all the countries in the Community, with relatively small differences among countries.

After that analysis of solidarity, let us now look at the aspect of *satisfaction*. All respondents were asked whether they felt satisfied with the life they are leading in the region. From the bottom row of Table 6.5 we see that the satisfaction felt by people in the seven types of regions shows no clear correlation with their opinion on their region's general socio-economic situation. In six regional types A to F people showed themselves more or less satisfied, in the middle group (type D) even more so than in the richest group (type A). That finding seems to indicate indeed that more money or more social services do not make a man happier. Only in group G, the most deprived one, is satisfaction also far below average. But, as this group contains only Italian regions, national differences (see Table 6.6) may have influenced the picture.

To compare subjective measures such as satisfaction with more objective indicators of wealth would be interesting. Unfortunately the lack of basic comparable data forbids such a comparison on the regional level. However, on the national level we have the relevant data available. Table 6.6 gives data on satisfaction by country (column 1); these figures differ somewhat from those from the regional survey owing to conceptual differences. To these are added data on Gross Domestic Product by head (column 2) and the share of social security in total GDP (column 3). From a comparison of the columns, satisfaction and income-by-head levels seem highly correlated, although some interesting national deviations can be observed. The correlation of satisfaction with the share of the welfare or social services is negligible. The degree of satisfaction has been followed for more than 10 years now (figures being available from 1973 to 1983); the figures reveal a remarkable stability through time; the ranking of the countries stays the same all through the period.

Table 6.6

Wealth and satisfaction: national comparisons, 1981
(EC = 100)

	% share satisfied 1	GDP/P 2	% social security in GDP 3
Greece	76	46	*
Italy	88	69	92
France	92	118	101
Germany	104	120	110
Italy	109	56	91
UK	111	97	88
Belgium	112	108	113
Netherlands	121	110	118
Luxembourg	124	160	109
Denmark	125	125	109

Sources: 1. Eurobarometer 1981; 2 and 3. Eurostat: Review 1972–1981, Luxembourg 1983.

The crude analysis of subjective elements permits only the fairly general conclusion that the figures confirm the popular wisdom that more wealth, more employment, more money do not automatically make for higher satisfaction.

Conclusions and outlook

The objective of the present chapter was to try to appraise the impact of the welfare state policies on regional equilibrium in the European Community in the last 30 years. Although no rigorous framework for testing certain hypotheses could be used, the evidence gathered on full employment, income inequality and access to social services strongly points to a highly equalitarian regional effect of macro welfare policies. Moreover the material suggests that when the welfare state becomes unable to attain its goals on the macro level, negative side effects on regional equilibrium ensue. Although surveys have shown that this need not result in an immediate loss of satisfaction or happiness, it may nevertheless imply that regions with low wealth levels intensify their claims on the richer ones to transfer some of their wealth to them. At the moment such claims do not yet reach much beyond the national boundaries, but as integration progresses they are likely to be voiced louder on the European level as well.

Notes

1 Note that nine out of ten respondents considered only other regions in their own country; only one in ten took other countries into account.

References

Achterhuis, H. (1979), *De markt voor welzijn en geluk* (The market for welfare and happiness), Ambo, Baarn.

Albeda, W. (1984), *The Future of the Welfare State*, Series Work and Social Change 14, ECWS, Maastricht.

Bohm, P. (1973), *Social Efficiency: A Concise Introduction to Welfare Economics*, Macmillan, London.

Camagni, R. and Cappelin, R. (1983), Structural change and productivity growth in the European regions (paper), Milano.

CERC (1980), *Deuxième rapport sur le revenu des Français*, no. spécial 1981, Paris.

CSO (Central Statistical Office) (1980), *Regional Statistics*, HMSO, London.

Easterlin, R.A. (1974), Does economic growth improve the human lot? Some empirical evidence, in P.A. David and M.W. Ruder (eds), *Nations and Households in Economic Growth*, Academic Press, New York/London.

EC (1980), *The Europeans and Their Regions*, Commission DG XVI, Internal Documentation.

EC (1984), *The Regions of Europe*, Com. (84)40 final, Brussels.

Haselen, H. van, c.s. (1983), *Analysis and projection of labour-market balances in Europe (LABEUR)*, Commission of the EC DG XVI Internal Documentation no. 14.

Haselen, H. van and Molle, W.T.M. (1984), Analyse et projection de marchés du travail en Europe: le modèle LABEUR, in Ph. Aydalot (ed.), *Crise et Espace*, Economica, Paris, pp.322–48.

Illich, I. (1971), *Deschooling Society*, Harper, New York.

Illich, I., et al. (1977), *Disabling Professions*, Boyers, London.

Klaassen, L.H. (1968), *Social Amenities and Area Economic Growth*, (OECD), Paris.

Klaassen, L.H. and Molle, W.T.M., (eds) (1983), *Industrial Mobility and Migration in the European Community*, Gower Press, Aldershot.

Lambooy, J. (1972), Redelijke regionale politiek (Reasonable regional policy), in L.H. Klaassen (ed.), *Regionale Economie* (Regional economy), Wolters Noordhoff, Groningen.

Molle, W.T.M. with B. van Holst and H. Smit (1980), *Regional Disparity and Economic Development in the European Community*, Saxon House, Aldershot.

Molle, W.T.M. (1983), Regional Policy, in P. Coffey (ed.), *Main Economic Policy Areas of the EEC*, Nijhoff, The Hague, pp.91–117.

Molle, W.T.M. and Beumer, L. (1984), Regional income disparity in the Netherlands, 1950–1975, *Tijdschrift voor Economische en Sociale Geografie*, vol. 75, no. 2, pp.82–99.

Moroney, J.R. (1980), *Income inequality: trends and international comparisons*, Gower Press, Aldershot.

Netherlands Economic Institute (1980), *Stage V of the FLEUR project; the quantification of the explanatory variables urbanisation, labour markets, regional policy, and output markets*, internal document, Rotterdam.

OECD (1976), Income Distribution in OECD countries, in *OECD Economic Outlook*, Occasional Studies, July, pp.3–35.

OECD (1981), *Welfare State in Crisis*, OECD, Paris.

Robson, W.A. (1970), *Welfare State and Welfare Society; Illusion and Reality*, Allen Unwin, London.

Rompuy, P. van, a.o. (1979), Determinante van de regionale inkomensverdeling (Determinants of regional income distribution), XIVe Vlaams Economisch Congres, *Referaten*, Brussels.

Ross, M. (1971), Methodology of personal income estimation by country, *ESRI paper* no. 63, Dublin.

Scitovsky, T. (1976), *The Joyless Economy*, Oxford University Press, Oxford.

Vanhove, N. and Klaassen, L.H. (1980), *Regional Policy; A European Approach*, Gower Press, Aldershot.

Veenhoven, R. (ed.) (1984), *Betere wereld, gelukkiger mensen?* (Better world, happier people?), Swets & Zeitlinger, Lisse.

7 A consistent model for regional-sectoral dynamics

J. H. P. PAELINCK*

Introduction

In a series of papers[1] we have tried to develop some concepts and models that should permit the dynamics of sectoral evolution to be studied across a system of regions.

The purpose of such a study is to systematise some of the material in continuous form. First the elements of a sectoral FLEUR[2] dynamics will be presented, followed by their integration in a complete multi-regional model. Necessary extensions will be suggested before a few conclusions are presented.

FLEUR-dynamics

Evolution of the regional equilibrium shares

We will start from the equilibrium location elasticity implicit in the FLEUR-model:[3]

$$E^0_{ir} = 2 - b^{-1} a^0_{ir} \tag{2.1}$$

* The author would like to thank M. Berliant, M.B.M. de Koster and M.H. ten Raa for critical remarks; all remaining errors are his own responsibility.

with

$$b \triangleq \sum_{r=1}^{r=R} a_{ir}^{0\,2} \leqslant 1 \tag{2.2}$$

In (2.1), E_{ir}^{0} is the equilibrium location elasticity of sector i in region r, a_{ir}^{0} the equilibrium share of region r in (national) sector i's production or employment, noted $y_{i.}$; of course, $\sum_{r} a_{ir}^{0} \equiv 1$. The relation was first derived in Gravesteijn c.s. 1983; from now on we will neglect the sectoral index.

Proposition 1: The right-hand side of (2.1) can become negative.
Proof:

Suppose first that:

$$\sum_{r=1}^{r=R} a_{r}^{0\,2} \geqslant \tfrac{1}{2}\, a_{s}^{0} \tag{2.3}$$

Now:

$$\sum_{r \neq s} a_{r}^{0\,2} \geqslant a_{s}^{0} (\tfrac{1}{2} - a_{s}^{0}) \tag{2.4}$$

is satisfied for a_{s}^{0}; supposing now $a_{s}^{0} < \tfrac{1}{2}$, let us formulate the following programming problem.

$$\min_{\forall a_{r}^{0}, r \neq s} \Sigma a_{r}^{0\,2} - \lambda \left(\sum_{r \neq s} a_{r}^{0} - c \right); \; c \triangleq 1 - a_{s}^{0} \tag{2.5}$$

giving as a solution:

$$\underset{r \neq s}{a_{r}^{0}} = \frac{1 - a_{s}^{0}}{R - 1} \tag{2.6}$$

R being the number of regions, from which there results:

$$\min \sum_{r \neq s} a_{r}^{0\,2} = (R-1)^{-1} (1 - a_{s}^{0})^{2} \tag{2.7}$$

and for $R > R^{*}$, sufficiently large, (2.7) can always be made smaller than $a_{s}^{0} (\tfrac{1}{2} - a_{s}^{0}) > 0$.

So, $\sum_{r=1}^{R} a_i^{0\,2} < \frac{1}{2} a_s^0$ is possible, and E_{ir}^0 can become negative, Q.E.D.

The following developments can be suggested.[4]
Let:

$$a_{max}^0 = \max_r \{a_r^0\} \; ; \; a_{max}^0 > a_r^0, \text{ for all } r \neq max \qquad (2.8)$$

The inequality implies:

$$F = a_{max}^{0\,2} - \tfrac{1}{2} a_{max}^0 + S < 0, \text{ where } S = \sum_{r \neq max} a_r^{0\,2} \qquad (2.9)$$

It is satisfied for:

$$\boxed{\frac{\frac{1}{2} - \sqrt{\frac{1}{4} - 4S}}{2} < a_{max} < \frac{\frac{1}{2} + \sqrt{\frac{1}{4} - 4S}}{2} \text{ and } S \leqslant 1/16 = 0.0625} \qquad (2.10)$$

[0, ¼] [¼, ½]

(See Figure 7.1).

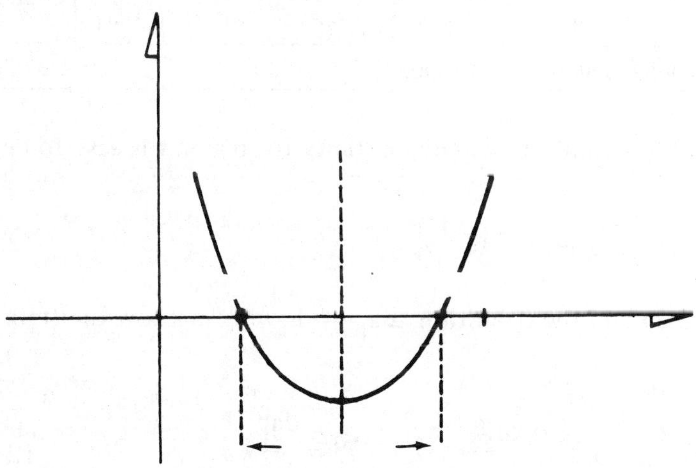

Figure 7.1

Moreover, from the inequalities $0 \leqslant a_r^0 \leqslant a_{max}^0 < 1$ $(r \neq max)$ follows that:

$$\text{the average of } a_r^0 = \frac{1 - a_{max}^0}{R^*} < a_{max}^0 \text{ or } R^* > \frac{1}{a_{max}^0} - 1, \; R^* = R-1 \qquad (2:11a)$$

and $$\sum_{r \neq max} a_r^{0\,2} < R^* a_{max}^{0\,2} \text{ or } R^* > \frac{S}{a_{max}^{0\,2}} \qquad (2.11b)$$

so:

$$\boxed{R > \max\left\{ \frac{1}{a_{max}^{0}} , \frac{S}{a_{max}^{0\,2}} + 1 \right\}} \qquad (2.12)$$

Table 7.1 gives an example.

Table 7.1

Numerical examples for (2.10) and (2.12)

S	Intervals for a^0_{max}	Corresponding intervals	Values of $a^0_r (r \neq max)$ if $a^0_r = a^0_s, \forall r,s \neq max$	
0.05	[0.138, 0.362]	[8, 3]	[0.108, 0.213]	orders of magnitude
0.03	[0.070, 0.430]	[15, 3]	[0.066, 0.285]	
0.01	[0.021, 0.479]	[48, 2]	[0.020, 0.174]	
0.0001	[0.0002, 0.4998]	[5000, 3]		

From (2.1) the equilibrium share elasticity for region r is easy to derive as:

$$E^0_{r,a} = 1 - b^{-1} a^0_r \qquad (2.13)$$

and from (2.2) and the condition $\sum_r a^0_r \equiv 1$ we also know that min b = R^{-1}.

If we define:

$$\rho \triangleq \frac{d\,\ell n\, y.}{dt} \quad , \quad \mathring{a}^0_r \triangleq \frac{da^0_r}{dt} \qquad (2.14)$$

the time path of a given a^0_r can be described by:

$$\mathring{a}^0_r = \rho a^0_r \,(1 - b^{-1} a^0_r) \qquad (2.15)$$

the sign of (2.15) depending on ρ and $1 - b^{-1} a^0_r$. With $\rho > 0$, α^0_r will increase or decrease according to whether a^0_r is smaller or larger than b.[5]

Evolution of the observed regional shares

In general one can postulate an adaptation mechanism in terms of the y_r as:

$$\mathring{y}_r = \alpha(y_r^0 - y_r) \tag{2.16}$$

leading to an adaptation equation in terms of the a_r, which is as follows:

$$\mathring{a}_r = \alpha[a_r^0 - (1 + \frac{\rho}{\alpha})a_r] \tag{2.17}$$

which is only additive (in the sense of $\sum_r \mathring{a}_r \equiv 0$)[6] if $\rho \equiv 0$. The reason is that (2.16) implies $\sum_r \mathring{y}_r = 0$, which in turn implies $\rho = 0$. An (arbitrarily) additive alternative to (2.16) would be:

$$\mathring{y}_r = \alpha(y_r^0 - y_r) + a_r \mathring{y} \tag{2.18}$$

a sort of shift-share equation (see the two terms of the right-hand side in (2.17)), which leads to the simple observed time path of the regional shares:

$$\mathring{a}_r = \alpha(a_r^0 - a_r) \tag{2.19}$$

The study of (2.18) is easy and will not be detailed here.

The time path of b

By taking the time derivative of b and substituting for $\mathring{a}_r^0$ from (2.15), one obtains:

$$\mathring{b} = 2\,\rho\, b(1 - b^{-2} \sum_r a_r^{0\,3}) \tag{2.20}$$

We now have:

Proposition 2: $1 - b^{-2} \sum_r a_r^{0^3} \leqslant 0.$

Proof: skipping the equilibrium ^{0} to ease notation, one would like to prove alternatively that:

$$(\sum_r a_r^2)^2 \leqslant (\sum_r a_r^3)(\sum_r a_r) \tag{2.21}$$

taking account of $\sum_r a_r \equiv 1$, and equality being reached if $a_i = 1$. It is easy to prove that $\alpha = 2$ is the minimum of:

$$(\sum_r a_r^{\alpha})(\sum_r a_r^{4-\alpha})$$

The first-order conditions are:

$$(\sum_r a_r^{\alpha} \ell n\, a_r)(\sum_r a_r^{4-\alpha}) - (\sum_r a_r^{\alpha})(\sum_r a_r^{4-\alpha} \ell n\, a_r) = 0 \tag{2.22}$$

leading, from symmetry, to $\alpha = 2$.

As to the second derivative, it can be computed as:

$$(\sum_r a_r^{\alpha} \ell n^2\, a_r)(\sum_r a_r^{4-\alpha}) - (\sum_r a_r^{\alpha} \ell n\, a_r)(\sum_r a_r^{4-\alpha} \ell n\, a_r)$$

$$- (\sum_r a_r^{\alpha} \ell n\, a_r)(\sum_r a_r^{4-\alpha} \ell n\, a_r) + (\sum_r a_r^{\alpha})(\sum_r a_r^{4-\alpha} \ell n^2\, a_r) \tag{2.23}$$

and for $\alpha = 2$ one has to prove:

$$\sum_r a_r^2 \ell n^2\, a_r \sum_r \alpha_r^2 - \sum_r \alpha_r^2\, \ell n\, a_r \sum_r a_r^2\, \ell n\, a_r \geqslant 0 \tag{2.24}$$

or, alternatively

$$\sum_r a_r^2 \ell n^2 a_r \geqslant \frac{(\sum_r a_r^2 \ell n\, a_r)^2}{\sum_r a_r^2} \tag{2.25}$$

or for $\beta_r \triangleq a_r^2$

$$\frac{\sum_r \beta_r \ell n^2\, a_r}{\sum_r \beta_r} \geqslant \left(\frac{\sum_r \beta_r \ell n\, a_r}{\sum_r \beta_r}\right)\left(\frac{\sum_r \beta_r \ell n\, a_r}{\sum_r \beta_r}\right) \tag{2.26}$$

and for $\omega_r \overset{\Delta}{=} \beta_r(\Sigma\beta_r)^{-1}$, $\sum_r \omega_r \equiv 1$, and $\ell n\, a_r \overset{\Delta}{=} x_r$

$$\sum_r \omega_r x_r^2 \geqslant (\sum_r \omega_r x_r)^2 \tag{2.27}$$

Now

$$\text{var } x_r = \sum_r \omega_r (x_r - \bar{x})^2 = \sum_r \omega_r x_r^2 - 2\bar{x}\Sigma\omega_r x_r + \bar{x}^2$$

$$= \sum_r \omega_r x_r^2 - \bar{x}^2 \geqslant 0 \tag{2.28}$$

Q.E.D.

An alternative proof[7] is the following.
Given $a_r \geqslant 0$ and $\sum_r a_r \equiv 1$, one has to prove

$$\sum_{r=1}^{R} a^3 \geqslant (\sum_{r=1}^{R} a_r^2)^2$$

$$\sum_{r=1}^{R} a_r^3 \geqslant (\sum_{r=1}^{R} a_r^2)^2 \Leftrightarrow \sum_{r=1}^{R} a_r \sum_{s=1}^{R} a_s^3 \geqslant (\sum_{r=1}^{R} a_r^2)^2 \tag{2.29}$$

$$\sum_{r=1}^{R} a_r^4 + \sum_{r=1}^{R} \sum_{s\neq r} a_r a_s^3 \geqslant \sum_{r=1}^{R} a_r^4 + \sum_{r=1}^{R} \sum_{s\neq r} a_r^2 a_s^2 \tag{2.30}$$

$$\sum_{r=2}^{R} \sum_{s<r} a_r a_s^3 + \sum_{r=1}^{R-1} \sum_{s>r} a_r a_s^3 - \sum_{r=2}^{R} \sum_{s<r} a_r^2 a_s^2 - \sum_{r=1}^{R-1} \sum_{s>r} a_r^2 a_s^2 \geqslant 0 \tag{2.31}$$

$$\sum_{r=2}^{R} \sum_{s<r} a_r a_s^3 + \sum_{s=2}^{R} \sum_{r<s} a_r a_s^3 - \sum_{r=2}^{R} \sum_{s<r} a_r^2 a_s^2 - \sum_{s=2}^{R} \sum_{r<s} a_r^2 a_s^2 \geqslant 0 \tag{2.32}$$

$$\sum_{r=2}^{R} \sum_{s<r} a_r a_s^3 + \sum_{r=2}^{R} \sum_{s<r} a_s a_r^3 - \sum_{r=2}^{R} \sum_{s<r} a_r^2 a_s^2 - \sum_{r=2}^{R} \sum_{s<r} a_s^2 a_r^2 \geqslant 0 \tag{2.33}$$

$$\sum_{r=2}^{R} \sum_{s<r} a_r a_s (a_r^2 + a_s^2 - 2a_r a_s) \geqslant 0 \qquad (2.34)$$

$$\sum_{r=2}^{R} \sum_{s<r} a_r a_s (a_r - a_s)^2 \geqslant 0 \qquad (2.35)$$

This means that for positive ρ, $\mathring{b} \leqslant 0$ (from (2.20).

A complete model

Let us now collect the results (see equations (2.15), (2.19) and (2.20)):

$$\dot{a}_r^0 = \rho a_r^0 (1 - b^{-1} a_r^0) \qquad (3.1)$$

$$\dot{a}_r^0 = \alpha (a_r^0 - a_r) \qquad (3.2)$$

$$\dot{b} = 2\rho\, b(1 - b^{-2} \sum_r a_r^{0\,3}) \qquad (3.3)$$

The system has the singular point

$$a_r^0 = b \qquad (3.4)$$

$$a_r = a_r^0 \qquad (3.5)$$

$$b^2 = \sum_r a_r^{0\,3} \qquad (3.6)$$

Let us first take the case of $\rho > 0$; in that case b tends towards its minimum, which we know to be R^{-1}, implying $a_r^0 = a_r = R^{-1}$, $\forall$ r, as a stationary point; this means an equalising multiregional tendency for a growing sector ($\rho > 0$).[8]

For $\rho = 0$, the system will converge to the prevailing a_r^0's (a_r^0 and b are zero, and only equation (3.2) is effective).

The case for $\rho < 0$ is more delicate. b will increase until it reaches its maximum value of 1 for one $a_r^0 = 1$, the others 0; this will be the a_{max}^0 as noted on p.93. This a_{max}^0 always exceeds b, so that a_{max}^0 will be increasing (expression (2.15)).

Proposition 3: $a_{max}^0 > b$.

Proof. From the definition of b

$$a_{max}^0 > \sum_{r \neq max} a_r^{0\,2} + a_{max}^{0\,2} \tag{3.7}$$

or

$$a_{max}^0 (1 - a_{max}^0) > \sum_{r \neq max} a_r^{0\,2} \tag{3.8}$$

$$a_{max}^0 > \frac{\sum_{r \neq max} a_r^{0\,2}}{\sum_{r \neq max} a_r^0} = \sum_{r \neq max} w_r a_r^0 \tag{3.9}$$

with $w_r \triangleq a_r^0 / \sum_{r \neq max} a_r^0$, which proves the proposition. Q.E.D.

The reverse case can be made for a_{min}^0 .

Furthermore

$$\frac{\partial \ln a_{max}^0}{\partial t} = \rho(1 - b^{-1} a_{max}^0) \tag{3.10a}$$

$$> \frac{\partial \ln a_r^0}{\partial t}, \quad r \neq max \tag{3.10b}$$

so that a_{max}^0 stays max; the constraint $a_r^0 \geqslant 0$, for all r, guarantees that finally $b_\infty = a_{max,\infty}^0 = 1$, so that $a_{max,\infty}^0 = 0$. If more than one a_{max}^0 occurs for a given t, the same constraint will guarantee that $a_{max,\infty}^0 = n^{-1}$, where n is the multiplicity of a_{max}^0.

In formal terms the system presents itself as follows: (3.11)

$$
\begin{pmatrix} \dot{a}_1^0 \\ \dot{a}_1 \\ \vdots \\ \dot{a}_R^0 \\ \dot{a}_R \\ b \end{pmatrix}
=
\begin{pmatrix}
\rho(1-b^{-1}a_1^0) & 0 & & & & 0 \\
\alpha & -\alpha & & \bigcirc & & 0 \\
 & & \ddots & & & \\
 & \bigcirc & & \rho(1-b^{-1}a_R^0) & 0 & 0 \\
 & & & \alpha & -\alpha & 0 \\
-2\rho b^{-1}a_1^{0\,2} & 0 & \cdots & -2\rho b^{-1}a_R^{0\,2} & 0 & 2\rho
\end{pmatrix}
\begin{pmatrix} a_1^0 \\ a_1 \\ \vdots \\ a_R^0 \\ a_R \\ b \end{pmatrix}
$$

a mixed linear–non-linear system of 2R + 1 differential equations.

The interregional links are formed by the equations for the b– variable, ensuring multiregional consistency. It should be added that the region-specific location functions g_r[9] are supposed to be constant.

Extensions

That takes us to the following point. In fact, the FLEUR locational g_r-functions have the various y_r's (or a_r's) as components in the form of a multiregional potential, so that the $\dot{a}_r^0$ time derivatives cannot be simply expressed as functions only of the corresponding a_r^0's (excepting the intervention of the b– variable); we will now address ourselves to that problem.

The FLEUR equilibrium values are of the form:

$$a_r^0 = by[y + g(\underline{y}_r)]^{-1} \quad , \underline{y}_r \triangleq [y_r] \tag{4.1}$$

from which it is easy to derive that [defining $g_r = g(\underline{y}_r)$] :

$$\dot{a}_r^0 = b^{-1} a_r^0 \sum_s g'_{rs} \dot{a}_s^0 + \rho a_r^0 \left[1 - b^{-1} a_r^0 (1 + \sum_s g'_{rs} a_s^0)\right] \tag{4.2}$$

which can be seen to be an extension of (2.15); moreover:

$$b = \sum_s a_r^{0\,2} (1 + \sum_s g^{\bullet}_{rs} a_s^0 E_s^0) \tag{4.3}$$

In particular (4.2) implies that system (3.11) should now be written as

$$B\ \underline{\mathring{a}} = A\ \underline{a} \tag{4.4}$$

or, provided B has an inverse

$$\underline{\mathring{a}} = B^{-1} A\ \underline{a} \tag{4.5}$$

with coefficients for equilibrium values a_r^0 this time appearing throughout the A-matrix. The additional difficulty, however, is the first right-hand side term of (4.2), which implies direct interdependence of the time derivatives; from spatial econometrics it is known that $g'_{rs} \leqslant 0$, for all r,s , so that the B^{-1}-matrix of (4.5) has not necessarily a dampening structure. Whether its structure will reverse the tendencies derived in the previous section is a problem left for further study.

Conclusions

Though the FLEUR-model has already been used empirically for programming purposes,[10] the study of multiregional-multisectoral dynamics remains complex. Indeed, additional difficulties to the ones just mentioned occur: discrete jumps,[11] mixtures of positive, negative and zero ρ_i's, changes in relative locational vectors, not to speak of consistency with interregional flows. It is the conjunction of all those factors that leads to regional cycles in the style extensively studied by Leo Klaassen, and which we should like to systematise as a conclusion to this study.

Consider the following model

$$\dot{y}_r \equiv \rho y_r(\gamma_r - 1) \tag{5.1}$$

$$\dot{\gamma}_r = \alpha(1 - y_r) \tag{5.2}$$

The variables are now defined as follows:

y_r = relative per capita income in region r (with respect to the national average);
γ_r = growth elasticity of y_r (with respect to the national rate of growth, ρ).

Equation (5.1) is an identity, equation (5.2) a hypothetical behavioural relation.

Take first the case $\rho > 0, \alpha > 0$; the following state-space Figure 7.2 represents the movement through time.

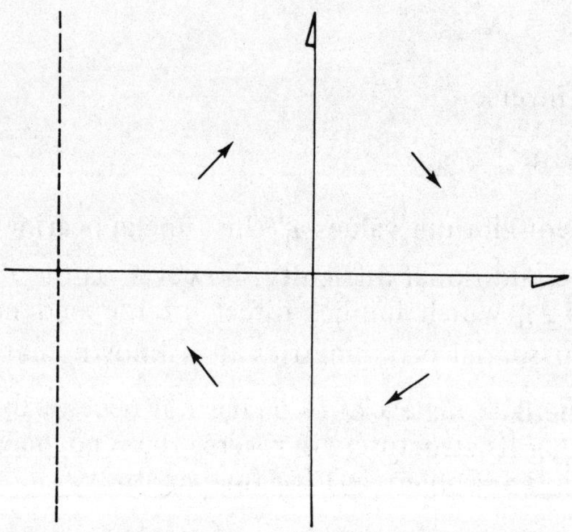

Figure 7.2

Model (5.1)–(5.2) belongs to the Lotka-Volterra family and can be solved as such; a slight respecification simplifies the solution and prevents negativity of y_r:

$$\frac{\dot{y}_r}{y_r} \equiv \frac{\partial}{\partial t}\ell n\, y_r \triangleq \dot{\eta}_r \equiv \rho(\gamma_r - 1) \tag{5.3}$$

$$\dot{\gamma}_r = -\alpha\eta_r \;,\; \eta_r \triangleq \ell n y_r \tag{5.4}$$

a linear differential model with characteristic values:

$$\lambda = \pm\, i\sqrt{\alpha\rho} \tag{5.5}$$

which is clearly oscillatory, non-damped and non-explosive in its endogenous part; in fact, η_r and γ_r oscillate permanently, the first around 0, the second around 1.

How about $\rho < 0, \alpha > 0$? Figure 7.3 pictures the situation.

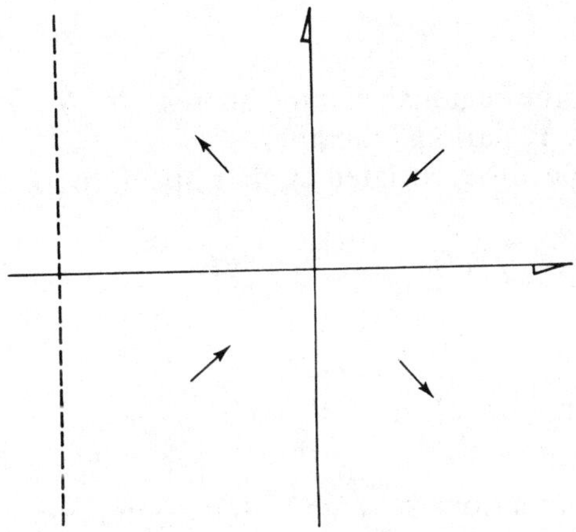

Figure 7.3

This is a diverging picture, initial 'faster' growers going down to zero per capita income, the others to 'large' relative per capita income, but with respect to an asymptotic zero national per capita income!

The following problems are mentioned:

1 Is model (5.1)–(5.2) reversible?
2 Is equation (5.2) always valid with $\alpha > 0$, or should one introduce α_r's $\gtrless 0$?
3 The model should further be checked for internal consistency, which is done hereafter.

On this internal consistency of the multiregional per capita income model the following can indeed be said.

Remember that in model (5.3) – (5.4) the first equation:

$$\dot{\eta}_r \equiv \rho(\gamma_r - 1) \qquad (5.6)$$

is an identity, valid for all r, r = 1, . . . , R, but that the second equation:

$$\dot{\gamma}_r = -\alpha\eta_r \qquad (5.7)$$

has to be consistent within the system.
The following identity is true:

$$\sum_r a_r\gamma_r \equiv 1 \qquad (5.8)$$

where the a_r's are now the regional income shares, $Y_r/Y.$, where Y_r is total income in region r, Y. national income.

Equation (5.8) can be differentiated with respect to time to give:

$$\sum_r a_r\dot{\gamma}_r + \sum_r \dot{a}_r\gamma_r \equiv \sum_r a_r\dot{\gamma}_r + \sum_r \dot{a}_r a_r^{-1} a_r\gamma_r \qquad (5.9a)$$

$$= -\alpha \sum_r a_r\eta_r + \sum_r a_r\gamma_r\dot{\eta}_r = 0 \qquad (5.9b)$$

at least for constant populations N_r and N. (or population shares η_r); hence

$$\alpha = \frac{\sum_r a_r\gamma_r\dot{\eta}_r}{\sum_r a_r\eta_r} \qquad (5.10a)$$

$$\rho\frac{\sum_r a_r\gamma_r(\gamma_r - 1)}{\sum_r a_r\eta_r} \qquad (5.10b)$$

$$= \rho\frac{\sum_r a_r\gamma_r^2 - 1}{\sum_r a_r\eta_r} \qquad (5.10c)$$

which shows that in terms of the original α the model is entirely interdependent. Mark, however, that the a_r's are themselves time-dependent; as

$$a_r \overset{\Delta}{=} w_r y_r \tag{5.11}$$

where the w_r's are the regional population shares $N_r/N.$, supposed to be constant, (5.10c) can be rewritten in terms of the original variables

$$\alpha = \rho \frac{\sum_r w_r \gamma_r^2 e^{\eta_r} - 1}{\sum_r w_r \eta_r e^{\eta_r}} \tag{5.12}$$

leading to a (partly) non-linear interdependent model, (5.6), (5.7) and (5.12).

Expression (5.12) can be linearised around $\underline{\gamma} = \underline{i}$ and $\underline{h} = \underline{0}$, giving

$$\alpha = \rho\,(2\sum_r w_r \eta_r - \sum_r w_r \gamma_r - 1) \tag{5.13}$$

which turns (5.7) into

$$\dot{\gamma}_r = \rho[1 + \sum_r \eta_r(\eta_r - 2\gamma_r)] \tag{5.14}$$

a bilinear (Lotka-Volterra) model.

Near the equilibrium values $\underline{\gamma} = \underline{i}$ and $\underline{h} = \underline{0}$, equation (5.14) becomes

$$\dot{\gamma}_r \simeq -\rho\eta_r \tag{5.15}$$

and system (5.6) – (5.15) can be shown to have 2R eigenvalues equal to $\pm i\rho$, which again means undamped cycling around $\eta_r^0 = 0$ and $\gamma_r^0 = 1$, for all r.

Notes

1 See the references.
2 On the FLEUR-model, see J.-P. Ancot and J.H.P. Paelinck, 1983; on general dynamics, see, e.g., S. Smale, 1980.

3 On the notion of location elasticity, equilibrium and adaptive, see J.H. Kuiper and J.H.P. Paelinck, 1981, and H. Gravesteijn a.o., 1984; on econometric tests of the relation derived, see J.H. Kuiper and J.H.P. Paelinck, 1982, and J.H. Kuiper, 1983. Note that (2.1) and (2.2) are approximations for large $y_{.}/g_r$-ratios, these variables to be defined further down.
4 They were, in fact, suggested by J.-P. Ancot.
5 For the discrete case, see H. Gravesteijn a.o., 1983.
6 That (2.15) is additive in this sense, whatever the value of ρ, is easy to check.
7 This proof is due to M.B.M. de Koster.
8 For an analysis in terms of densities, see H. Gravesteijn a.o.
9 See H. Gravesteijn a.o., 1983.
10 See J. Paelinck, 1983.
11 G. den Broeder and J.H.P. Paelinck, 1983 (a) and (b).

References

Ancot, J.-P. and Paelinck, J.H.P. (1983), The Spatial Econometrics of the European FLEUR-model, in D. Griffith and A. Lea (eds), *Evolving Geographical Structures*, Martinus Nijhoff Publishers, The Hague, pp.229–46.

Broeder, Guido den and Paelinck, J.H.P. (1983a), Some multiregional dynamics, paper presented at the 8th *PRSC*, Tokyo, 17–19 August.

Broeder, G. den and Paelinck, J.H.P. (1983b), Discrete Dynamics for Multiregional Developments, paper presented at the joint *ASRDLF-RSA Conference*, Poitiers, 29 August – 3 September.

Gravesteijn, H., Guesnier, B., Kuiper, J.H. and Paelinck, J.H.P. (1984), Un modèle d'évolution conjoncturelle pour un système de régions, in Ph. Aydalot (ed.), *Crise et espace*, Economica, Paris, pp.285–96.

Kuiper, J.H. and Paelinck, J.H.P. (1981), Macro, Sectoral, Regional Policies and Regional Growth, *Revue d'Economie Régionale et Urbaine*, no. 4, pp.517–34.

Kuiper, J.H. and Paelinck, J.H.P. (1982), Implémentation empirique d'élasticités de localisation, *Revue d'Economie Régionale et Urbaine*, no. 4, pp.235–46.

Kuiper, J.H. (with the assistance of H. Gravesteijn and J. Prins) (1983), Further evidence on location elasticities: the French case, paper presented at the joint *ASRDLF-RSA Conference*, Poitiers, 29 August – 3 September.

Paelinck, J.H.P. (1983), Investment and the Development of Backward Regions, in A. Heertje (ed.), *Investing in Europe's Future*, Basil

Blackwell, London, pp.152–87.
Paelinck, J.H.P. (1983), Regional Cycles, Erasmus University, Faculty of Economics, Department of Theoretical Spatial Economics, *Working papers*, Rotterdam, 19 September.
Smale, S. (1980), *The Mathematics of Time*, Springer-Verlag, New York–Heidelberg–Berlin.

PART II
LOCATION THEORY, GENERAL AND PARTIAL

8 On the timing of investment to maximise spatial diffusion

L. S. BURNS

Introduction

Explaining differences among territorial units, and the identification of their causes, is a central task of regional analysts. Appropriately, worrying about remedies for these differences is the policymaker's concern.

Regional differences are the result of many factors, and high on that list are the impediments to the spatial flows of trade, labour, activity and capital. Unblocking bottlenecks, or encouraging the conditions for regional integration, paves the way for encouraging the flows that help homogenise national and, indeed, world systems of production and consumption. Falling transport and communication costs, for example, have shrunk the economic size of the world by improving access to once-distant places and making the production of goods and services more universally and uniformly available. Put another way, removing impediments to activity flows strengthens interregional linkages and facilitates the spatial diffusion of activity. Thus, integration relies on strong linkages between territorial units.

It is argued in this chapter that the strength of interregional linkages, a necessary condition for the diffusion of growth, varies as a cyclical phenomenon driven by national growth. The empirical evidence presented later reveals that interregional linkages are tighter during periods of slack national economic growth. Similarly, as macroeconomic growth rates accelerate, subnational economies grow less in tandem. The empirical testing is prefaced by a verbal model elaborating the rationale.

The model and illustrations

To facilitate the description of the model and its later testing, the following symbols are defined:

Y = annual per capita personal income, national average;
Y_r = annual per capita personal income, region r;
$\tilde{\Delta} Y, \tilde{\Delta} Y_r$ = five-year growth rates of Y and Y_r, respectively;
$\approx\!\!\!\Delta Y_r$ = relative five-year growth rate of regional income, obtained as $\dfrac{\Delta Y_r}{\tilde{\Delta} Y}$.

The model is demand-oriented and operates this way. Firstly, an autonomous change occurs in the growth rate of Y. Secondly, this leads to a change in the mix of goods and services demanded, with those having highly income elastic demands changing the most. Thirdly, total regional output changes with the magnitude of response depending on both the composition of regional product and its income elasticity of demand. Fourthly, altered demands for factor inputs such as labour and capital will affect regional output. Fifthly, while changed materials requirements will be reflected outside as well as within a region, wages and salaries will translate directly into a change in regional per capita personal income (Y_r). The distribution of responses throughout the set of regions comprising the national territorial system reflects the degree that the system's units are linked: the more equal the spatial distribution of responses, the more highly linked are the regions.

The transmission of macroeconomic growth to the regions, and the regional impact, is illustrated by a comparison of income growth in two US regions. The regions, the East North Central (ENC) and West North Central (WNC), though adjacent to each other, differ markedly in their industry mixes. The ENC includes most of the manufacturing belt, and durable goods production generates 29 per cent of its labour and proprietors' income, compared to 18 per cent earned from this source in the nation; the region also accounts for more than three times the national share of income earned from automobile manufacturing (Browne, 1978). In contrast, the WNC, often characterised as 'the nation's breadbasket', has an intensely agricultural economic base: food products grown in the seven states comprising the region account for three times the national share of income from agricultural production (Browne, 1978); with only 8 per cent of US population, the region in 1969 accounted for more than a quarter of the nation's total farm output (US Bureau of the Census, 1972).

Given the extreme differences in the income elasticity of demand for manufacture and agricultural production, we would expect substantially different responses to overall changes in Y_r. Estimates of the demand elasticities for durables are well over unity and range upward from 1.2 (Harberger, 1960) to as high as 3 (Chow, 1957); elasticities of the demand for food, on the other hand, generally fall well below unity (Mack, 1952; Morgan, 1958). During accelerated macroeconomic growth, manufacturing-dependent regions such as the ENC, with a relatively elastic demand for its output, should fare well compared to the WNC and other rural regions where output is relatively insensitive to income fluctuations.

The period running from the late 1950s to the mid-1960s, when the economy was growing at a particularly rapid pace, illustrates the point well. During the five-year period 1955–60, real income grew by a total of 7.9 per cent, and the rate increased consistently until, by 1962–67, the five-year rate had climbed to 21.6 per cent, the highest in the entire postwar period. While the rate of growth expanded rapidly for the nation, income grew even faster in the ENC region; the ENC's rate at the beginning of the interval was about three-quarters (74 per cent) of the rate for the nation, but it had attained a rate equal to the nation's when the national rate reached its peak. During the same time interval, the WNC's growth rate dropped from 115 per cent of the nation's to 107 per cent; throughout the period since 1950, the WNC has tended to fare relatively well during periods of slack national activity, but to lose its comparative edge as shares of consumer expenditure shift from basic commodities in favour of durables during national upswings. Based on these examples, differing growth rates between regions can be attributed to the dissimilarities of their industry mix and the income elasticity of demand for their output.

The question before us deals not so much with the behaviour of specialised regional economies or with regional *vis-à-vis* national growth rates as it does with the performance of the entire system of regions under differing macroeconomic growth conditions. Still, it should be noted that parallels in the behaviour of regions may result either as effects transmitted from the national level (vertically) or as spillovers from other regions (horizontally). For our purposes, the distinction is irrelevant; the key question is what macroeconomic growth conditions promote the more integrated, or linked, response from the regions. The empirical testing that follows addresses that question.

The data and testing

As its chief descriptive measure, the analysis relies on annual per capita personal income estimated by the US Department of Commerce for states and regions and reported annually since 1948. The data have been smoothed to five-year moving averages to remove erratic annual fluctuations. From the 28-year series running from 1950 through 1978, five-year growth rates spanning the period from 1950–55 to 1972–78 are calculated for each territorial unit. As such, the growth rate, $\widetilde{\Delta Y}_r$, to some extent incorporates both future and historical elements and excludes the transitory element characteristic of annual income data. Finally, to correct for the substantial influence of macroeconomic activity on regional growth, the rates for individual states are analysed as ratios to national totals to produce estimates of $\widetilde{\widetilde{\Delta Y}}_r$; thus, when $\widetilde{\widetilde{\Delta Y}}_r > 1$, the region's individual well-being on the average is increasing relative to the nation's and, when $\widetilde{\widetilde{\Delta Y}}_r < 1$, the region lags national growth.

The empirical test involves estimating the strength of linkages between states and regions separately for periods of accelerated (1955–60 to 1962–67) and decelerated (1950–55 to 1954–59 and 1963–68 to 1973–78) national growth. Linkages are proxied by correlations between each pair of states' $\widetilde{\widetilde{\Delta Y}}_r$ for the acceleration and deceleration phases; positive correlations indicate pairs of economies' similar response at similar times. Although no valid inferences can be made about one $\widetilde{\widetilde{\Delta Y}}_r$ series 'causing' the other, the existence of a significant, positive correlation infers that the two states' economies are associated or are linked.

Separate Pearson rank-order correlations were obtained between each pair of states during each of the growth phases. The results, displayed in matrix form in Table 8.1, show the interstate correlations, with states grouped by region. Each 'X' in the table signifies a positive correlation significant at the 0.05 level or higher.

Comparison of the matrices shows that the absolute number of linkages and their pattern differs between growth phases. The lower overall level of integration occurs during acceleration and the only generalisation that can be made about the pattern is that it appears highly atomised, for the X's are few and unclustered. Of all regional cores, the industrialised ENC tops the list as the least integrated for its states show the fewest number of linkages to other states. The New England (NE) region, second in production of durables to the ENC, also ranks as the second least linked.

Table 8.1
Linkages during accelerated growth

	New England						Mid-Atl.			East North Central					West North Central							South Atlantic									East South Central				West South Central				Mountain								Pacific				
	ME	NH	VT	MA	RI	CT	NY	NJ	PA	OH	IN	IL	MI	WI	MN	IA	MO	ND	SD	NB	KS	DE	MD	DC	VA	WV	NC	SC	GA	FL	KY	TN	AL	MS	AR	LA	OK	TX	MT	ID	WY	CO	NM	AZ	UT	NV	WA	OR	CA	AK	HI
ME																																																			
NH																																																			
VT																																																			
MA																																																			
RI																																																			
CT	X																																																		
NY				X																																															
NJ				X			X																																												
PA						X																																													
OH																																																			
IN					X																																														
IL				X																																															
MI																																																			
WI																																																			
MN				X			X	X																																											
IA					X						X																																								
MO							X								X																																				
ND															X		X																																		
SD		X		X			X	X							X																																				
NB		X																	X																																
KS		X																	X	X																															
DE										X																																									
MD					X											X																																			
DC		X	X	X			X	X							X				X	X	X																														
VA					X						X					X							X																												
WV	X								X				X																																						
NC					X						X					X							X		X																										
SC											X		X																																						
GA													X													X		X																							
FL	X								X																																										
KY				X			X	X							X		X	X	X					X																											
TN										X			X									X				X			X																						
AL	X																																																		
MS							X								X		X	X													X																				
AR															X		X	X													X			X																	
LA									X																	X				X		X	X																		
OK			X																	X																															
TX	X								X	X												X				X						X				X															
MT							X			X												X																													
ID																																																			
WY		X		X			X												X	X				X																											
CO				X															X	X	X			X																	X										
NM		X																	X	X				X														X			X	X									
AZ																				X																		X					X								
UT				X			X	X							X		X		X					X							X			X							X										
NV		X		X			X	X							X				X					X							X										X	X			X						
WA											X																													X											
OR																	X	X																X	X																
CA		X					X	X							X				X					X							X										X	X			X	X					
AK																																																			
HI				X			X	X							X		X		X					X							X			X											X	X			X		

Accelerated Growth

As hypothesised, specialisation and growth unique to individual states and their industries accompanies accelerated growth. Those producing for inelastic demand emerge during a macroeconomic growth upswing as the most differentiated. The overall pattern of sparse linkages, shown in the matrix, is one of low integration and from this it follows that growth cycles are moving out of phase with one another as leading industries expand production more rapidly than others.

The system as a whole becomes more integrated during deceleration (Table 8.2): more linkages appear as macroeconomic growth slows and, in response, industries and states that grew the fastest during the acceleration phase become more similar to the others; in short, regional homogeneity increases. The three chief automobile producing states (Michigan, Ohio, Indiana) are now linked to each other whereas, during the acceleration phase, none of them were. The two North Central Regions (ENC and WNC), each with their specialised economies, now show internal cohesion as shown by the large number of linkages between their states.

Summary statistics more clearly reveal the shifting patterns of integration between growth phases. Two tables, based on the detailed information displayed in the matrices, show these data. Linkage coefficients, defined as the ratios of statistically significant linkages to the total number of possible interstate linkages, are shown by phase and by region in Table 8.3. Intraregional coefficients appear along the diagonals and interregional coefficients account for the remainder. Analysing raw numbers rather than coefficients would have distorted the results since an area's number of linkages is related to its size. The coefficient scales to size by adjusting the raw numbers by the number of possible cases; as such, they measure the actual probabilities of a statistically significant correlation occurring. The linkage coefficients, like an index, theoretically run from zero to unity: zero indicates no linkages and a coefficient of one indicates that all units are linked. Moreover, since the nation is the sum of its regions, a coefficient of one would mean complete homogeneity in the responsiveness of the system with no deviations from the national norm. According to the coefficients, the regional system is more highly integrated during deceleration than during acceleration: one-quarter of the states are linked during the former phase or twice the proportion as during acceleration.

More descriptive of the dynamics are the changes in coefficients between phases shown as first-differences in Table 8.4. The coefficients show that, during both phases, the agricultural WNC remains more integrated into the national system of regions than does the ENC. The overall coeffient increases only from 0.18 during the acceleration

Table 8.2
Linkages during decelerated growth

Decelerated Growth

	New England						Mid-Atl.			East North Central					West North Central							South Atlantic									East South Central				West South Central				Mountain								Pacific				
	ME	NH	VT	MA	RI	CT	NY	NJ	PA	OH	IN	IL	MI	WI	MN	IA	MO	ND	SD	NB	KS	DE	MD	DC	VA	WV	NC	SC	GA	FL	KY	TN	AL	MS	AR	LA	OK	TX	MT	ID	WY	CO	NM	AZ	UT	NV	WA	OR	CA	AK	HI
ME																																																			
NH																																																			
VT	X																																																		
MA	X		X																																																
RI		X																																																	
CT		X			X																																														
NY	X		X	X																																															
NJ	X		X	X			X																																												
PA																																																			
OH					X																																														
IN									X	X																																									
IL									X		X																																								
MI					X					X	X																																								
WI									X		X	X	X																																						
MN																																																			
IA												X																																							
MO									X	X	X	X	X	X																																					
ND															X	X																																			
SD															X	X		X																																	
NB															X	X		X	X																																
KS												X				X		X	X	X																															
DE												X				X		X	X	X	X																														
MD	X			X			X	X																																											
DC																X		X	X	X	X	X																													
VA	X			X				X							X				X	X			X																												
WV									X		X	X		X		X		X			X	X		X																											
NC	X		X	X			X	X															X																												
SC	X		X	X			X	X															X																												
GA	X		X	X			X	X															X				X	X																							
FL	X		X	X			X	X															X		X		X	X	X																						
KY	X		X	X			X	X															X		X		X	X	X	X																					
TN	X		X	X			X	X															X				X	X	X	X	X																				
AL												X				X		X	X		X	X		X		X																									
MS	X		X	X			X	X															X		X		X	X	X	X	X	X																			
AR																		X			X	X		X		X							X																		
LA					X					X	X		X	X			X																																		
OK									X	X	X	X	X	X			X																			X															
TX					X					X			X				X																			X	X														
MT												X				X		X	X	X	X	X		X		X							X		X																
ID																X		X	X	X	X	X		X		X							X		X				X												
WY									X		X	X		X			X									X											X														
CO															X	X		X	X	X	X	X		X		X							X						X	X	X										
NM									X		X	X		X			X									X											X				X										
AZ	X		X	X			X	X															X		X		X	X	X	X	X	X		X																	
UT									X		X	X		X			X				X	X				X							X				X		X		X		X								
NV																																																			
WA					X					X	X		X	X			X																			X	X	X													
OR									X		X	X		X			X									X											X				X		X		X						
CA									X		X	X		X			X									X											X				X		X		X			X			
AK									X		X	X		X			X				X	X				X							X				X		X		X		X		X			X	X		
HI	X		X	X			X	X															X				X	X	X	X	X	X		X										X							

Table 8.3

Linkage coefficients during accelerated and decelerated growth, by regions

Region	NE	MA	ENC	WNC	SA	ESC	WSC	Mtn	Pac
				Acceleration					
NE	0.07								
MA	0.17	0.33							
ENC	0.07	0	0						
WNC	0.14	0.24	0.03	0.33					
SA	0.15	0.15	0.16	0.11	0.14				
ESC	0.08	0.25	0.10	0.25	0.11	0.17			
WSC	0.08	0.17	0.05	0.14	0.11	0.31	0.17		
Mtn	0.15	0.25	0.03	0.23	0.08	0.09	0.06	0.29	
Pac	0.07	0.27	0.04	0.20	0.04	0.25	0.05	0.18	0.10
Total	0.11	0.19	0.06	0.18	0.12	0.16	0.12	0.15	0.12
				Deceleration					
NE	0.04								
MA	0.33	0.33							
ENC	0.07	0.20	0.70						
WNC	0	0.05	0.20	0.62					
SA	0.30	0.44	0.09	0.25	0.39				
ESC	0.38	0.50	0.05	0.14	0.56	0.50			
WSC	0.08	0.08	0.55	0.18	0.08	0.06	0.50		
Mtn	0.06	0.21	0.25	0.36	0.26	0.22	0.16	0.29	
Pac	0.13	0.33	0.52	0.14	0.20	0.20	0.30	0.28	0.30
Total	0.18	0.27	0.26	0.24	0.28	0.29	0.20	0.24	0.25

Table 8.4

Changes in linkage coefficients between accelerated and decelerated growth, by regions

	NE	MA	ENC	WNC	SA	ESC	WSC	Mtn	Pac
NE	+0.33								
MA	+0.16	0							
ENC	0	+0.20	+0.70						
WNC	–0.14	–0.19	+0.17	+0.29					
SA	+0.15	+0.29	–0.07	+0.14	+0.25				
ESC	+0.30	+0.25	–0.05	–0.11	+0.45	+0.33			
WSC	0	–0.09	+0.50	+0.04	–0.03	–0.25	+0.33		
Mtn	–0.09	–0.04	+0.22	+0.13	+0.18	+0.13	+0.10	0	
Pac	+0.06	+0.06	+0.48	–0.06	+0.16	–0.05	+0.25	+0.10	+0.20
Total	+0.07	+0.08	+0.20	+0.06	+0.16	+0.13	+0.08	+0.09	+0.13

phase to 0.24 during the deceleration (Table 8.3), or the change of 0.06 shown in Table 8.4. The ENC's coefficient, however, jumps from 0.06 to 0.26 to yield a change of 0.20. The intraregional coefficients relating a region's states to each other show that the economy of the WNC remained relatively stable, increasing from 0.33 to 0.62 as the economy moved from acceleration to deceleration, in comparison to the ENC, which rose dramatically from 0 to 0.70 between phases. Of all regions, the largest overall change in inter- and intraregional coefficients was registered for the ENC (+0.20), the regional example producing for elastic demand; the WNC, the region responding to inelastic demand, produced the smallest change (+0.06) of the nine regions.

Conclusions for policy

The existence of viable linkages is a necessary condition for regional interaction. Similarly, the diffusion of growth throughout a regional system is facilitated during periods when regions are most tightly connected. These connections vary with macroeconomic growth cycles, stronger during decelerated growth than during accelerations, as this chapter attempts to show.

The conclusions derived from this suggest that the preferred timing for placing spatially focussed investments intended to have spread effects, as for example in growth pole policy, is during periods of slowed economic growth, linkages are weakest, and chances for diffusing the benefits of growth through regional systems poorest, when the national economy is making its most rapid advances.

References

Browne, L.E. (1978), Regional Industry Mix and the Business Cycle, *New England Economic Review* (November–December 1978), Table A1, p.5; originally from unpublished data supplied by the Bureau of Economic Analysis, US Department of Commerce.

Chow, G.C. (1957), *The Demand for Automobiles in the United States*, North-Holland Publishing Co., Amsterdam.

Harberger, A.C. (1960), *The Demand for Durable Goods*, University of Chicago Press, Chicago.

Mack, R.P. (1952), Economics of Consumption, in B.F. Haley (ed.), *A Survey of Contemporary Economics*, vol II, Richard Irwin, Homewood, I1 l., pp.39–78.

Morgan, J.N. (1958), A Review of Recent Research on Consumer Behaviour, in L.H. Clark (ed.), *Consumer Behaviour: Research on Consumer Reactions,* New York University Press, New York, pp.13–37.

US Bureau of the Census (1972), *Statistical Abstract of the United States: 1972*, US Government Printing Office, Washington DC.

9 Self-organisation: the foundation of spatial order of economy and society

R. DOMAŃSKI

Introduction

The central planner may influence the spatial order in the economy and in society, but cannot arbitrarily form the socio-economic space, for that is subordinated to objective economic and social laws showing up as natural spatial tendencies. The role of a central planner is:

1 To define the spatial objectives of society, taking the natural tendencies into consideration;
2 To create conditions in which the objective economic and social laws coincide approximately with the spatial objectives of society;
3 To correct natural tendencies and achieve the objectives.

The range of corrections – interventions of the central planner – varies and depends on the level of ordering of the spatial organisation of an economy or society. If the ordering level is low – showing disorganisation – restructuring the existing spatial patterns may be necessary; in such a case the intervention range of the central planner must be wide. At a high ordering level it can be much narrower. The central planner's instruments vary too: in the former situation large investments to change the original spatial structure are indispensable; in the latter instruments of a 'regulation' type – taxes, subsidies, credits – suffice.

Theory of spatial self-organisation

To determine the natural spatial tendencies which show the workings of objective economic and social laws, a theory of spatial self-organisation can be useful. The notion of self-organisation has become popular lately because of the work for which I. Prigogine received a Nobel Prize. It is primarily known in thermodynamics, but is inspirational in chemistry and biology as well as in physics. Recently, some researchers into social problems and specialists in systems analysis have begun to apply to social systems Prigogine's theory of the behaviour of physical systems.

Prigogine's theory (G. Nicolis and I. Prigogine, 1977) shows how complex systems pass from one structure to another, or from one order to another. It considers systems which are:

1 Open to transmission of energy and matter (exchanges with their environment);
2 Far removed from an equilibrium;
3 Characterised by non-linearities.

Prigogine assumes that open systems under certain conditions develop into more and more complicated structures. He studies the influence of these conditions – departure from equilibrium and existence of non-linearities – and indicates that if they occur, the systems may, or even must, undergo evolution. The structures evolving under such conditions are called 'dissipative structures' by Prigogine, from the Latin word 'dissipatio', because they collect and disperse energy and matter from and into their environment.

Complex systems pass from one structure to another as follows. At a time of stability, the system may undergo a sudden perturbation, to which it responds by fluctuations. After exceeding a certain gradient, the fluctuations intensify, causing macroscopic movements; these bring about a new order, a new structure, which is supported by the exchange of energy and matter with the environment. Fluctuations that do not reach the marginal value of the gradient damp and vanish. The next wave of perturbation and fluctuation will lead to more complicated structures.

The first attempts at applying the notion of spatial self-organisation to spatial-economic systems have been very promising (P.M. Allen and M. Sanglier, 1979; R. Domański and A.P. Wierzbicki, 1981 and 1983). Needless to say that these efforts did not constitute a mechanical transfer of thermodynamic notions to the domain of spatial planning, but were rather inspired by a conception (R. Domański, 1983, RSA) of which the multidisciplinary range had been proved.

In the present contribution we shall express the characteristic behaviour of spatial-economic systems in terms of self-organisation theory; such systems are dissipative structures in that they are connected with their environment by flows of goods, persons and information. In geographic and economic science the term disequilibrium has another meaning to that used in thermodynamics: thermodynamical disequilibrium denotes the state of a system which in economic geography is called *differentiation*. Non-linearities are common in spatial-economic systems: large-scale and agglomeration economies are of special importance to the development of cities and regions.

In spatial-economic systems, innovations or impulses, broadly speaking, are the parallels of perturbations. For instance, new investments in poorly developed regions, modernisation of the sectoral structure of a regional economy, new technologies and products, new methods of environmental protection and organisational progress. Reforms in the functioning of a socio-economic system are innovations of an organisational character. Sudden breaks in the economy from domestic or international causes are yet another type of perturbation.

The term 'fluctuation', which is incongruous with the situations considered and moreover has a specific meaning in business-cycle theory, will be abandoned and replaced with the expression 'change of relations'; the nature of these relations may vary; they can be quantitative (enlarging or adding fixed assets) and qualitative (raising efficiency), functional and structural, and spatial and non-spatial. There may be relations between production and infrastructure, between town and country, among the socio-economic levels of different regions. In particular, there are relations of spatial interaction between elements and systems (feedback). All these relations are often beset with non-linearities.

A new order established as a result of strong impulses (innovations) and changes of relations, always manifests itself in the change of sectoral and spatial structures of systems. Such an order is maintained by differentiated flows of goods, persons and information; it is disturbed only when new strong impulses (innovations) occur.

Three hypotheses may be put forward:

1 Spatial organisation results from the functioning and developing of an economy subject to non-linear interactions, or from specialisation and differentiation among people, business companies and territorial units. Such specific conditions bring about the flow of goods, persons and information that is indispensable to build up and preserve the functional and spatial order, that is, organisation.
2 Transformation of the spatial organisation, in other words spatial reorganisation, results from fundamental changes in economic and spatial relations under the influence of very strong impulses.

3 Spatial organisation and its transformations reveal a tendency towards growing complexity; parallel to this, however, there are tendencies towards a simpler organisation (limits to complexity).

We will now give some examples from which the role of interactions among people, business companies and territorial units with respect to spatial self-organisation become apparent; because these interactions can be expressed by functional dependence, we shall use the term 'dependence', some having the qualities of production functions. The following dependences (aggregated to spatial units) are essential:

1 Dependence of an urban economy on the size of the urban population (and its professional activity) as well as on the attractiveness of cities, expressed by net migration and the value of fixed assets; the level of employment or the value of production may serve as a measure of the size of the urban economy;
2 Dependence of agricultural production on the size of the rural population, the area and fertility of the cultivated land and the level of equipment in production means;
3 Dependence of the size of the urban and rural population on the level of employment and the family model adhered to;
4 Dependence of urban and rural infrastructures on the scale and structure of the economy and the size of the population;
5 Dependence of environmental transformation on the scale and structure of the economy and on the size of the population;
6 Dependence of the flows of goods, persons and information on the potentials of interacting regions.

One other factor shaping the spatial development of a country is the regional differentiation of the relation 'consumption versus accumulation'.

To each of the above mentioned dependences, if considered on a regional level, should be added another causal agent, namely, the impact of other regions, that is to say, the rest of the system.

New spatial order

Changes in the relations caused by impulses lead to changes in spatial tendencies, and to a new spatial order or reorganisation of spatial systems. Theoretically, this new order can be deduced in a conclusive and precise manner by the application of bifurcation theory, catastrophe theory, phase transitions, Markov chains, diffusion theory, thermodynamics of ecosystems, and many other methods.

To lay an intuitive basis for modifying the layout of spatial development in Poland, one has to plot the direction of coming changes in the non-linearities of interactions among people, enterprises and territorial units, their differentiation and specialisation, the flows of people, goods and information, the kind and force of impulses that stimulate spatial-economic development, basic economic and spatial relations. From these changes one should intuitively deduce the directions of changes in spatial organisations, among them changes of the tendency towards growing complexity and the parallel simplification of the organisation.

In the economic and spatial interactions where non-linearities occur, agglomeration multipliers may be expected to weaken and local and regional multipliers to strengthen. That will restrain the growth of urban-industrial agglomerations, reduce the backwash of the hinterland by agglomerations, intensify the cumulative processes in the outside areas; as a consequence of all that, the development of the local and regional economies will be speeded up. Such multiplier effects will be conditioned on the one hand by environmental constraints and the internalisation of social costs in the costs of companies (reduction in external economies), on the other by the intensification of farming and agricultural-processing industry and by more favourable conditions for the expansion of small industry and services.

A restructuring of the national economy aiming at better adjustment of production to social needs (development of agriculture and food industry, home building, production of consumption and export goods), will affect sectoral differentiation and specialisation. It will exert a differentiating influence on the regional patterns of the economy, because the preferential sectors are not evenly distributed; however, interregional differences in socio-economic levels are likely to be reduced somewhat, because the preferential trends of development will activate the common factors of regional growth at a faster rate than sporadic factors would. That tendency will manifest itself in the activation of small towns.

As far as the flows of goods, persons and information are concerned, one could predict that local and regional flows will be revived relatively faster than countrywide flows, a phenomenon which could be interpreted as a transitional move towards 'closer' regional economies. Migration from country to city will decline, and the role of households as a locational factor for industry will increase.

The impulses stimulating socio-economic development will change. Restructuring of the national economy will involve changes in the sectoral structure of investments. The shares of preferential sectors of production, home building, infrastructure and environmental protection in the total volume of investments will increase.

The spatial structure of the economy is characterised by a heavy inertia. Great changes are possible only when the growth impulses are very strong; when they gather enough force, they are additionally intensified by the influence of cumulative feedbacks and multiplier effects. Recently there have been lively discussions in economic geography and spatial economics about the influence which the rising cost of energy may exert on the spatial systems of cities, regions and countries. Developments in the years which have passed since the oil crisis of 1973 seem to indicate that, at least in most cases, the national economies have absorbed the shock and damped its effects: no essential spatial changes have occurred, however, such changes cannot be completely excluded.

The restructuring of the economy will produce one more spatial effect: as functions change while locations do not, the spatial system of activities will alter while the spatial system of fixed assets remains the same.

Apart from the changes in the above mentioned economic and spatial relations (the restructuring of sectors, relatively faster growth of local and regional economies, restrained agglomeration growth and activation of small towns), an attenuation of conflicts between the economy and the natural environment, better adjustment of production and infrastructure, especially in urban-industrial agglomerations, diminished disparities among regions and between town and country are predictable.

Spatial interactions will change with regard to direction, distance, intensity and time. The spatial system of a country being basically durable, no greater changes are to be expected; the anticipated restructuring, however, may modify the network of supplies and sales to some degree.

Spatial interactions, considered in terms of inputs and outputs, will probably become more effective; that development, intensified by cumulative feedbacks and multiplier effects, results in the change of elements and links in spatial-economic systems. Such changes lead to a new order, that is, a new organisation; the new order will be in accordance with certain principles constituting the mechanism of spatial organisation. These principles comprise: centrality of the spatial system, urban and regional daily cycles, inflow of growth factors into attraction niches, locational changes in the ripening process of new activities, life histories of individuals and their families, the gravitation principle, intervening opportunities, dependence of the organisation of spatial movements on the structure of institutions, spatial coincidence, hierarchic diffusion of socio-economic phenomena, spatial barriers, growth of connectivity, limits to complexity, agglomeration, incomplete decomposition, re-integration of given hierarchical levels with higher levels, indispensability of intermediate organisational levels, anisotropic deviations, equifinalism.

In long-term spatial planning one needs to know whether the spatial-economic system, always more or less in disequilibrium, can be coached to a state of equilibrium, or whether the existing spatial deviations will widen in the future. To answer the question, one should find out how susceptible the system is to transformations, and what direction such transformations are likely to take; it is physically a question of 'stability versus complexity'.

Objectives, evaluation of natural tendencies, and planning solutions

The general socio-economic aims to be achieved by spatial planning, already suggested previously (Domański, 1982), are:

1. To raise the quality of life in regions to the social optimum;
2. To improve access to opportunities by spatial organisation;
3. To increase the economic effectiveness of spatial structures and processes.

Will the natural tendencies resulting from spatial self-organisation converge to these objectives under new conditions? The answer is: to a degree, yes; but not satisfactorily so without a national plan. The tendency for local and regional economic elements to grow relatively faster than national ones is consistent with the first objective; to achieve it, however, the national income will have to be centrally redistributed among regions. The second objective will be favoured by the self-government of cities, communities and voivodeships; unless local and regional activities are supplemented by central ones, however, the development of infrastructure, especially supra-regional ensuring better accessibility, will not be possible. The natural tendency of companies to acquire the highest economic effectiveness, and the economic activity of cities, communities and voivodeships, will lead to the third objective; achieving it will also depend on employees' engagement in economic reform. The strongest impulses to economic effectiveness in the country, including major innovations, should be encouraged by central planning and governing bodies; that does not exclude initiatives from people, companies and territorial units.

The general objectives must be specified and given a measurable form; to that end one can use functions expressing dependences which will most significantly shape the country's spatial development. To approach the first objective, regional incomes may be maximised. Regional incomes depend on employment, the productivity of labour, and the relative value of production in industry, agriculture and services; they are highest when the first two functions reach their maximum (see p.126). The arguments in these functions should be connected with the instruments of regional policy on the central level. By studying the third function we can determine the future population of cities and villages; again the arguments of the relevant function should be shaped so as to limit the increase of urban population and maintain the rural one at the required level. The two postulates are quite commonly accepted in discussions of population problems. Studying functions 4 and 5 one should look for the maximum increase of infrastructure, and minimise harmful influences on the natural environment, this being in agreement with the second as well as the first objective. Infrastructure is understood here to include, apart from municipal infrastructure, also service facilities and services on a higher level as well as transport and communication systems. Achieving the third objective requires, among other things, decreased transportation requirements of the national economy; suggestions in that directions may result from studying function 6. One should also determine the regional differentiation of investment and exploitation costs connected with the production of certain goods, or groups of goods, and try to minimise costs given required levels of production.

From the many quality measures of spatial order possible, those should be chosen, and submitted to deep analysis, which express important socio-economic dependences; by such analysis should be identified the main factors forming spatial arrangements and the most effective ways to influence the arrangements through those factors, the choice of these ways being a steering problem. Among such quality measures are:

1 Marginal products in cities and in the country, in other words: determining what results can be expected from pumping successive millios of zlotys into the development of industrial and agricultural production in chosen cities and rural areas;
2 Marginal effects of expenditures for improving the quality of life in cities and in the country, especially in urban-industrial agglomerations;
3 Marginal effects of expenditures for improving the human environment;
4 Transportation requirements of the national economy. By these measures the quality of the national plan and its particular solutions can be evaluated.

Steering of spatial development of the country

In spatial economics, a full set of steering instruments should be used, including administrative, financial, investment and social instruments.

To ensure the internal logics of the national plan, steering instruments and the factors determining the course of development processes should be matched. For example, should we employ a coefficient of marginal capital requirements to explain the development of a given industrial sector, then we should include that same coefficient in the set of steering instruments. By steering we aim at improving this coefficient, that is to say, at decreasing the fixed assets for successive units of production; such matters belong to the realm of marginal programming.

In spatial steering use could be made of the concept of Pareto-optimality; it would rely on the shift of steering instruments among regions (cities, voivoideships) as a function of changing results. The shifting would cease as soon as no shift would give better results than those already observed; in the case of non-comparable effects, the notion of shadow prices could be used intuitively. Let us assume that in a given region total investment resources have to be distributed among four objectives: industry, infrastructure, residential construction and environmental protection. In the mathematical programming sense distribution is optimal if it minimises a weighted sum of balance limits; in non-mathematical terms it is optimal if it minimises the sum of vexations connected with investment constraints. A few versions of investment distribution should be compared, and specialist help should be recruited to determine the vexations appearing in each of the four domains in spite of the investments. An agency authorised to make decisions should make the choice, keeping the principle of minimising all vexations in mind; such matters belong to the realm of optimisation of multiple objectives, which spatial planning is often dealing with.

The effectiveness of steering may be increased by the synergism of instruments, that is, the co-operation of two or more instruments to obtain the same objective.

The national plan should identify spatial tendencies in the economy and in society springing from spatial self-organisation processes, stimulating them when they are heading in the direction agreeable to social aims, and correcting them if they disagree. It should assume especially strict requirements and instruments with regard to protection of the natural environment. More self-government of voivoideships will raise the rank and also the difficulty level of interregional co-ordination; within the co-ordinating function the regional consequences of the restructuring of the economy should be studied (which regions will gain and which will lose), and, in view of expected increased voivoideship pressure on the central investment fund, a distribution procedure of investments among voivodeships should be established to ensure impartial distribution of the fund and to reconcile conflicting goals. Such a procedure would act as an impartial redistributor of national income, and, if necessary, as a referee.

Through conscious and planned activity in space and environment, society and state should strengthen their control of resources, and above all, periodically redefine environment and space so as to achieve harmonious economic and spatial development.

References

Allen, P.M. and Sanglier, M. (1979), A dynamic model of growth in a central place system, *Geographical Analysis*, vol. 11, no. 3, pp. 256–72.

Domański, R. (1982), *Teoretyczne podstawy geografii ekonomicznej* (Theoretical foundations of economic geography), Państwowe Wydawnictwo Ekonomiczne, Warsaw.

Domański, R. (1983), Self-organisation in spatial systems: evolutionary problems for regional science, *Papers of the Regional Science Association*, Twenty-Ninth North American Meetings, Pittsburgh.

Domański, R. and Wierzbicki, A.P. (1983), A simulation model for developing service centers in a rural settlement network, *International Institute for Applied Systems Analysis, Working Paper*, WP 81–58, Laxenburg, Austria.

Domański, R. and Wierzbicki, A.P. (1981), Self-organisation in dynamic settlement system, *Papers of the Regional Science Association*, Seventh Pacific Regional Science Conference, Surfers' Paradise, vol. 51.

Nicolis, G. and Prigogine, I. (1977), *Self-organisation in nonequilibrium Systems*, Wiley, New York.

10 The role of political bodies in the allocation of produced locational qualities

D. BÖKEMANN

The problem

This chapter deals with locations as elements of regional systems. Locations are regarded as complexes of natural and artificial properties, bound together by a well-defined ownership. Each complex of locational properties enables a firm to produce more or less profitably, or a household to consume more or less usefully. Locations in private ownership are considered as an important part of individual wealth thus, we understand the quality of a location to enable its owner (or user):

1 To save more or less on transportation costs or gain more or less leisure time in realising a certain sequence of activities;
2 To realise a certain production or consumption from a set of alternatives, each associated with a certain change of profit or utility.

In that view, whether a firm can produce successfully, or the members of a household can realise their dreams of social exchange and cultural activities, depends essentially on their location.

We consider locations to be produced by public and territorial authorities such as communities (producing plots of land) and states (producing communities). It means that the quantities and qualities of locations are not constant through time, but are variables continuously influenced by public investments and interventions. From that point of view, a basic political question of regional policy is how to allocate the locational qualities produced to the inhabitants (social groups) and firms (industrial sector) of a certain territory. For political evaluation of regional development this question seems to be more important than the traditional and more geographical one which deals with the distribution of population and firms among the locations of a particular area.

This chapter consists of three parts:

1 The main hypotheses of the author's theory on the production of locations are put forward;
2 The problem of allocating the locational qualities produced in agreement with the governments' interests is explained;
3 How to aggregate indicators of individual locational qualities to obtain a measure describing the political success of a regional plan defined as an allocation programme of locations, is demonstrated by a specific interpretation of an urban interaction model; this model for measuring the political effects (as aggregated from private effects) of public investments is based on empirical research carried out for the City of Vienna.

Production of locations

Locations are considered to be products, their producers pursuing certain objectives within their production possibilities. To that end, they combine factors of production accessible to them; the result of their production is normally sold.

Given the above concepts, the following questions arise:

1 *Who is the producer of locations?*
The public administrative units within territorial authorities (on the national, provincial and local levels) responsible for regional planning are regarded as firms that produce locations, the 'owners' of these 'public firms' are the politicians in power, responsible for a specific regional policy.
2 *What are the objectives of production?*
It seems obvious that the objectives of producing locations can be related to the utility function of the politicians – or, alternatively, a specific political party – responsible for a specific policy.
3 *What are the factors of production?*
Land, access to regional infrastructure, and locational boundaries are assumed to be the categories of production factors for locations.

(a) *Land*: the term 'land' stands for the resources of a location and its potential for absorbing environmental disturbances; goods obtained from some other location may be substituted for the resources of any specific location. For locational absorbing potential may be substituted special measures to avoid environmental disturbances.
(b) *Access to regional infrastructure*: the term 'access to regional infrastructure' stands for all the different communication facilities at a location, to be regarded as links to interlocational communication and supply systems; goods, persons, information may be obtained or passed on through these facilities across the boundaries with adjoining locations. These facilities make it possible for goods to be acquired from, transported to, and exchanged with all simultaneously 'connected' users in other locations; thus, infrastructural facilities replace property rights on land resources, a situation that requires division of labour.
(c) *Locational boundary*: the term 'locational boundary' should characterise the territorial structure of individual property rights and includes the whole set of barriers associated with a certain location; barriers (as elements of the locational boundaries) prevent unregulated and thus uncontrollable movements to and from the location. Barriers safeguard and protect the property rights with respect to a location as well as the rights of control and disposal; for the owner they safeguard the exclusive right of disposal of a well-defined set of facilities and resources. The right of disposal can be safeguarded by material barriers (for instance, protective constructions against natural disturbing factors such as floods; another example is border walls) and/or immaterial barriers of a legal, economic or social nature (for instance, boundaries of plots of land or provincial boundaries, building regulations, zoning laws).

As we are considering the values of a location in terms of its usability, or evaluating a location's quality, we are less interested in the 'mediating' factors necessary to produce a location (land, infrastructure, boundaries) than in those that can be combined and transformed at the locations (in the sense of producing or consuming final goods). Land, infrastructure and boundary, as production factors for locations, describe a set of locational properties, all of which can be related to 'mediated' consumption goods and production factors: land as the 'bearer' of natural resources, infrastructural facilities as 'procurers' of the exchange of goods, and barriers as 'safeguards' of the property rights on these goods.

All the technically possible combinations of the mediated goods and factors available in a location constitute its 'technical-usage potential', and all the combinations that can be realised economically constitute its 'economic usage potential'. Elements of the economic usage potential of locations are the production and consumption functions that can be realised there.

4 *What are the characteristics of the production function for locations?*

We start from the assumption that public authorities produce locations by combining defined quantities and specifications of factors concerning the categories land, access to regional infrastructure, and boundaries. The output of production is measured by the locational usage potential, which describes the whole set of land use alternatives. Each type of land use can be evaluated by the relative amount of costs saved, in particular on transportation costs; in the case of consumption-oriented land use like housing, the location quality can be evaluated by the leisure time gained by the population.

We take, therefore, the locational usage potential as an objective of production. Our first question is what characteristics of a location's production factors must be combined to produce consumption goods? Without going into details the following assumptions are made.

(a) Our hypothesis is that there is a time sequence in the location of facilities (or barriers) from universal multipurpose facilities (or barriers) to specialised single purpose facilities (or barriers). It follows that each new facility (or barrier) diminishes the increase in the mediated goods and factors that may be acquired or disposed of in a location ('excludable' factors, 'disturbing' factors).

(b) To obtain a certain locational usage potential, facilities and barriers cannot substitute each other. Hence, in the production of locations only one production method is efficient; any deviation from the efficient relation means wasting one of the two production factors. If the production method is efficient, the more facilities and barriers there are at a location, the more uses may, *ceteris paribus*, be obtained. The locational combination potential will marginally increase more than proportionally, and there will be increasing returns of scale.

Locations with a high usage potential not only offer a multitude of land use alternatives, but are also as a rule the locations of the technologically more complex types of land use. The complexity of the uses depends on the number of combinable factors in the broadest sense: the higher number, the more complex the use technology.

(c) To obtain a certain locational usage potential, the production factors land and infrastructure facilities can be substituted for each other within limits, as the resources of a piece of land and the goods and factors mediated by infrastructure facilities may be the same. On the other hand, the production factors land and boundaries may also be substituted for each other. That becomes clear from the barriers' function to safeguard property from external (environmental) disturbances; land is also characterised by its potential to absorb environmental disturbances (for instance: noise, waste water, etc.); more land requires more energy to overcome distance; safeguarding barriers have the same effect.

The conclusion is that a certain locational quality can be produced by varying the relations between infrastructure and boundary investments on the one hand, and the quantity of land on the other. That idea might be a basic concern of regional planning activities in the public sector. From the production function of locations, we can derive the 'management problem' of regional planning; it is not a political but a technical economic problem.

Allocation of produced locations

The allocation of locations is a political problem: governments realise their regional policy by redistributing the existing locational quality among, and allocating additionally produced locational quality to the inhabitants and firms of their territories. In that view, the fundamental question of regional politics is: how much locational quality should be allocated to the individual inhabitant (social group) and to the individual firm (branch, sector)?

First, some remarks are in order about the allocation mechanism by which the utility of the individual suppliers of and demanders for produced locations is co-ordinated.

As a first approach, we consider the market for land to be such an allocation mechanism. The land market, however, deals only with the exchange of already existing plots of land in private property. The question is how a good location and the additional locational quality produced by public authorities comes into the possession of its first private owner. The suppliers of additional locations and locational qualities are the politicians in power, in their role as 'owners' of the producing 'public firms'; the final demanders are the private firms and households using the produced good i.e. the 'location'.

In that context, landowners fulfil the role of retailers of locations, transferring property rights from the producer(s) to the user(s).

We know that land has a price on the market when property rights of locations change hands; however, no market price emerges between the producers of locations on the one hand, and the owners and users of locations on the other. In that context, the allocation mechanism seems to be based on the exchange of goods which are, in a more abstract sense, arguments in the actors' utility function: private goods are exchanged for political goods, and vice versa.

Politicians in power make available locations as an investment good produced by their public firms to private households and private firms, who in turn pay taxes, fees etc. as private contributions to the public budget and express private votes as contributions to the public loyalty.[1]

We assume as a first approximation that the public budget, as aggregated from the results of using the produced locations, must balance their production costs, and that the voters' loyalty as aggregated from the satisfaction of the owners and users of the produced locations must exceed a minimum level (determined by law).[2] Thus, each regional plan represents a certain production function for each location to be produced as well as an allocation programme by which additional locational qualities produced are allocated to certain private subjects, who become the owners and/or users.

Next we consider the political utility associated with alternative allocation programmes for produced locations, each represented by a potential regional plan. If politicians wish to maximise their utilities, they have to evaluate and select the allocation programme of locations that best expresses their preferences.

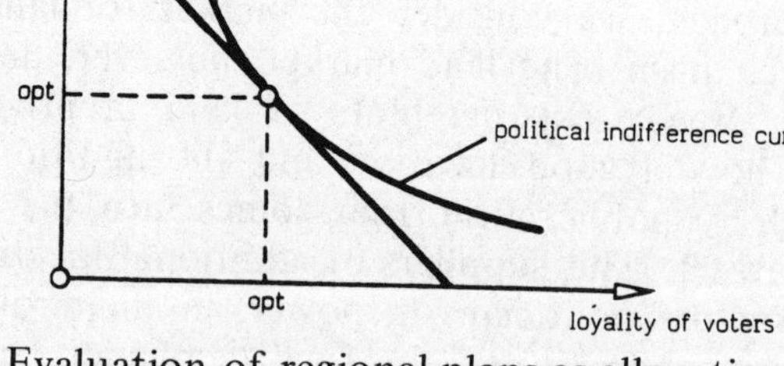

Figure 10.1 Evaluation of regional plans as allocation programmes for produced locations related to politicians' utility

Figure 10.1 demonstrates the political utility of alternative programmes to allocate locational quality. On the iso-potential curve each point represents a specific regional plan as an allocation programme for locational qualities, each combining determined sets of the political goods budget revenues and voters' loyalty. The political iso-utility curve (indifference of political utility) is assumed to be convex, because budget revenues and voters' loyalty can substitute each other in the case of existing political power; there are, however, limits to that substitution, because political activities require a minimum of budget revenues as well as a minimum of voters' loyalty. In realising a certain programme (at certain costs) the maximum of political utility is reached when the marginal utilities of the available political goods are equal.

To explain the optimisation problem, we will discuss the private and political efforts of two allocation programmes of produced locations; firstly the levelling programme, and secondly the exclusiveness programme.

In the *levelling programme* the existing infrastructure and borderline systems are extended, so that an increasing number of lower ranking locations is connected to systems of progressively higher ranks (see Figure 10.2). It means that a growing number of equally equipped locations is available on the market for locations and that the relations among the sets of locations are changing in favour of the (previously) lower ranking ones: the additionally produced locational quality is proportionally distributed among an increasing number of private firms and households. In that case the landowners' revenue for each additionally produced location of a particular quality will decrease. Similarly the profitability of the extended infrastructural and safeguarding systems decreases and the returns on the budget drop, diminishing the public and political investment potential.

Under the *exclusiveness programme* new infrastructural facilities and new safeguarding barriers are invested first at the best equipped locations; this programme progressively concentrates locational quality with fewer firms and households (see Figure 10.3).

We assume that only under the exclusiveness programme do public investments encourage technical innovation by land users, thus inducing firms and households to intensify settlement. We assume further that when there is competition for the few upgraded locations, the more efficient (and more solvent) users will displace others. This implies that with each investment the returns to the landowners of such locations increase, and the revenues of the budgets of public authorities increase more rapidly in relation to their investments. Because competition will ensure a growing proportion of efficient and solvent users paying higher taxes, public authorities will also own

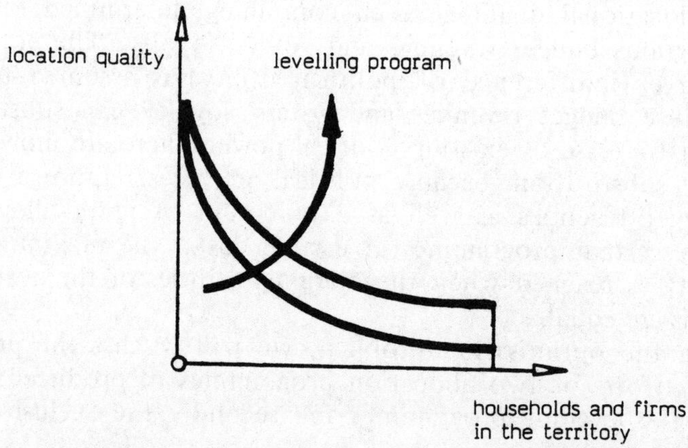

Figure 10.2 Effects of the levelling programme on the rank size distribution of locational qualities among households and firms in a (politically defined) territory

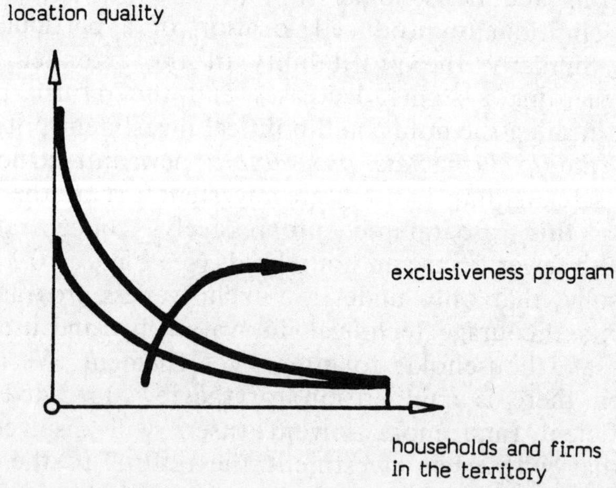

Figure 10.3 Effects of the exclusiveness programme on the rank size distribution of location quality among households and firms in a (politically defined) territory

an increasing investment potential.

So far we have discussed the first argument in the politicians' utility function: the effects of the production activities on the budget; we now turn to the voters' loyalty to the politicians in power. The political survival of an individual or a party depends mainly on how voters judge their policy, in particular their allocation programme for produced locations. We assume that voters judge the individual effects of the programme by its marginal utility, and that their judgement depends mainly on how their position in the rank sequence of locational qualities changes relative to that of their neighbours.[3]

Under the levelling programme the locational differences are diminished, so that voters living outside the previously favoured centres are initially satisfied. In view of the diminishing returns on their budget, the investment efforts of the public authorities will presumably slacken. Under those circumstances voters' loyalty in the whole territory will increase for as long as they ignore the symptoms of future decay; with improved knowledge, loyalty to the governing politicians will rapidly decrease after a phase of stagnation.

Under the exclusiveness programme locational differences increase, so that growing prosperity in agglomerations favourable to innovations is accompanied by relative economic stagnation of lower ranking locations. With growing budgetary funds, total public investment activities will probably increase. While the favoured population in the agglomeration will judge positively of their improved situation, the rest of the population will generally regard the increasing disparities as unfair. Under those circumstances, loyalty in the entire territory will continue to rise (as it did with the levelling programme) as long as the situation is not considered too unfair. When the concentration of benefits becomes so great as to be thought unfair, loyalty will rapidly decrease.

From that point of view, a government cannot maintain either of these extreme regional investment programmes for a long period of time. To survive, governments must find a realistic compromise between extreme exclusiveness and levelling programmes, the precise nature of which depends on the specific starting position. Generalising that idea, we conclude that over a long period of time, the distribution of produced locations among economic subjects tends to a dynamic equilibrium, satisfying Pareto-distribution conditions which can be described by the Rank-Size Rule (Beckmann, 1957; Berry, 1964; Zipf, 1949).

Political effects of public investments

Public investments in infrastructural and property safeguarding systems change the territorial structure of locational qualities in general; they change in particular the distribution of locational qualities among the private subjects in the territory under consideration. The locational utility effects of each public investment spread out among the private subjects in a specific coherence determined by spatial neighbourhood and technological functions. How to ensure that they reach the subjects who should be favoured politically, is therefore a serious problem of regional planning. Before a regional plan can be formulated, the question must be raised how to measure the political effects of public investments as derived from the contribution made to individuals' locational qualities. It can be adequately answered by a land-use interaction model describing locational quality as determined by (among other things) infrastructural (transportation) and borderline (property safeguarding) networks.

The following empirical results are based on such a model, constructed by the author, to derive the distribution of an indicator of locational quality for consumption among the population of Vienna. This model deals with 1,265 intra-urban regions (each of about 1,000 inhabitants); 127 intra-urban service centres and 3 transportation models (walking, public transport, private cars).

The graphs describing the transportation systems include about 2,000 vertices and about 7,000 edges.

The models define locational quality for consumption as 'leisure time gained' or 'time saved' in realising the individual's consumption function by providing goods from supply centres. In this model, locational quality for consumption depends on:

1 The set of establishments offering the goods demanded;
2 The time necessary to reach these establishments (by coupling different supply activities).

Comparison of different locations firstly by the time needed to provide a person with a well-defined vector of goods, or secondly by the set of complementary establishments which can be reached within a given amount of time, gives an idea of what we have called locational quality for consumption.

To evaluate the leisure time gained by supply activities, we first need a matrix of shortest paths between all pairs of locations under consideration, this in the dimension 'transportation time'. Within transportation networks people link their destinations without returning after each activity; thus, we must describe the linking behaviour by macro-assumptions, which have to be tested in terms of an individual's function describing the transportation time spent on a marginal activity.

1 Supply activities from home locations to centres (agglomerations of supply establishments) are the more frequent and intensive the larger the centres (measured by the number of employees).

2 Supply activities from home centres are more frequent and intensive the greater the purchasing power of the home location considered.

3 Supply activities from home to a given centre are modified by the alternatives available in the shape of competing centres.

The individual's utility function (describing consumption behaviour in space) is expressed by supply preferences p_{ij}, in which people relate home locations i to centre locations j; thus, the supply preference values inform us how people in i divide their purchasing power among different centres j ($\sum_j p_{ij} = 1$). That problem was first tackled by Huff (1964) and Lakshmanan-Hansen (1965); to evaluate centre j's utility for the residential location i, the benefits of the quantity and assortment of the goods offered must be compared with the costs associated with the time spent on transportation.

We adopt an exponential function to describe the utility u_{ij} which a centre j has for a residential location i depending on travel time d_{ij} (see Figure 10.4).

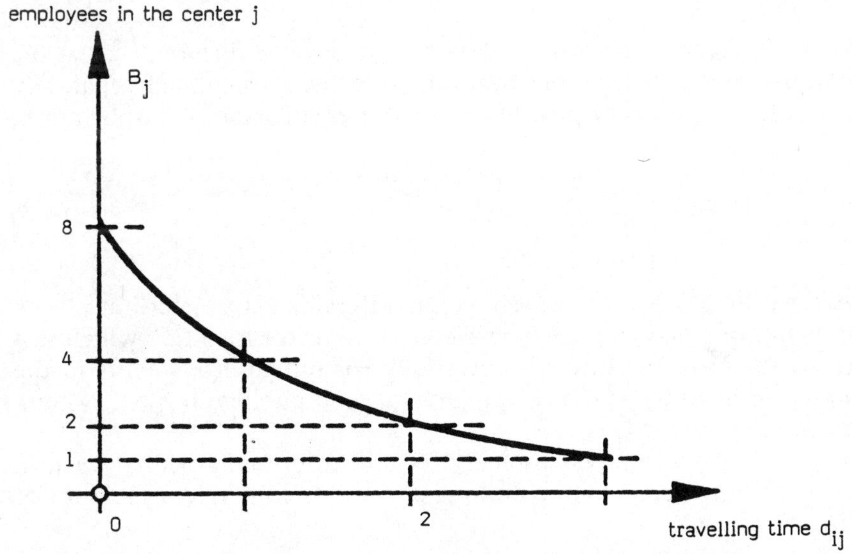

Figure 10.4 Indifference of the consumer's utility depending on travel time to, and employees in, the centres.

$$u_{ij} = e^{\beta b_j - \alpha d_{ij}} \qquad (4.1)$$

where b_j is the number of employees in centre j;

d_{ij} is transportation time between i and j;

α is a parameter describing the value of time to the individual;

β is a parameter describing the value of intra-centre organisation of establishments.

Testing this function for the City of Vienna, we have calculated the following parameter values: the utility of the centres is halved in about three minutes (α = 0.13) when private cars are used, and in about five minutes (α = 0.25) when public transport is used. To test the model, an equilibrium between total purchasing power and total number of employees in the centres was assumed. The flows of purchasing power have been determined by interviews covering one per cent of the population; they refer only to consumption goods, not to industrial and commercial sectors, and to an aggregated regional level.

On the basis of the individual utility functions, the locational quality for consumption (LQC_i) is defined as follows:

$$LQC_i = \sum_j p_{ij} \cdot e^{\beta b_j - \alpha d_{ij}} \qquad (4.2)$$

Because different means of transportation involve different costs, the locational qualities for consumption have been calculated separately for pedestrians, users of private cars, and users of public transportation, as follows:

$$LQC_i^k = \sum_j p_{ij}^k \cdot e^{\beta b_j - \alpha_k d_j^k} \qquad (4.3)$$

After calibration on the basis of the interview data describing shopping behaviour in Vienna, we derived our indicator for LQC, which was sensitive to infrastructure variations such as public investments in the intra-urban highway systems, the underground public transport system, and others.

The LQC values as micro-analytic indicators of individual wealth, were then aggregated in the following manner to derive a measure of political success:

1 The location specific indicator values LQC_i were transformed into rank sequences;

2 The sequence of locations, ranked by their locational quality indicators, LQC_i, were transformed into an inhabitant sequence ranked by locational quality indicators;
3 The indifferent alternative programmes of public investments and the sequential stages in the realisation process were calculated and compared to produce a set of different rank size distributions of the LQC_i values for the Viennese population;
4 These rank size distributions of the LQC_i values among the Viennese population formed the basis for calculating Lorenz-Gini coefficients, the differences of the coefficients in the regional plan as compared to the starting situation being used as a macro-analytical indicator of political success in the allocation activities;
5 The Lorenz-Gini index, however, does not account for the very serious political problem of social justice, which calls for stable rank size distributions in terms of changes in the position of individuals (see Figure 10.5).

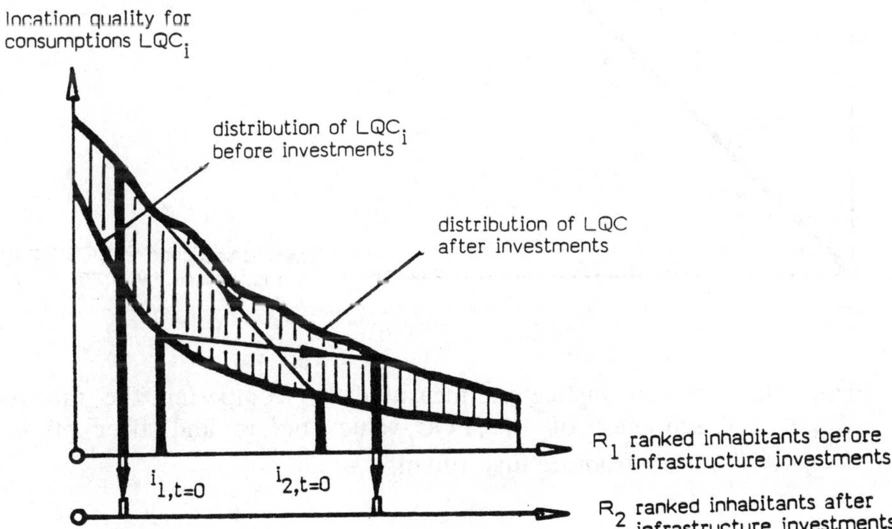

Figure 10.5 Changes in the individual position in the rank distribution of locational quality affected by infrastructure investments

The following remarks address the problem of social justice in regional politics in methodological terms. Each public investment affects a larger or smaller set of people; apparently, public investments in infrastructure systems in particular cannot be associated exactly with specific locations because there are so many side effects. Thus the number of locations and their inhabitants changing their position in the rank sequence of locational quality owing to public investments, can be considered a measured deviation from social justice.

The effects relating to social justice can also be looked upon as deviations from a specific Pareto-optimum; the aggregate of the deviations can be measured by the Spearman rank-correlation coefficient ρ (see Figure 10.6).

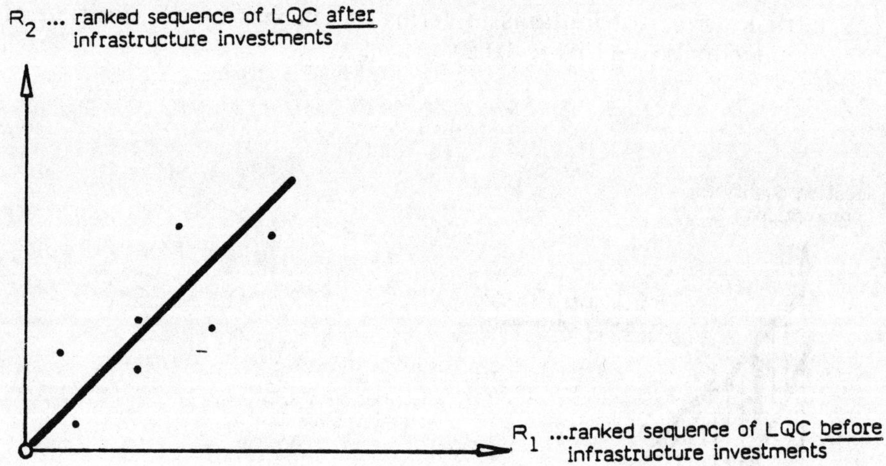

Figure 10.6 Social justice as measured by comparing the ranked sequence of the LQC_i-values before and after public infrastructure investments

Empirical results

The following empirical results of our Vienna model may be regarded as an evaluation of the potential success derived from the execution of the urban development programme (Stadtentwicklungsplan). After the execution of the urban-development programme, the concentration of the LQC_i values, as distributed among the inhabitants of Vienna (no change in the existing geographic distribution of the population being assumed), will decrease between 1977 and 1995 (measured by Lorenz-Gini coefficient):

- from 0.40 (1977) to 0.35 (1995) for private car ownership;
- from 0.52 (1977) to 0.48 (1995) for public transportation.

Taking into account the forecast (continuing) trend of the Viennese population to migrate from the high density urban core to the periphery, we find an increasing concentration of the LQC_i values:

- from 0.40 (1977) to 0.42 (1995) for private car ownership.
- from 0.52 (1977) to 0.54 (1995) for public transportation.

It means that the allocation effects towards levelling may be more than counteracted by the trend of people to migrate to the periphery.

Changes of the individual positions in the rank sequence of the LQC_i values as affected by public investments have also been calculated for the Viennese population. The new underground public transport systems in Vienna as well as the major investments in its intra-urban highway systems alter the rank sequence of LQC_i values between 1977 and 1995 (after the complete realisation of the urban development programme under consideration, and intra-urban migration effects being left aside):

- by $_{pc}$ (Spearman) = 0.932 for users of private cars;
- by $_{pt}$ (Spearman) = 0.925 for users of public transport systems.

These values suggest that the regional policy of the city of Vienna has had relatively strong social effects.

Notes

1 In reality, time lags have to be recognised between the production and use of locations, as well as cognitive dissonances everywhere.

2 Because the production of locations is not the only productive activity of politicians, the private subjects' satisfaction and payments relate in reality to a combination of public goods.

3 Here we do not consider the problem of changes in the position within the rank sequence.

References

Beckmann, M.J. (1957), City Hierarchies and the Distribution of City Size, *Economic Development and Cultural Change*, Chicago, vol. 6, pp.243–8.

Berry, B.J.L. (1964), City Size Distribution and Economic Development, in J. Friedman and W. Alonso, *Regional Development and Planning*, The MIT Press, Cambridge, Mass.

Bökemann, D. (1974), A Framework of Technological Theory of Regional Development, *RSA-Papers*, vol. 33, pp.33–56.

Bökemann, D. (1982), *Theorie der Raumplanung, regionalwissenschaftliche Grundlagen der Stadt-, Regional- und Landesplanung*, Oldenbourg, Munich.

Bökemann, D. (1981), Distributive Effects of Infrastructure Investments, *Sistemi Urbani*, vol. 2, pp.165–79.

Bökemann, D. (1983), Zentralitätsgefüge und Versorgungsqualität, Grundlagen zu einem Zentrenkonzept, in Geschäftsgruppe Stadtentwicklung und Stadterneuerung, *Beiträge zur Stadtforschung, Stadtentwicklung und Stadtgestaltung*, Band 12, Magistrat der Stadt Wien, Vienna.

Demsetz, H. (1974), Towards a theory of Property Rights, in E. Furobotn and S. Pejovich, *The Economics of Property Rights*, Ballinger Publishing Company, Cambridge, pp.31–42.

Downs, A. (1967), *Inside Bureaucracy*, Little and Brown, Boston.

Frey, B. (1977), *Moderne politische Oekonomie*, Munich.

Furobotn, E. and Pejovich, S. (1974), *The Economics of Property Rights*, Ballinger Publishing Company, Cambridge.

Huff, D.L. (1973), A Probability Analysis of Shopping Center Trading Areas, *Land Economics*, vol. 39, 1963, pp.81–9.

Lakshmanan and Hansen (1965), A Retail Market Potential Model, *Journal of the American Institute of Planners*.

Lösch, A. (1963), *Die räumliche Ordnung der Wirtschaft*, third edition, Fischer Verlag, Stuttgart.

Zipf, G.K. (1949), *Human Behaviour and the Principle of Least Effort*, Addison Wisley Press, Reading.

11 Locational decisions and regional structure

J. G. LAMBOOY

Introduction

Many regional studies stress the relation between the locational choice of industries and the regional structure. Classical location theory recognised two possibilities: (1) that a regional structure was the outcome of a series of independent locational decisions taken with a view to optimising transportation costs; (2) that the decision to locate was determined entirely by the spatial structure of natural resources. Classical authors, while undoubtedly accepting a more complex reality, did not explicitly include it in their theories. Theory building often demands starting from a strongly reduced complexity. However, for theory to enter a new stage of development, higher levels of complexity need to be included.

The complexity of location theory can be increased in three directions. The first complication is to include more variables, which can either be interrelated or not; the second is to acknowledge that the decision making process is more complicated than is assumed in the traditional location theories; and the third and most recent one is to include the life-cycle concept.

The first step has been taken in many studies. Klaassen (1965, 1967, 1968) has developed several new ideas in that direction, for instance about the role of amenities and the influence of urbanisation economies on regional growth. He has shown that location theory, thus enriched, could become a more fruitful planning instrument.

The second complication was emphasised in particular by authors who, like Pred (1967 and 1969), made use of theoretical work done by Herbert Simon. The main point was that not maximising, but satisficing behaviour was 'normal' in decision making. Another important element introduced by this school of thinking was differentiation among industries, in particular the distinction between one-product/one-location firms and multi-product/multi-location firms.

The third and most recent complication was introduced into the theories of international trade, industrial organisation, and location, by Vernon (1968), and elaborated on by – among others – Scott (1980). Its main contribution to location theory is the idea that an industry will find its market position changing as its products mature and are imitated, and often will have to adapt its location. That idea can be linked with Schumpeterian innovation theory and mobility studies.

In the pages to follow some recent adaptations of location theory will be commented on and evaluated, the emphasis being on the second category of changes.

The choice of variables

Among the most complicated parts of theory construction and empirical analysis is to choose the set of variables to be included. Indeed, the set of variables chosen and the set of causalities assumed largely determine the character of the theory. If a variable is not included in the selected set, no causalities involving that variable can be assumed or found on empirical testing. Indeed, the feature that distinguishes regional economics from 'general' economics is that the latter's set of relevant variables does not include spatial variables, which are fundamental to regional economics. That was a major reason for creating 'regional science' some thirty years ago, and starting to integrate regional economics with economic geography, regional sociology, human ecology, and parts of political science. Later on, environmental and energy issues were also included.

Location theory in the strict sense has also become more complicated in the course of time. Some of the variables that used to be assumed away through the *ceteris paribus* clause, are now incorporated; the question 'which factors determine the location of firms?' remained central, however.

Once the variables have been chosen, the research process remains fraught with methodological troubles. The first question that arises is whether a differentiation among industries is opportune. The second is whether to concentrate on the motivations and intentions of the decision maker(s), or rather on the 'objective, structural' conditions. The choice is fundamental because the two options require different sets of variables and govern different directions of causality.

Most traditional location studies focus on motivation and start without a prior classification of types, thus favouring 'methodological individualism' rather than 'structuralism'. The basic assumption of methodological individualism is that the entrepreneur, from his central position, maximises utility and/or profits, being free to choose from alternative solutions for his location problem, but under certain restraining conditions, such as budget or information constraints. Consumer sovereignty and equilibrium situations are accepted as normal (Earl, 1983).

The basic sets of variables to be included in all location studies are shown in Figure 11.1. If the causal chain starts with motivations and intentions, the basic question is: which motivation or intention explains the choice of a location, and which is the stronger factor? In that approach the assumption must be that individuals are the essential elements for the analysis; from a set of possibilities and constraints they choose on the basis of either maximising or satisficing behaviour. Neo-classical reasoning is the most typical example of maximising behaviour.

The other extreme is the structuralistic approach: not individuals, but the 'objective' structural conditions are taken as the starting point for the analysis, the implicit hypothesis being that individuals adapt completely to pressures from outside; classical Marxism is most typical of that direction. This deterministic approach is essentially holistic and historic; it is based on historical laws of evolution, in which the class struggle and the development of the productive forces are decisive elements: the structure develops, and individuals adapt.

In the structuralistic approach, locational developments are logically connected with the historical evolution of the productive forces governed by the laws of capital accumulation. With those ideas in mind, Harvey (1973) and Gordon (1978) explained the spatial developments of agglomerations and industrial sectors in the USA. Their contributions are not very convincing because their approach is very general: locational problems are regarded as the shift of capital from areas where labour has too much influence to areas where profits can be increased thanks to the absence of well-organised labour unions. They fail to explain the rise of new sectors in areas of the former type, such as New Jersey and Massachusetts; the rise of the Sunbelt-cities could be fitted within their framework, but only in a very general sense. Differences in locational behaviour among sectors cannot be explained in a strictly structuralistic approach; the role of individual

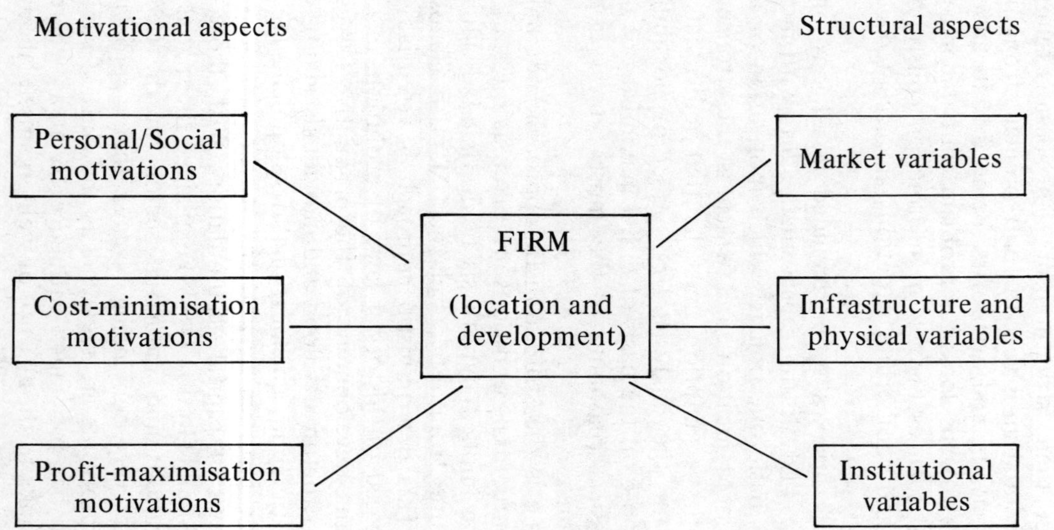

Figure 11.1 Locational variables

entrepreneurs and governments has to be acknowledged. Locational problems can be looked at from at least two sides; reality is so complicated that one method cannot be judged in advance to be 'better' than the other. Let it be stressed, however, that the choice of either filters the selection of variables.

To us, the choice of method appears to depend in part on the scale of the analysis. If the problem is how to explain interregional movements of industries, or how to analyse differences in growth potentials, then the method can be more structuralistic (Massey, 1979; Hilhorst, 1981); if one is primarily interested in the locational problems of a particular industry or category of industries, an approach oriented directly to the decision making individual(s) and the relevant constraining conditions is quite acceptable.

Would it be necessary, however, to push the problem one step ahead, asking what determines the motivations (or intentions, or goals)? The answer will no doubt be found to depend on:

1 The decision maker's social and institutional position (for instance in institutional economics; see also Hirsch, 1977);
2 The economic-technological position of the firm (see, for instance, Vernon, 1966, and De Jong, 1983 and 1984);
3 The characteristics of the physical environment (for instance in the school of Physical Determinism).

From a methodological point of view, our main problem is not whether motivations depend on such structural positions – that cannot be denied – but firstly whether the individual decision maker has freedom to make totally unexpected ('creative', 'innovative') decisions not logically springing from the structural position; and secondly whether raising the question of the structural dependence of the decision maker is methodologically necessary.

In our opinion, the answer is yes to both questions, which means that neither extreme – methodological individualism or radical structuralism – can be used as the exclusive methodological approach. Therefore, many studies of locational dynamics – concerning both relocation and new location – have been too restricted in their choice of variables and methodology. Most are based on neoclassical views of the rational decision making procedure. Accepting a certain degree of irrationality is not enough; the methodological basis has to be broadened. That assertion can be elaborated on with the help of the results of work by Nelson and Winter (1982).

Decision making and institutional aspects

In a recent publication, Nelson and Winter develop a theory of the decision making process of organisations, especially business companies. Their starting point is that theories are constructions to explain reality and that all too simple theories cannot explain complicated reality. To understand economic reality complex theories may be needed, that is, heterogeneous theories containing many variables. Nelson and Winter (1982) focus on decision making in a context of uncertainty; part of individuals' and organisations' behaviour consists in predictable, standard acts called 'routines'; another part, however, is unpredictable. The latter part of human behaviour should not be understood to be totally involuntary and irrational; it may be the result of a lack of information, or spring from values or conditions which have not (yet) reached consciousness. A very important argument of the authors is that such unpredictable activities are often stochastic, and related to conditions not directly but indirectly, through a stochastic process, which indeed may be strongly associated with the situation the relevant structure has started from.

Not only individuals but also organisations are active; neither of them are fully informed. The conditions do not fit the assumptions of neoclassical economics; the main difference is that, while neoclassical economics presupposes a static world in which equilibrium is the ultimate result of rational behaviour, in fact the conditions in which man decides and acts may change drastically. In neoclassical theory, man behaves with 'unbounded rationality', but its results cannot be used in the real world where there are many 'bounds'.

Nelson and Winter stress the fundamental significance of *technological change* and *institutional/political developments* for the understanding of behaviour. A theory that does not acknowledge that conditions and man's 'action environment' are changing continuously without everybody being fully informed, would be irrational. The 'homo economicus' cannot exist in a dynamic context, *dynamic* to be explicitly understood not to refer to 'more or less of the same as time goes on' but to a change of the composition of basic elements. A fundamental requirement is the willingness to accept a greater complexity of the real world as well as of the theory (Nelson and Winter, 1982, p.402). Evolutionary economics, for example, no longer falls into the trap of regarding prices and markets as the only social mechanism that actively transmits information and determines communicative and social relations. Another principle is that 'the conditions of each day arise from the actual circumstances of the preceding day and in which uncertainty abounds' (Nelson and Winter, 1982, p.404). There are 'patterns of differential survival and growth in a population of firms', a selective process in response to sometimes very rapid technological and institutional changes. Nelson and Winter's theory both 'contemplates the "inheritance" of acquired characteristics and the timely appearance of variation under the stimulus of adversity' (Nelson and Winter, 1982, p.11); further on (pp.14/15) the authors state that routines 'are a persistent feature of the organism and determine its possible behaviour (though *actual* behaviour is determined also by the environment)'. Firms and other organisations develop learning processes and 'search activities' to adapt as quickly as possible to changed conditions. There are *transition processes* from one state of affairs to another; adaptations failing to adapt 'properly' will lose substance or disappear altogether, the best innovators and adaptors surviving.

As to governmental organisations, Nelson and Winter (1982, p.384) contend that:

> policy making is a continuing process, the organisational and institutional structures involved become critical. Public policies and programmes, like private activities, are embedded in and carried out by organizations. And, in a basic sense, it is the organizations that learn, and adapt. The design of a good policy is, to a considerable extent, the design of an organizational structure capable of learning and of adjusting behaviour in response to what is learned.

Thus relating evolutionary economics with the institutionalist approach, Nelson and Winter (1982, p.356) introduce the term 'institutional ecology'. Economic development springs not only from individual activities, but also from organisational conditions. Omitting institutional reality is a major flaw of the neo-classical approach. In economic theory there are several approaches that do not consider institutional aspects. Marxism reduces social relations to two classes only, regarding the state as the representative of the capitalist class. Nowadays, that is too simplistic a view for many countries; Giddens (1978) for instance argues that more 'classes' have to be distinguished. Power is in fact based not only on landownership (as in feudal times), or capital (as in the period of the Industrial Revolution), but also on other factors (labour unions, science, information, etc.). The mainstream Institutionalists like Myrdal, Kapp and Galbraith stress the importance of interest groups for the development of the economy. Value systems are inherited from the past or have the function of maintaining the power of certain interest groups (such as 'national pride' for the military, and religious beliefs for churches). Decision making related to economic processes cannot be isolated from 'institutional ecology': economics, values and institutions are intricately interwoven.

In this chapter, an institution is defined as:

1 A group or organisation that is held together mainly by the object of maintaining or improving its position, and/or regulated by laws, rules and values; examples are political parties, business groups, neighbourhood groups, churches, governments and labour unions; or as
2 A commonly accepted set of values or accepted and codified rights that regulate a certain part of society, such as the 'property rights', and 'marriage'.

The concept of an institution entails a certain tension between 'organisation' and a set of values.

A very important problem is whether such emphasis on the 'institutional ecology' of decision making leaves an entrepreneur free to show 'creative, innovative' (in the sense of unpredictable) behaviour, provided complete information were available to researchers, as opposed to the 'routinised innovation' by organisations (Nelson and Winter, 1982, pp.133–4); choosing an unexpected location can be either a creative act or mere coincidence.

To relate the number of starting firms with regional growth, it is essential to look not only at the number of 'starters', but also at the number of successful entrepreneurs after a period of five to ten years. Quite possibly, only firms in 'expected locations' are successful, while others failed because their 'creative behaviour' did not fit that particular regional structure. The structure of the region's 'production environment' may thus be more decisive than the abilities of the entrepreneur (Van Duijn and Lambooy, 1983; Van Duijn, Lambooy and Paelinck, 1983; Pollard, 1981). A safe assumption is, nevertheless, that extremely gifted entrepreneurs can make such an impact on their environment as to make the structure adapt; once that has happened, other entrepreneurs cannot but adapt themselves. That phenomenon leads to another approach, namely the one using the concept of a 'life-cycle'.

Location and the life-cycle of products

The decision to locate a firm anywhere depends on many conditions; among the most dominant are the state of the life-cycle, the formal position of the firm (whether or not part of a multi-locational concern), and the sector to which the firm belongs: starters in the biotechnology sector behave differently from starters in the grocery branch. The location and relocation of firms through time and across space is a continuous process of adaptation to internal and external forces.

The adoption of new technologies or a change in the organisational structure may lead to locational changes. External pressure may be exerted by all three legs of the relation between business and environment: (1) the market; (2) the institutional structure; (3) the physical environment and the infrastructure (see again Figure 11.1 above).

If the market forces change (more competitors, less demand, for instance), internal changes can be made, but sometimes, to influence the cost structure, relocation is required. If the institutional structure changes (owing to fiscal measures, action by neighbourhood groups, deterioration of the 'business climate'), relocation may be the best solution. A change in the infrastructure: a new road, a new airport, can offer new chances of business.

With the introduction of the concept of product life-cycles, also called growth-cycles, a pattern becomes visible in the continuously adjusting spatial structure of towns and regions. To explain change is very important, and, as Schumpeter once stressed: 'Capitalism is change! To analyse locational changes the concept is very useful, because firms have to deal with a dynamic market environment, competition being the key word. Competition, broadly understood, is rivalry, a continuous struggle to preserve the lead' (De Jong, 1979, p.40); Clark speaks of 'competition as a dynamic process' (De Jong, 1981). The product life-cycle also serves to indicate a firm's position in the business/environment relation; Figure 11.2 shows its basic form.

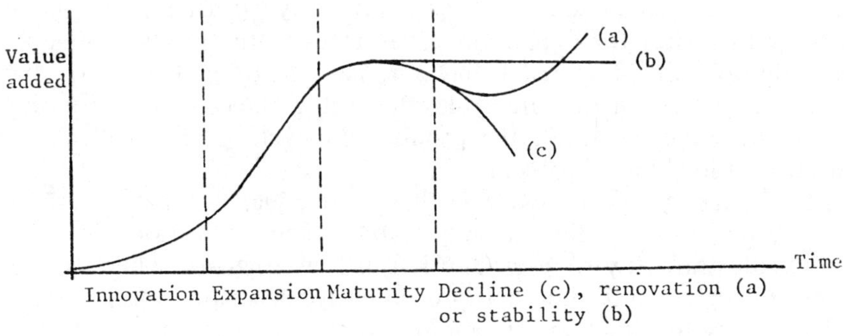

Figure 11.2 The product life-cycle

Figure 11.2 illustrates how a firm, manufacturing one newly developed product, starts production. On the market, the product has an advantage because it is innovative, but initially demand is very low, and in spite of its monopolistic market position the firm will not yet generate profits. Gradually the turnover may increase if the product is successful; expansion occurs, but at the same time imitation creates competition. How much the initial advantage is lost depends on the firm's ability to buy out new successful companies or compete successfully by price and/or quality policies; often, however, new rivals, learning from the leader's mistakes, or perhaps because they have a better location, manage to produce more cheaply. As the production passes from expansion to maturity, there will be strong rivalry, mergers and (partial) relocations; profitability first stabilises and then declines, which leads to more cost awareness and stronger internal control.

Location costs – in particular the costs of real estate and transportation, institutional and environmental costs – are regarded as impediments to profit; locational adjustments can be of different kinds:

1 Total relocation: for manufacturing industry and some wholesale branches to move from urban areas either to adjacent metropolitan areas or to other regions is quite common;
2 Partial relocation: a phenomenon that can be observed mostly with large companies, which move the production units to cheaper sites while keeping their headquarters in, or moving them to, the cores of agglomerations. Small firms tend to relocate as a whole.

Empirical studies have shown moving firms to be often more dynamic (in terms of employment growth) than non-moving ones (SEO, 1978). The picture is incomplete for lack of studies of *intra-urban* movements, movers seeming in that case primarily to attempt to reduce costs or find sites for expansion. The stages of the product life-cycle can help to explain spatial behaviour; next to other factors (in particular the entrepreneur's life-cycle, the sector, the economic situation, and institutional pressure), the product life-cycle is an excellent first indicator of locational problems.

The final stage of the cycle is that of decline. Actually, there are two alternatives to decline, namely stability and renovation. The latter is aptly illustrated by shoe production in New England, where specialisation in high-quality shoes has proved quite successful.

There is some uncertainty about whether to use the concept of product life-cycle for firms or for sectors. Individual firms tend to differentiate so much around the average that speaking of 'the' entrepreneur is virtually impossible. The concept may be a useful device to explain the locational dynamics of sectors, especially the interregional relocation processes of new sectors (Perry and Watkins, 1977; Aydalot, 1984).

For the concept to be useful to location theory, it has to be combined with sectoral and organisational variables. Heuss (1965) announces good results in particular for manufacturing industries; in our opinion, application to service industries is more difficult, because their relationship with the environment is different from that of manufacturing industries. At any rate some kind of a growth-cycle can be observed whenever there is innovation and market saturation, and success remains commonly imitated. The spatial impacts of the different cycles possible still have to be studied in more detail, especially the impact of innovations in transportation, communication, and data processing which tend to affect the size of market regions: indeed, success in business may depend on the size of the market region and an optimum location.

Business environment and regional structure

Regional structure is a heterogeneous concept, containing socio-economic as well as cultural and physical variables. In search of a location, an entrepreneur or manager can compare several regions, but in most cases he will make his decisions with only the region where he lives in mind. Of course, the large multinationals behave more 'rationally', but imitation and fashion have their way with them, too. Most locational decisions are based on the outcome of regional accretion and the cumulative development of the regional structure. The structure of economic space is not stable in itself, but the dynamics of economic development keep mostly within the existing structures; new structures tend to be created in periods of strong technological change and economic growth. Keeble (1978) has shown that in periods of rapid growth, many industries moved part of their companies from the South-East of England to the 'assisted areas' in search of labour and cheap sites.

An interesting question is whether regional structures also pass through a life-cycle. Forrester (1969) contended that cities and regions have indeed a cycle of economic development of about 150 years. Other scientists, urban planners for instance, recognise a development from Eopolis through Neopolis and Metropolis to Necropolis; Norton (1979), having compared the gradual decline of the economic position of the Snowbelt as contrasted with the Sunbelt, believes that it is impossible and 'unnatural' to 'rejuvenate' the 'old cities' of the North of the USA: it would be better to relocate the workers to the job, that is to the South. He bases his opinion on data of the 1960s and the 1970s till about 1975. From about 1975 onward, however, several Snowbelt-cities have shown a remarkable 'rejuvenation', among them New York and Boston; the latter has achieved it by the tremendous increase of the 'high-technology' sectors (De Jong, 1983). Indeed, Norton's thesis fails because it is based too much on the 'iron law' that the older regions have become less suitable for 'young industries'; regional structures have proved to be strong and fertile enough for fast new developments.

The examples of successful rejuvenation show that a region with a differentiated labour market, good accessibility for air transportation, and abundant educational and leisure facilities, remains attractive to investments. Back in the 1960s Klaassen had already stressed that amenities and qualified labour are very important locational factors.

Let us now return to our methodological problem: whether to use a structuralist approach or an approach based on methodological individualism. Of course, our survey is short and incomplete, but still warrants the conclusion that neither approach needs to be excluded. We should point out, however, that at least in locational studies, goals and motives have been emphasised more than structural conditions. Goals and motives often spring from structural developments in the business environment: decisions are commonly made under a given set of conditions. On the other hand, human beings have a happy tendency not to conform to set conditions and theories: innovation is not only creative destruction (Schumpeter), but also creative obstruction to general theories. The silent majority simply adjusts.

References

Aydalot, P. (1984), Reversal of spatial trends in French industry since 1974, in *IRPA-Yearbook*, vol. 1, Finnpublishers, Tampere.

Duijn, J.J. van and Lambooy, J.G. (1982), Technological innovation and regional economic growth: a meso-economic analysis, Research memorandum, no. 8207, Department of Economics, University of Amsterdam.

Duijn, J.J. van, Lambooy, J.G. and Paelinck, J.H.P. (1983), *Wegen van de doelmatigheid; Rapport inzake het regionaal sociaal-economisch beleid* (Roads of efficiency; Report with respect to regional socio-economic policy), SER/Staatsuitgeverij, The Hague.

Earl, P. (1983), *The Economic Imagination: Towards a Behavioural Analysis of Choice*, M.E. Sharpe, New York.

Forrester, J.W. (1969), *Urban Dynamics*, MIT-Press, Cambridge, Mass.
Giddens, A. (1978), *Class Structure of Advanced Societies*, Hutchinson, London.
Gordon, D.M. (1978), Capitalist development and the history of American cities, in W.K. Tabb and L. Sawers (eds), *Marxism and the Metropolis*, Oxford.
Harvey, D. (1973), *Social Justice and the City*, Arnold, London.
Heuss, E. (1965), *Allgemeine Markttheorie*, Mohr, Tübingen.
Hilhorst, J.G.M. (1981), *Territory and Function: A new Paradigm?*, Institute of Social Studies, The Hague.
Hirsch, F. (1977), *The Social Limits to Growth*, Routledge-Kegan Paul, London.
Jong, H.W. de (1979), *Paradoxale Economie* (Paradoxical Economy), Stenfert Kroese, Leiden.
Jong, H.W. de (1981), *Dynamische Markttheorie* (Dynamic Market Theory), Stenfert Kroese, Leiden.
Jong, M.W. de (1983), Regionale condities voor nieuwe hoogwaardige bedrijvigheid; industriële vernieuwing in Greater Boston (Regional conditions for new high quality activities; industrial renovation in Greater Boston), *ESB*, no. 3431, pp.1059–63.
Jong, M.W. de (1984), *Ruimtelijke dynamiek van het midden – en kleinbedrijf; het lokatiepatroon van kleine industriële ondernemingen in de Noordvleugel van de Randstad* (Spatial dynamics of small and medium-size enterprise; the location pattern of small industrial companies in the northern part of the Randstad), Economisch Geografisch Instituut, Universiteit van Amsterdam.
Keeble, D. (1976), *Industrial Location and Planning in the United Kingdom*, Methuen, London.
Klaassen, L.H. (1965), *Area Economic and Social Redevelopment*, OECD, Paris.
Klaassen, L.H. (1967), *Methods of Selecting Industries for Depressed Areas*, OECD, Paris.
Klaassen, L.H. (1968), *Social Amenities in Area Economic Growth*, OECD, Paris.
Lambooy, J.G. (1983), Urban theory and urban planning: the choice of a 'problematic', *Research Memorandum* no. 8319, Department of Economics, University of Amsterdam.
Massey, D. (1979), In what sense a regional problem? *Regional Studies*, vol. 13, pp.233–43.
Nelson, R.R. and Winter, S.G. (1982), *An Evolutionary Theory of Economic Change*, Belknap Press, Cambridge, Mass.
Norton, R.D. (1979), *City Life Cycles and American Urban Policy*, Academic Press, New York.
Perry, D.C. and Watkins, A.J. (1977), *The Rise of the Sunbelt Cities*,

Sage Publications, Beverly Hills/London.
Pollard, S. (1981), *Peaceful Conquest: The Industrialisation of Europe, 1760–1970*, Oxford University Press, Oxford.
Pred, A.R. (1967 and 1969), *Behaviour and Location*, 2 volumes; University of Lund, Lund.
Scott, A. (1980), *Locational Patterns and Dynamics of Industrial Activity in the Modern Metropolis*, University of Toronto.
Stichting voor Economisch Onderzoek (1978), *Bedrijfsmigratie uit Amsterdam* (Industrial migration from Amsterdam), Amsterdam.
Vernon, R. (1966), International investment and international trade, *Quarterly Journal of Economics*, May, pp.190–207.

PART III
URBAN TRENDS

12 Processes of urban development

R. H. FUNCK AND U. BLUM*

Introduction

Over the last decades in West Germany, but in other highly developed European countries as well (van den Berg, Drewett, Klaassen et al., 1982), urban development has been characterised by tendencies which influenced and changed the structure of large agglomerations to a considerable extent – an end to these tendencies is not yet to be seen. Some major symptoms are:

1 A continuing out-migration from city cores to the urban fringe and the suburbs which reached its peak in the 1970s;
2 Immigration from rural areas into the cities in the 1950s and 1960s, and an increasing remigration into the city core in the 1980s (Klaassen, Scimemi, 1981);
3 Changes in the economic, spatial and demographic structure of cities;
4 Repositioning of the administrative-political rank of cities in the national city hierarchy.

The underlying causes of the emergence of new urban and inter-urban structures are severe alterations in the values that are being attached by individuals as well as by the society as a whole to the respective merits of country versus city living, of closeness to nature

* The authors are indebted to Jan S. Kowalski, University of Karlsruhe, for valuable comments.

versus easy accessibility of cultural and other urban activities, and the related questions of environmental impacts and excessive energy consumption of a widely scattered settlement system and the resulting mobility patterns (van den Berg, Klaassen, 1984). Other causes lie in technological progress and the consequential changes of industrial and locational structure which tend to make job opportunities less dependent on raw material concentrations, and increase the attractiveness of centres of high infrastructural quality.

All of these tendencies are interwoven in a network of urban interrelationships. They may have different and even opposing effects on the development of various urban agglomerations. Some cities will experience a positive, others a negative migration balance; the economic performance of some cities will improve, it will deteriorate in others; some cities will increase their rank in the national city hierarchy, others will suffer a loss of importance as central places.

Based on this general description it seems adequate to assume that urban development is not a strictly monotonous growth process. Changes in growth rates over time, sudden breaks in the development direction, and – in the long run – cyclical processes (Funck, Blum, 1981) may be expected.

The urban system

The city can be defined[1] as a system consisting of three subsystems:

1 The urban population as the number of people living in the city and the balance of commuters;
2 The private and public capital assets;
3 The natural resources, especially air, water, land (including raw material deposits, forests etc.).[2]

The city, in a geographical sense, is incorporated in a metasystem which includes all other communities and rural areas of the country (see Figure 12.1). In its social and political meaning the metasystem represents the technological, institutional and behavioural structures which prevail in the society as a whole, and thus have to be considered as exogenous with respect to one particular urban society.

The three subsystems are realised in space which in turn is characterised by an economic, a geographic and a political dimension.[3] The interrelationships between the subsystems and toward the environment of the system (the metasystem) are defined as processes. It seems adequate to distinguish three urban processes:

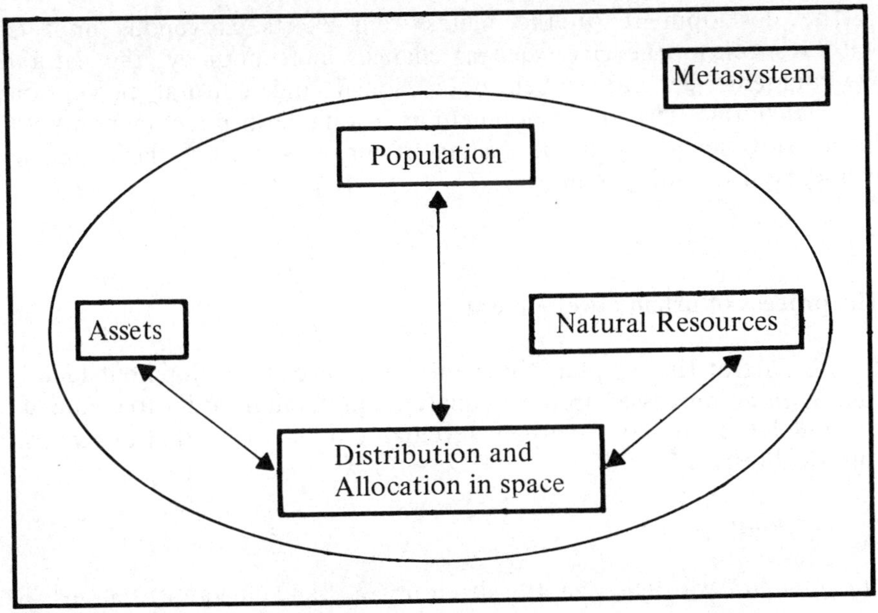

Figure 12.1 The city as a system

1 *The economic process* in relation to which the three subsystems may be identified as production factors;
2 *The social and cultural process*; the three subsystems in this respect are identified as factors of urban quality;
3 *The political and administrative process*; the three subsystems are identified as political and institutional factors.

The three processes and their interrelationships and interactions which will be subject to more detailed analysis in this chapter constitute the *process of urban development.*

The city as a special type of settlement is characterised by the specific way the three processes are realised in space, which means that the spatial organisation and structure of a city's social, economic and political activities differ considerably from those carried out in other types of settlements, especially those occurring in rural areas. Every city is a centre of attraction for its geographical, economic and political environment. This implies a circular relationship between the city and its metasystem which leads to positive as well as negative impacts on the urban processes.[4] In order to include these relationships the analysis of urban development should rely on a dynamic theory and dynamic models, even to the inclusion of structures as modelled by catastrophe theory (Orishimo, 1982).

The development of the metasystem exerts exogenous impacts with respect to the city, such as changes in technology, the natural environment, generative behaviour, social and cultural perception or legal norms. Urban development is a long term phenomenon with rather slow reactions in the system of interrelationships between the elements of the subsystems.

The process of urban development

In this part of the chapter, the elements of urban development identified as three processes are being analysed in detail in order to enable us to model the process of urban development in a way that allows for empirical testing.

The economic process

The population The size, the structure and the behaviour of an urban population influences the urban economy to a large extent. Consumer preferences determine the way private incomes are spent and, thus, influence the structure of urban production. This is of special importance for cities in their function as centres for the supply of spatially immobile goods, especially tertiary services of public and private origin. These in turn influence the exchange with the metasystem, predominantly the import of resources and the export of intermediate and final goods as well as capital. In addition, the level of qualification of the urban population should be noted; in most cases, a strictly increasing relationship between the ability of a city to cope with economic change and the level of qualification of its population can be observed.[5]

Capital assets Public capital assets are mainly incorporated in elements of infrastructure. The infrastructure is defined as a set of special categories of assets, the availability of which is a necessary precondition for making productive or consumptive use of other types of capital assets. We can distinguish between material and immaterial infrastructure, the latter consisting of institutional infrastructure and personal infrastructure.

The bulk of public capital assets belongs to the category of material infrastructure which is characterised by spatial immobility. Thus, it can be considered as an input potential (Blum, 1982a, 1982b) while spatially mobile factors are called attractable factors. The distinction between input potentials and attractable factors is most useful in the analysis of urban or regional production (Funck, Blum, 1983); however, it will also prove helpful for identifying the effects of the other urban processes. Some types of material infrastructure in a city are roads, railway tracks and stations, communication systems, schools, theatres, hospitals, recreation facilities etc.[6]

Private capital assets may be put to either productive or consumptive use. Where spatial immobility is given for the assets, they can be considered as an input potential, e.g. urban land, buildings, most industrial facilities etc.

Natural resources The qualities and sizes of different locations are of utmost importance for the distribution of capital assets and activities in urban geographical space. With respect to production, all kinds of natural resources have to be considered as spatially immobile production factors, the use of which in production has, among other effects, an impact on environmental quality. Predominantly though, the degree of availability of certain natural resources determines the economic structure of a city. As an example: rivers which can be used as waterways or as a source of energy have, in many cases, been responsible for the founding and the direction of the economic development of a city.

The importance of input potentials in the economic process Input potentials influence the economy of a city in two different ways (Blum, 1982a, pp.20–35):

1 The urban equipment with input potentials to a large extent determines the locational structure and, thus, the types of economic activities as well as the level of income in the city. This is due to the fact that the capacity for utilising an input potential is limited, and, with regard to a given technology, input potentials are limitational with respect to the input of attractable factors.
2 There is no free market for input potentials since public authorities control the supply of and the access to input potentials and have the power of determining their prices; it can be assumed that in most cases these prices do not reflect marginal costs, thus preventing a clearing of the market in the Walrasian sense.[7]

Due to the limitationality between input potentials and attractable factors, the latter are always fully employed as they are being purchased at marginal costs according to the economic necessities. The urban equipment with input potentials thus determines the economic suprastructure.

The social and cultural process

Population The following phenomena linked to the size and the structure of the population are to be noted in the West German context:

1 The age distribution and the size of the German population are changing rapidly due to changes in generative behaviour; the age median will be 65 years in 2030, should the present birth and death rates remain constant.
2 The decrease in the size of the population, and the increase in average age will reduce the dynamics of social and cultural behaviour, and thus will probably lead to more conservative attitudes with respect to social change, and to more stable consumer preferences.
3 Differences in the generative behaviour of the German population and of foreign worker families, especially from the Near East, may decidedly change the ethnic structure of the society in Germany.
4 Changes in the structure of the workforce, especially an increase in unemployment of unskilled labour, will have a stronger impact on urban areas than on rural areas: in rural areas the unemployed have better opportunities of spending their free time in a productive way, e.g. by joining the underground economy. Female participation in the labour force is highest in urban areas.
5 A high degree of urban segregation, especially prevalent in suburbs designed in the 1960s and 1970s as 'dormitory cities' reduces the coherence and increases the social strains in a city.
6 The urban population is a carrier of education in a broad cultural sense as compared to instruction which is relevant for creating human capital in a purely economic sense.

Assets Assets relevant for the social and cultural process of a city are very often identical to the assets relevant for production, as social and economic effects are often closely linked. Facilities for instruction, education and recreation, institutions of social service or cultural institutions are typical examples in this sense. Social and cultural assets which are not directly relevant for production lie in the historic heritage of a city, as it is mainly represented in buildings (castles, historic town halls etc.).

Natural resources Urban quality factors related to natural resources can be named as follows:

1 The geomorphological structure of a city which influences the zoning within the city area, i.e. the distribution of social

and cultural activities in geographical space, and thus mobility and communication behaviour.

2 The historic heritage of a city, as expressed in distinct places in the city where certain historic events occurred which are considered relevant by the city population for their urban identity.

Effects of urban quality factors on the social and cultural process
The quality of living experienced by the urban population is the most important effect of urban quality factors. The following aspects are worth noting:

1 Territoriality defined as a level of consciousness through which the urban population develops a feeling of identification with its neighbourhood, its city district or the city as a whole (Newman, 1972).

2 The social and cultural life of a city expressed in mobility, communication, arts etc.

Thus, the quality of urban life is not an objective phenomenon; on the contrary, it is distinctly dependent on the perception of the urban population. This perception will vary strongly from one citizen to the next. The perception revealed in social and cultural preferences is a cause but also an outcome of urban cultural and social development.

The political and administrative process

Population The importance of the population in the political and administrative process lies in the attitude of urban citizens toward their political institutions and the question of how to structure them, as expressed in voting participation, citizens' initiatives etc.

Assets and natural resources The relevance of assets and natural resources in the political and administrative process can be expressed in property rights which can be exerted by land owners but also by non-owners, especially by political institutions. Among the most important property rights is the legal competence to delineate a piece of land and to use the resources which it harbours as well as certain categories of material infrastructure (roads, water, energy and sewage systems) which are related to it within the legal norms. These property rights constitute a location (see Bökemann, 1982, pp.64ff).

The effects of political and institutional conditions on the political and administrative process The power which a city is able to exert with respect to the city area and into the metasystem is the most important result of the three political and institutional factors which are combined in the political and administrative process. Several aspects of this power have to be considered:

1 The legitimacy of the political process in a city;
2 The degree of control which a city exerts over a certain area in a legal sense, and as a supply site for public goods, especially infrastructure services;
3 The authority of the political institutions of a city with respect to zoning and the creation of guidelines for future city developments;
4 The direct interference of political institutions as the public sector in the economic process through investments and public consumption and in the social and cultural process through subsidies, social security systems etc.;
5 The ability of institutional conflict resolution within the political process.

In recent years political power has shown the tendency to shift away from cities to state or federal governments because of the fact that an increasing number of political and administrative decisions as well as an increasing share of financial resources were subjected to legal norms established by central governments. The cancellation of certain urban taxes[8] and, consequently, the increasing dependence on revenue sharing with respect to federal taxes and on project-related federal and state subsidies is an example of this development. Thus, urban institutions are increasingly losing their capacities to influence urban development.

Description of a dynamic model of urban development

The structure of the model

In Figure 12.2 a model of urban development is outlined which includes all aspects of urban development described in the first four sections. The following general assumptions are needed to define such a model:

A1: The city as a system is constituted by the three subsystems urban population, assets and natural resources and is incorporated in a metasystem which includes other cities, rural areas and exogenous structures.

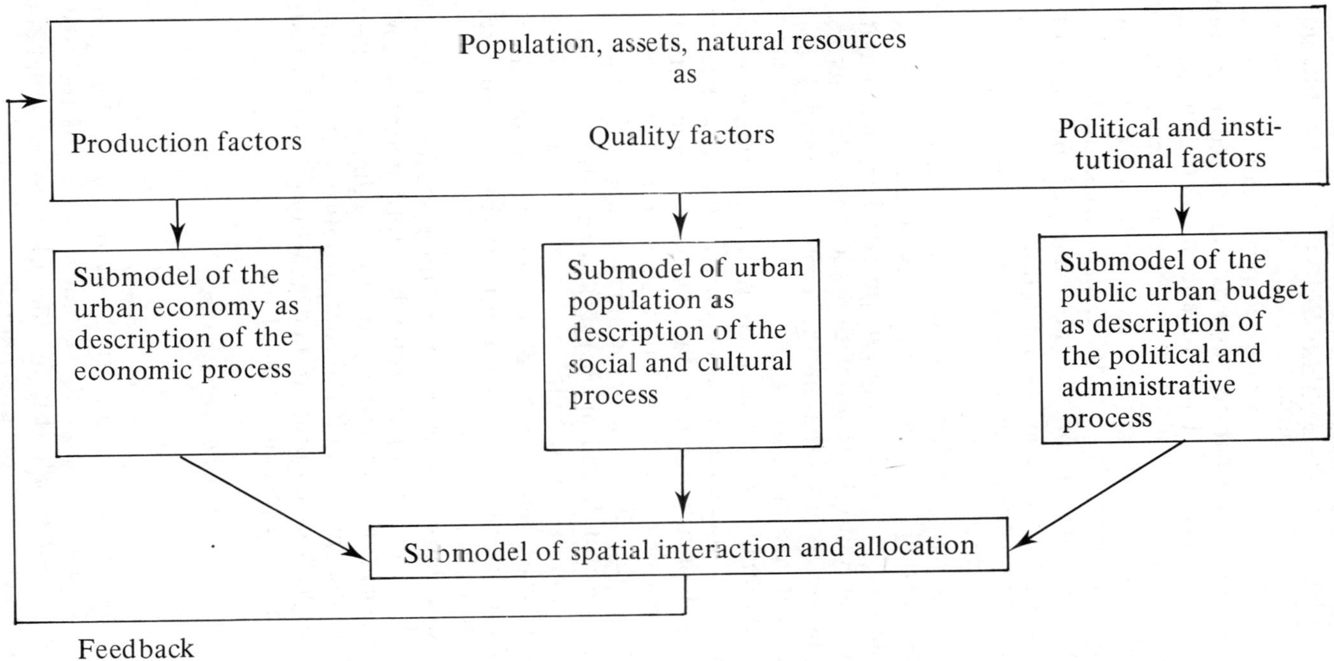

Figure 12.2 Diagram of a model of urban development

A2: Three processes take place in the city and are fed by the elements of every subsystem: (a) the economic process; (b) the social and cultural process; and (c) the political and administrative process.

A3: The combination of the three production factors population, assets and natural resources in an economic process can be directly related to the urban production level.

A4: The combination of the three quality factors population, assets and natural resources in a social and cultural process can be directly related to the level of urban quality of living.

A5: The combination of the three political and institutional factors population, assets and natural resources in a political and administrative process can be directly related to the level of urban power.

A6: All subsystems or factors which are – in a medium to long term period – characterised by spatial (geographical) immobility are called input potentials. They are limitational with respect to the input of all other attractable factors.

A7: Input potentials used in the economic process are not priced at marginal costs.

A8: The economic process in a city is subject to outside control (from the metasystem) according to the degree to which a city is incorporated in the system of commodity flows and thus dependent on an outside supply of attractable factors, the degree of exogenous company management, the degree of technical change and the ability of the city population to cope with it.

A9: Urban space and thus land use can be described in three dimensions: (a) geographical space; (b) economic space; (c) political space.

A10: The distribution in space of the three subsystems is determined in the economic sector by profit maximisation, in the social and cultural sector by maximising collective utility and, in the political-administrative sector, by maximising the long term urban budget within the set of restrictions valid in a certain period of time.

Operationalising the subsystems and processes

Production factors

1 Urban population may be quantified by the size and age structure, and the educational and sectoral structure of the labour force on the supply side, the number of consumers and their preference structures on the demand side.

2 Urban assets should be classified in the following way:

(a) Public assets

(i) Material infrastructure may be quantified by using capacity indicators.

(ii) Immaterial infrastructure (e.g. the influence of the rank of a central place) may be quantified by using the attributed average income value which can be estimated using regression techniques (Funck, Blum, 1984).

(b) Private assets may be quantified using their market values.

3 Natural resources should be classified in two groups according to their degree of spatial (geographical) mobility. They can be quantified by their market values, the value of the amount of the resource extracted over the period analysed or by estimating opportunity costs, especially in the case of environmental resources.

Quality factors

1 Population as a quality factor is important with respect to age structure, educational structure and the social and cultural perception of the city; through these aspects the scale and the range of social and cultural interactions within the set of neighbourhoods or city districts is defined as well as the ambience as a set of spatially indetermined social coherences (Orleans, 1973).

2 Assets as quality factors should again be classified according to their degree of spatial (geographical) mobility. They may be quantified by capacities on the supply side, the degree of utilisation (number of visitors, students, etc.) on the demand side.

3 Natural resources as quality factors should also be classified according to their degree of spatial (geographical) mobility. They may be quantified by defining certain standards accepted by the urban society and estimating the actual deviation from these standards (e.g. a standard of 40 db(A) as an acceptable noise level in a residential area during night-time).

Political and institutional factors

1 Population is relevant to the political and administrative process as the number of tax payers and the amount of tax revenues which can be collected.

2 Assets and natural resources are relevant as a tax base and as a strategic instrument of shaping a city and its locational structure. The latter has repercussions on the economic sector; the effects

are to be quantified as changes in land prices (assets), infrastructure equipment, etc.

Operational definitions of the three dimensions of urban space

Urban space contains the outcomes of the three processes which have, until now, been considered separately even though they share a common set of three factors with three different characteristics.

1 The result of an urban production process may be quantified as the gross value added of a city or the gross urban product.
2 The result of the social and the cultural process may be quantified in levels of attractivity, e.g. as number of citizens enjoying certain social or cultural services or the aggregate attractivity of the city as indicated by the commuter balance. These approaches probably offer the best opportunities to solve the measuring problem. To try and describe personal preferences or utilities and to aggregate them into a collective indicator of attractiveness would pose difficult theoretical (Arrow, 1951) as well as empirical problems.
3 The result of the political and administrative process can be quantified in the size of the urban budget and in election participation rates.

Spatial interaction

In a spatial allocation model, every geographical location defined as a certain zone in the city can be related to the urban population residing or working and to the assets localised in that zone, to the value of production, investment and consumption, the social and cultural attraction and the balance between the taxes collected and the share of the budget spent in relation to that zone.

According to technology, preferences and quality perception, the system has an economic, a social and cultural as well as a political and administrative suprastructure which is restricted due to assumption (A6): As input potentials are limitational with respect to the input of attractable factors, economic output, the attractivity of the city or the size of the budget has an upper limit once the capacities of input potentials are exhausted; e.g. all roads are fully congested, all theatre seats are taken, all the land is zoned and occupied.

Having quantified all necessary indicators of the model, these indicators can be related to each other in a mathematical model according to cause-effect relationships established in additional assumptions. Most of these relationships can best be formulated using systems of difference equations in a population model, an economic model, a model of the public budget, a model of spatial interaction and allocation. The following sections give a brief survey of such a model (for a more detailed description see Blum, 1984).

A model of cyclical urban development

The economic process

The economic submodel is an extension of the Samuelson-type accelerator-multiplier model and is characterised by the following properties:

- E1: Private households, private firms and public urban institutions are actors in the economic process.
- E2: Investments create a capacity and an income effect.
- E3: Consumer demand depends on the disposable income of the urban population in the preceding period.
- E4: Ex post savings equal investments.
- E5: Inputs may be related to production levels by a Cobb-Douglas-type function.
- E6: Private firms maximise profits.

Urban income, YU(t), is defined as the sum of consumer demand, CU(t), and urban investments, IU(t). Disposable income may be computed by subtracting taxes, TU(t), from urban income and by adding the income of the balance of commuters given by the product of their number, CBU(t), and the urban wage level, WU(t). Urban investments, IU(t), depend on private autonomous investments, IUA, public investments IPU(t) as determined by the political process, and the change in private consumption, CU(t)–CU(t – 1). Hence, the first part of the model reads:

$$YU(t) - b.(1+d).YU(t-1) + b.d.YU(t-2)$$

$$= IUA + IPU(t) - b.TU(t-1) + c.WU(t-1).CBU(t-1) \qquad (5.1)$$

This inhomogeneous difference equation has cyclical, unsteady or monotonic solutions depending on the values of the marginal consumption rate, b, and the value of the accelerator, d.

The most probable solutions are the cyclical ones due to $b \in (0,1)$.

The cyclical development is divergent $\sqrt{b.d.} > 1$, constant if $\sqrt{b.d} = 1$ and convergent if $\sqrt{b.d} < 1$. Solving the inhomogeneous equation, we obtain the equilibrium urban income and the urban investment multiplier, $(1-b)^{-1}$.

Urban savings are supposed to equal urban investments:

$$SU(t) = IU(t) \tag{5.2}$$

Producton factors are given in the urban labour force, LU(t), the stock of private capital assets, KU(t), and the stock of public capital assets, KPU(t). Then:

$$YU(t) = f_0.\exp(f_1.t).LU(t)^{f_2}.KU(t)^{f_3}.KPU(t)^{f_4}, \quad f_0, f_1, f_2, f_3, f_4, > 0 \tag{5.3}$$

Demand for urban labour for given levels of income, and stocks of private and public capital assets, may be computed by inverting formula (5.3). The first derivative of urban income with respect to urban labour renders the urban wage level.

Urban private and public investments increase the stocks of capital assets:

$$KU(t) = KU(t-1) + IU(t-1) \tag{5.4}$$

$$KPU(t) = KPU(t-1) + IPU(t-1) \tag{5.5}$$

The social and cultural process

This submodel is defined by the following properties:

- Q1: The balance of urban migration depends on the (relative) quality of living in the city as described by the factors of urban quality. The economic strength of a city influences the balance of commuters.
- Q2: The size of urban population depends on the size of the urban population in the preceding year, on birth and mortality rates and the migration balance.

The migration balance, MU(t), depends on the quality of living inside and outside the city, QU(t–1) and QA, the size of the city population, PU(t–1) and the size of the outside population, PG(t–1), in the preceding year:

$$MU(t) = a_2 \,.\, QU(t-1) - a_3 \,.\, QA + a_4 \,.\, PG(t-1) - a_5 \,.\, PU(t-1) \,,$$

$$a_2\,,\; a_3,\; a_4,\; a_5 > 0 \text{ as perception parameters,}$$

$$a_4\,,\; a_5 < 1 \tag{5.6}$$

The commuter balance, CBU(t), depends on the labour market situation and the labour force participation rate of the city residents:

$$CBU(t) = \begin{cases} 0 & \text{if } LU(t) \leqslant a_1 \,.\, PU(t) \quad (5.7a) \\ LU(t) - a_1 \,.\, PU(t) & \text{if } LU(t) > a_1 \,.\, PU(t) \quad (5.7b) \end{cases}$$

where $a_1 \in (0,1)$ is the labour force participation rate.

Urban quality with respect to urban assets is given as

$$QU(t) = \frac{KBU(t)}{FU \,.\, PU(t-1)} \tag{5.8}$$

where FU is the urban area.

The total model thus reads:

$$\begin{aligned} & PU(t) - (1+g-m) \,.\, PU(t-1) + a_5 \,.\, PU(t-2) \\ & = a_2 \,.\, QU(t-2) - a_3 \,.\, QA - a_4 \,.\, PG(t-2) \end{aligned} \tag{5.9}$$

where g and m are the birth and the mortality rates.

Depending on the values of the parameters, the solution of this inhomogeneous difference equation may either have cyclical, unsteady or monotonic solutions. A cyclical development is most probable if the total urban population stagnates while the levels of in- and out-migration are very high; then, a divergent solution is not possible as divergence is dependent on $a_5 > 1$, which is ruled out.

The political and administrative process

This submodel is characterised as follows:

P1: Public urban revenues consist of business, property and income taxes, revenues from public services and the increase of public debts.

P2: Public urban capital expenditures consist of public urban investments, backpayments of loans and payments of interest on loans; a surplus of the public urban budget is needed to pay for all other public urban activities.

P3: Loans are granted for two years and are paid back in the second year; interest payments are due both years.

P4: Public urban investments earn revenues in the consecutive two years; they are part of total urban investments.

P5: Loans and investments are proportional to the surplus of the urban budget.

If the increase in urban public debt, DPU(t), and the level of urban public investments, IPU(t), both depend on the size of the surplus of the urban public budget, BPU(t), then

$$DPU(t) = h_2 \,.\, BPU(t) \;, \; h_2 \in (0,1) \qquad (5.10)$$

$$IPU(t) = h_3 \,.\, BPU(t) \;, \; h_3 \in (0,1) \qquad (5.11)$$

Taxes, TU(t), are proportional to urban income, YU(t–1), and the size of the urban population, PU(t–1) of the preceding year:

$$TU(t) = h_4 \,.\, YU(t-1) + h_5 \,.\, PU(t-1), h_4 \in (0,1), h_5 > 0 \qquad (5.12)$$

For an interest rate on public debt z, and a rate of revenues for investments h_1 the total model reads:

$$\begin{aligned} BPU(t) = {} & DPU(t) - IPU(t) + h_1 \,.\, IPU(t-1) + h_1 \,.\, IPU(t-2) \\ & - z.DPU(t-1) - z.DPU(t-2) - DPU(t-2) \\ & + h_4 \,.\, YU(t-1) + h_5 \,.\, PU(t-1) \qquad (5.13) \end{aligned}$$

If formulae (5.9) through (5.13) are combined, the result is:

$$\begin{aligned} (1-h_2) \,.\, BPU(t) & - (h_1 .h_3 - z.h_2) \,.\, BPU(t-1) \\ & - (h_1 .h_3 - z.h_2) \,.\, BPU(t-2) + h_2 \,.\, BPU(t-2) \\ & = h_4 \,.\, YU(t-1) + h_5 .PU(t-1) \qquad (5.14) \end{aligned}$$

The solution of equation (5.14) is either cyclical, unsteady or monotonic depending on the value of the parameters. Complex solutions occur if public authorities increase the level of new loans above the level of new investments – which is illegal in the case of the Federal Republic of Germany – or if investments are completely unprofitable and the interest rate on public debt is high.

The realisation of the three processes in urban space influences the processes themselves by changing the quantities and the structures of the subsystems and by reshaping behavioural and technological side-conditions and patterns.

The quantities and the structures of the subsystems are changed at the end of every period according to the relationships established in the three submodels; the behavioural and technological patterns and relationships are reflected by the coefficients in the submodels. It is assumed that some of them are fixed and can only be affected exogenously, that is through influences from the metasystem; in the model, the respective parameters can be changed numerically as it is implemented in an interactive way on a computer. Other influences are endogenous to the urban development and are subject to changes depending on the degree of urban congestion:

S1: Parameters reflecting changes of behavioural and technological patterns are endogenous to urban development and, thus, depend on the level of urban congestion and agglomeration in the influencing variable.

S2: The distribution of endogenous parameters is symmetric and triangular (see Figure 12.3).

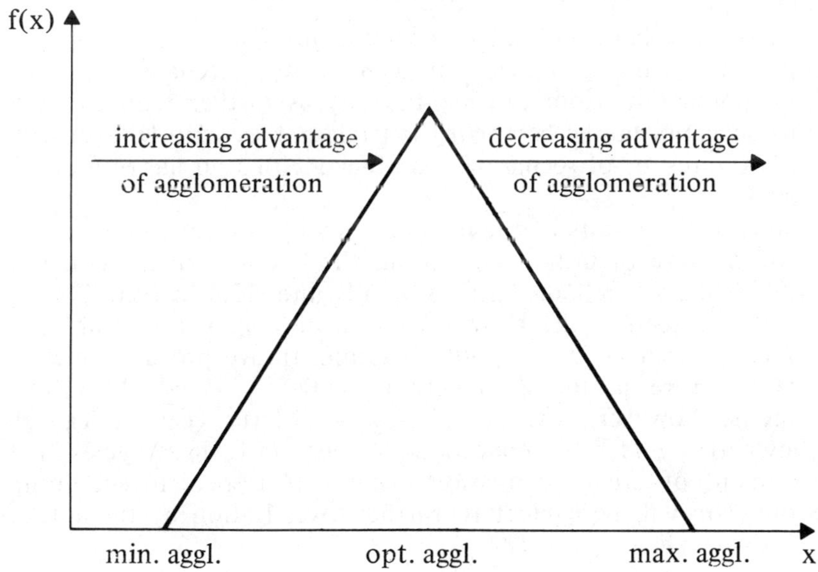

Figure 12.3 Distribution of endogenous parameters as determined by the degree of urban agglomeration and congestion
(x: Level of agglomeration or congestion;
f(x): density function)

Urban production elasticities (f_2, f_3, f_4) are related to their production factors; labour force participation rates (a_4) and the rate of urban demographic pressure (a_5) are related to the size of urban population; the value of the accelerator (d) is related to the stock of private urban capital, the earning ratio of public investments (h_1) is related to the stock of public urban capital.

Empirical evidence

Based on data of the city of Karlsruhe and the Federal Republic of Germany for the years 1980 and 1981 for the values of the elements of the subsystems and on data estimated with econometric models for the parameters (every endogenous parameter was described by two values: its optimal level and its worst level), a set of scenarios was computed.

Scenario A, proposed as a reference, describes the situation as perceived in the years 1976–82; the situation is economically depressed, the lack of investments and excessive economic congestion keep the level of urban income at constant levels. The size of urban population increases due to a positive balance of migration, mostly encouraged by increases in urban attractivity. The city budget is stable due to a surplus of investments over new debt.

Scenario B is characterised by a decrease of the perception of population pressure to half of its value in scenario A; in scenario C the pressure of population from outside the city is further reduced. Based on this scenario, public borrowing is tripled in scenario D. Scenario E presents the results of scenario D combined with a surplus of mortality over births.

Graphs of the results of these scenarios with respect to the development of the size of urban population, the level of urban income and the level of the urban budget are given in Figures 12.4 to 12.6.

As can be seen in the figures, cyclical developments occur in the economic as well as in the political-administrative process which are especially severe in the extremely pessimistic scenario E. Cyclical movements, however, ease out after about thirty years. It can also be shown that under the conditions of scenario E slight cycles in the development of urban population occur with respect to age groups. This question will be subject to further investigation by the authors.

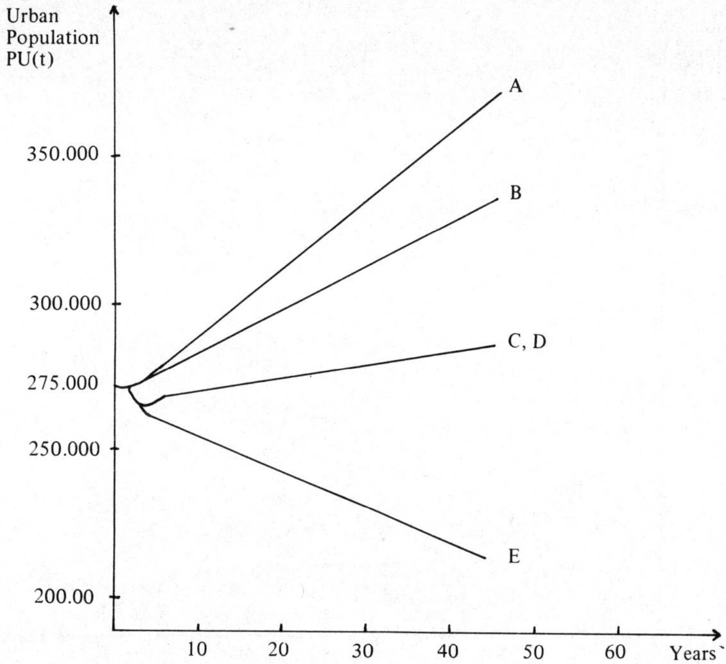

Figure 12.4 Development of urban population

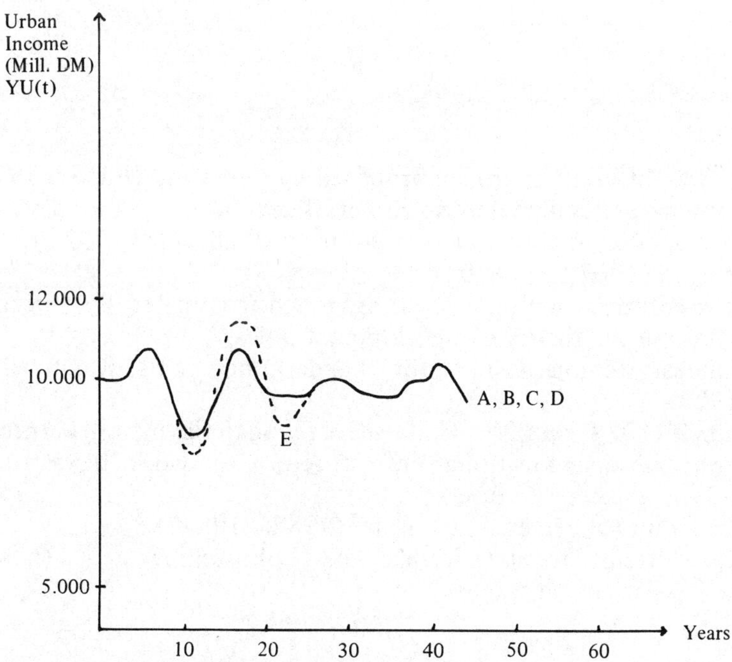

Figure 12.5 Development of urban income

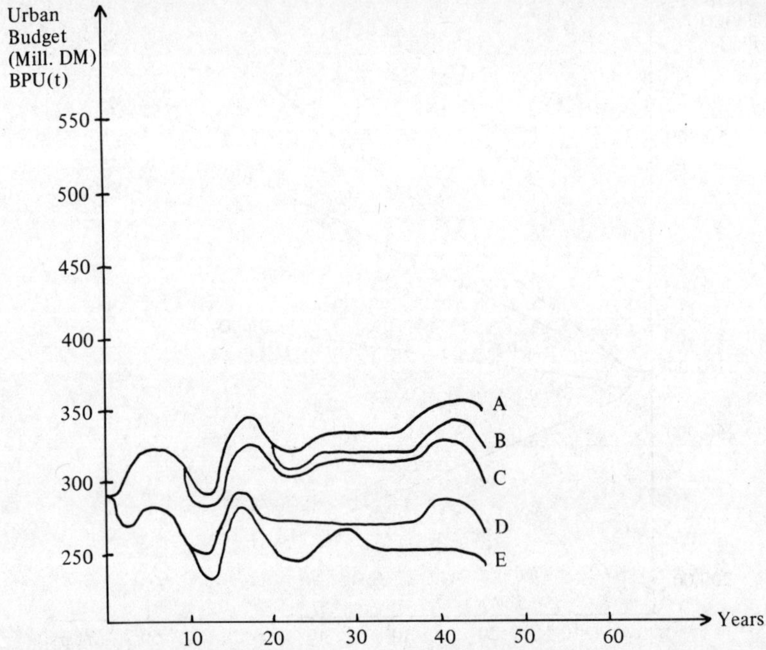

Figure 12.6 Development of the urban budget

Notes

1 Cf. the different approach proposed by Berry and Horton, 1970.
2 For a more detailed description cf. Blum, 1984.
3 As opposed to the approach given by Boudeville (1972, pp.17ff) or Isard (1967, pp.647ff).
4 This contrasts with the dual approach formulated by Hirschman (1958) in the theory of development poles.
5 Bundesforschungsanstalt für Landeskunde und Raumordnung (1982).
6 Funck (1978, pp.290–4) classifies the material infrastructure into three subsets: locational infrastructure, network infrastructure and nodal infrastructure.
7 For empirical evidence, see Blum (1982a, 1982b).
8 E.g. Getränkesteuer (beverage tax), Lohnsummensteuer (business tax on the sum of wages).

References

Arrow, K. (1951), *Social Choice and Individual Values*, John Wiley, New York-London-Sydney (1964).

Berg, L. van den and Klaassen, L.H., Economic Cycles (1984), Spatial Cycles and Transportation Structures in Urban Areas, Netherlands Economic Institute, Rotterdam, *Series: Foundations of Empirical Economic Research*, 1984/1.

Berg, L. van den, Drewett, R., Klaassen, L.H., Rossi, A. and Vijverberg, C.H.T. (1982), *Urban Europe, A Study of Growth and Decline*, Pergamon, Oxford.

Berry, B. and Horton, F. (1970), *Geographic Perspectives on Urban Systems*, Prentice Hall, Englewood Cliffs.

Blum, U. (1982a), Regionale Wirkungen von Infrastrukturinvestitionen (Regional Effects of Investments in the Infrastructure), in R. Funck (ed.), *Karlsruher Beiträge zur Wirtschaftspolitik und Wirtschaftsforschung*, Karlsruhe.

Blum, U. (1982b), Effects of Transportation Investments on Regional Growth – A Theoretical and Empirical Investigation, *Regional Science Association Papers*, vol. 49, Urbana (Ill.), pp.169–84.

Blum, U. (1983), Bestimmungsgründe der regionalen Wirtschaftsstruktur (Determinants of Regional Economic Structure), *Discussion Paper*, Institut für Wirtschaftspolitik und Wirtschaftsforschung, Karlsruhe.

Blum, U. (1984), Stadtentwicklung als unstetiger Prozess im Raum (Urban Development as an Unbalanced Process in Space), *Discussion Paper*, Institut für Wirtschaftspolitik und Wirtschaftsforschung, Karlsruhe.

Bökemann, D. (1982), *Theorie der Raumplanung* (Theory of Spatial Planning), Oldenbourg, München, Wien.

Boudeville, J.R. (1972), *Aménagement du territoire et polarisation*, Paris.

Bundesforschungsanstalt für Landeskunde und Raumordnung (1982), *Qualifikation und Innovation als Strategie der Raumplanung* (Qualification and Innovation as a Strategy of Spatial Planning), Bonn.

Funck, R. (1978), Multidimensionale Entscheidungsfunktionen in der Planung der regionalen Infrastrukturausstattung (Multidimensional Decision-functions for Planning the Regional Equipment with Infrastructure), in W. Buhr, P. Friedrich (eds), *Wettbewerb zwischen kleinen Regionen* (Competition among small Regions), Nomos, Baden-Baden, pp.289–304.

Funck, R. and Blum, U. (1981), Urban Policy Analysis, in P. Nijkamp, P. Rietveld (eds), *Problems and Policies*, Alphen aan den Rijn-

Rockville (Md.), pp.243–55.
Funck, R. and Blum, U. (1983), Regional Development and Investments in the Infrastructure – The Evaluation of Conflicting Impacts, in W. Isard, Y. Nagao (eds), *International and Regional Conflict*, Ballinger, Cambridge, Mass., pp.91–116.
Funck, R. and Blum, U. (1984), Zentralörtlicher Status, Verkehrsinfrastruktur und regionales Einkommen (Central Place Status, Transport Infrastructure and Regional Income), in H.J. Ewers, H. Schuster (eds), *Probleme der Ordnungs- und Strukturpolitik* (Problems of Economic Policy and Structure), Vandenhoeck and Ruprecht, Göttingen, pp.223–33.
Hirschman, A. (1958), *The Strategy of Economic Development*, New Haven-London.
Isard, W., et al. (1967), *Methods of Regional Analysis: An Introduction to Regional Science*, Cambridge, Mass.
Klaassen, L.H. and Scimemi, G. (1981), Theoretical Issues in Urban Dynamics, in L.H. Klaassen, W.T.M. Molle, J.H.P. Paelinck (eds), *Dynamics of Urban Development*, Gower, Aldershot, Hants.
Lynch, K. (1960), *The Image of the City*, MIT Press, Cambridge.
Newman, O. (1972), *Defensible Space: Crime Prevention through Urban Design*, Macmillan, New York.
Orishimo, I. (1982), *Urbanization and Environmental Quality*, Kluwer-Nijhoff, Boston-The Hague-London.
Orleans, P. (1973), Cognition of Urban Residents: Effects of Social Scale on Mapping, in R. Downs, D. Stea (eds), *Image and Environment: Cognitive Mapping and Spatial Behaviour*, Aldine, Chicago, pp.115–30.
Statistisches Bundesamt (different years), *Statistisches Jahrbuch für die Bundesrepublik Deutschland*, Kohlhammer, Stuttgart-Mainz.

13 An analysis of recent urban development trends in Japan

H. YAMADA

Introduction

The rapid mass urbanisation which Japan has experienced in the post-war period of high economic growth is probably unrivalled anywhere else in the developed countries. Up to the late 1960s the most significant feature of this urbanisation was the concentration of population and industry in a limited number of metropolitan regions such as Tokyo, Osaka and Nagoya. Indeed, with the larger urban centres growing faster than average, until 1970 the whole Japanese urban system tended to centralise. Within these metropolitan regions there was at first a tendency to concentrate in the central cities. But the 1960s saw a marked decentralisation, the suburbs growing faster than the central city. The large metropolitan areas suffered from many urban problems inherent in such a process: housing shortages, traffic congestion and degradation of the environment.[1] Most studies of Japanese urban development have tended to focus on these large metropolises, but in two important recent studies attempts have been made to analyse the development of the Japanese urban system as a whole. First, N.J. Glickmann (1979) set out to analyse the entire system of Japanese cities and understand the nature of urban development in Japan. For the purpose of his research he defined the 'Regional Economic Cluster (REC)', an urban unit composed of a core city and its commuting field, as a measure of a unified economic region. His definition of a functional urban area is similar to the United States' 'Standard Metropolitan Statistical Area (SMSA)' or the British

'Standard Metropolitan Labour Area (SMLA)'. Trying to develop Glickmann's ideas, T. Kawashima called this unit the 'Functional Urban Core (FUC)', and then extended the analysis using a new definition of the 'Functional Urban Region (FUR)', which is the whole region composed of a functional urban core and its hinterland (Kawashima, 1981).

The second study is the one made by the Mitsubishi Research Institute (MRI) under the sponsorship of the National Institute for Research Advancement (NIRA), in which we ourselves collaborated in its early stages (MRI, 1981). This study also defined an urban unit composed of a central city and its commuting area, calling it 'Toshiken' (Urban Area). The new definition covers more central cities, and hence more urban areas and a broader commuting area than either the REC or the FUC; it also differs from the latter two in that the urban areas are not exclusive, because an administrative area included in one urban area can also be included in others.

There is every reason to continue such research, especially in view of recent indications of changes in urban development. The shift of people from peripheral to central areas has gradually lost its momentum; net migration to the three largest metropolitan regions has almost stopped, and some old urban centres are losing population. So, the pattern of urban development may shift in the direction which has brought about 'inner city problems' or 'urban decline' in many developed countries.[2]

This chapter is an attempt to analyse the evolution of the Japanese urban system and to gain a deeper insight into the nature of the urban development process in contemporary Japan, with the so-called 'stage model of urbanisation' as a framework. This model, proposed by Drewett, Goddard and Spence (1976), postulates that centralisation and decentralisation in urban systems depend on the stage reached in the 'life cycle' of individual cities.[3] It has recently been developed by Klaassen et al., (1979, 1981) into the 'spatial-cycle model', which characterises the whole process of urban development as consisting of the following stages: urbanisation, suburbanisation, disurbanisation, and, possibly, reurbanisation. On the basis of that model we shall examine recent urban change in Japan.

As an analytic unit for our research we introduce a new definition of the metropolitan area, using a measure based on functionally integrated economic regions; it is a new definition of the Japanese version of the SMSA or SMLA. This urban unit will be called the 'Standard Metropolitan Employment Area (SMEA)', being more similar to the SMSA or SMLA than to the REC (FUC) or 'Toshiken'; the word 'employment' is added to emphasise the importance of employment to any definition of the metropolitan area.

The definition of the Japanese urban system

The definition of an individual SMEA contains two elements: first, a city of a specified population constituting the central city, and second, economic relations with contiguous administrative areas of a metropolitan nature.

To choose a set of central cities, four criteria for selecting a potential central city were adopted:

- 1a The city must have more than 50,000 inhabitants.
- 1b At least 75 per cent of the resident employed population must be non-agricultural.
- 1c The ratio of day-time to night-time resident population must be greater than 1.
- 1d The proportion of the resident employed population of a central city commuting to other central cities and other administrative areas must be less than 15 and 30 per cent, respectively (this condition has been added to eliminate satellite cities).

To identify administrative units (cities, towns and villages) as lying within the commuting range of central cities and thus qualifying for incorporation in the metropolitan ring, three criteria were adopted:

- 2a At least 75 per cent of the resident employed population must be non-agricultural.
- 2b The proportion of the resident employed population commuting to the central city must be greater than 10 per cent.
- 2c If an administrative area is eligible for incorporation in more than one potential central city, it is grouped with the central city to which most commuters travel.

Finally, the following criterion was added as a minimum agglomeration requirement:

- 3a To be regarded as a SMEA, the whole group should have an enumerated population of at least 100,000.

By applying the same criteria to 1965 and 1975 data sets of population, employment, and journey-to-work data for about 3,000 local authority areas (cities, towns and villages), adjusted for boundary changes, we have identified 87 SMEAs in 1965 and 104 in 1975. Table 13.1 shows the selection of the central cities of SMEAs; the number of cities where the population satisfies the minimum criterion (1a) and where employment was urban in character (1b) greatly increased through the period, while that of cities meeting the centrality criterion (1c) decreased. The considerable number of cities satisfying

Table 13.1

The numbers of cities and central cities of SMEAs

	1965 (% of total)	1975 (% of total)
All cities	561(100.0)	634(100.0)
Cities meeting 1a	291(51.9)	376(59.3)
Cities meeting 1b	291(51.9)	496(78.2)
Cities meeting 1c	372(58.3)	319(50.3)
Cities meeting 1a, b, c	126(22.5)	180(28.4)
Central cities (meeting 1a, b, c, d, 3a)	87(15.5)	104(16.4)
SMEAs with metropolitan ring	43	80

these three criteria was significantly reduced by the minimum-agglomeration criterion of 100,000 population (3a), namely, from 126 to 87 for 1965 and from 180 to 104 for 1975. In the course of the ten-year period, 19 new SMLA cores emerged, but of the 87 SMEAs in 1965, two had disappeared in 1975, their central cities having been absorbed into the metropolitan rings of other SMEAs. That leaves 85 SMEAs for a comparison of 1965 and 1975. Of the 85 SMEAs, 44 had no metropolitan ring in 1965; in 1975, no more than 16 were still without a ring. The spatial configuration of the SMEAs in 1975 is given in Figure 13.1: out of 104 SMEAs, seven are on the northern island Hokkaido, 74 on Honshu, six on Shikoku, and 17 on Kyushu.

Urban change on the national level

By comparing the two descriptions of urban Japan for 1965 and 1975, we can obtain a broad picture of urban developing in the decade.

Firstly, the increase in the number of SMEAs from 87 to 104 suggests that the population had grown not only in existing urban areas but also around a number of previously non-metropolitan cores. Many new SMEAs emerged simply because they crossed the minimum agglomeration threshold, though some areas also entered the SMEA-ranks because they had become increasingly urban or through annexation or amalgamation. Strikingly, most new SMEAs emerged in the

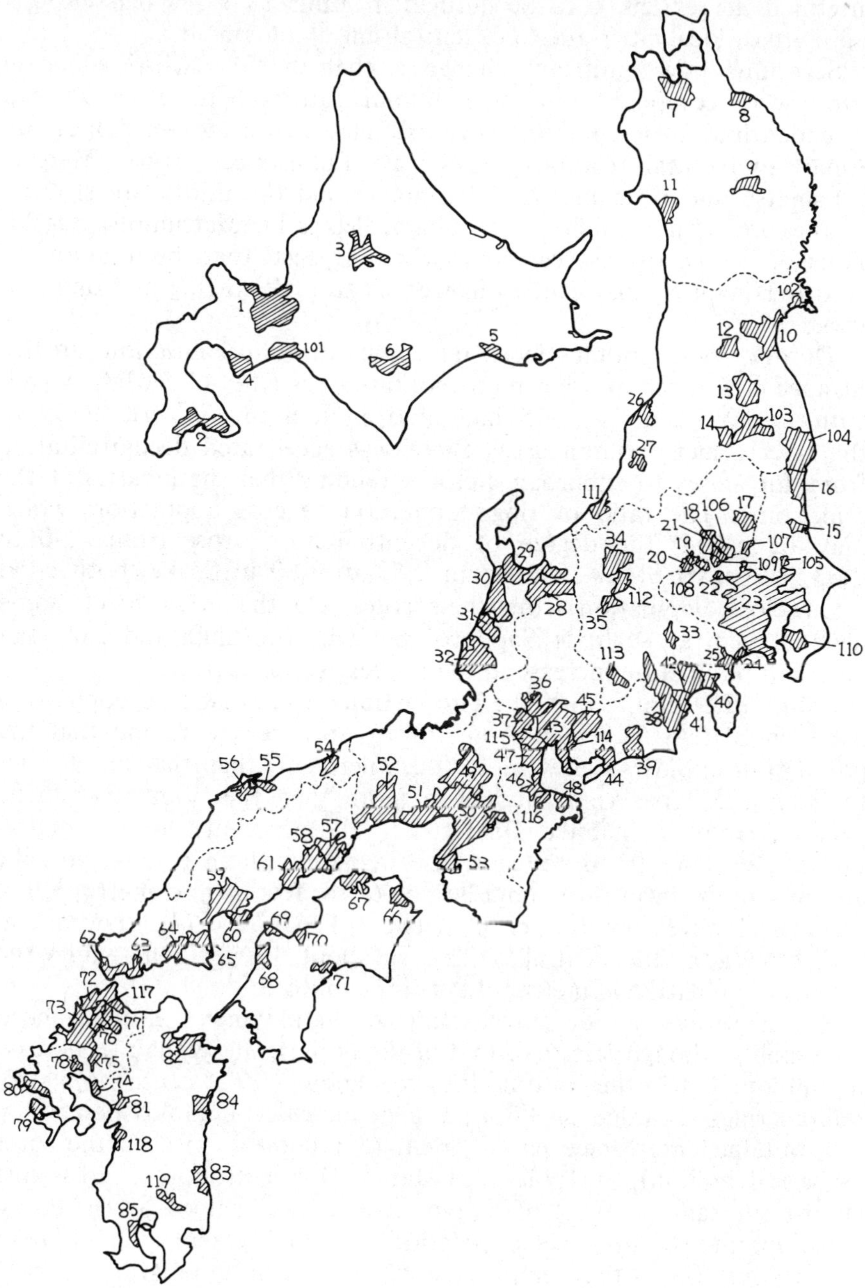

Figure 13.1 Standard Metropolitan Employment Areas, 1975

intermediate regions – to be defined in Table 13.6 – which suggests a growth of local cities due to decentralising employment.

Secondly, one significant change is that the 28 SMEAs which in 1965 were composed of single administrative areas, by 1975 had extended into adjacent areas previously classified as non-metropolitan. Some prefectural capitals, such as Fukushima, Mito, Matsue, Takamatsu and Kumamoto, and some second (or third) largest cities in the prefectures, such as Hakodate, Takasaki, Matsumoto, Ogaki, Yonago, belong to that category, which suggests that suburbanisation occurred in provincial centres as well as around existing metropolitan areas.

Thirdly, metropolitan decentralisation, or suburbanisation, greatly advanced in most existing metropolitan areas (the 43 SMEAs which both in 1965 and in 1975 had metropolitan rings). Particularly in the largest metropolitan areas there was accelerated decentralisation from the cores to suburban areas, extending their boundaries at the same time. The ratio of ring population to core population, which may be called 'the degree of decentralisation', rose from 1.90 to 2.63 in Tokyo SMEA, and from 2.52 to 3.80 in Osaka, both cities having lost population from their cores. On the other hand, some regional centres such as Sapporo, Sendai, Hiroshima and Fukuoka saw their population increase in their cores as well as rings.

Table 13.2 shows that the proportion of the nation's population living in SMEAs increased from 53 to 66.7 per cent, and that the population in SMEAs grew more (42.2 per cent) than that in all cities together (25.9 per cent) and even more than the population living in the Densely Inhabited Districts[4] (33.9 per cent). In the period up to 1965 the trend to centralise in metropolitan regions brought an enormous influx of population to a few major metropolitan regions. However, in the period between 1965 and 1975, the population growth in the central cities was about 15 per cent, while the national population in metropolitan rings doubled.

The metropolitan decentralisation of employment also advanced remarkably, though less than that of the population. While the increase in employment in the central cities was about 20 per cent, the metropolitan rings recorded an 88.4 per cent increase in employment; they also obtained more new employment (5 million jobs) than the cores (nearly 4 million), as Table 13.3 shows. Non-metropolitan areas lost almost the same amount of employment as was gained by the cores.

Comparing the shares of population and employment in component zones, one finds that employment more than population is concentrated in the cores, the respective shares in 1975 being 45.5 and 37.3. For the cores, the ratio of the population and employment shares was 0.82; the value of less than one means that the core is a

Table 13.2

Population and population change, 1965 to 1975

	Population				Population change	
	1965	% of total	1975	% of total	absolute change	relative change (%)
SMEAs	52,048	53.0	73,994	66.7	21,946	42.2
cores	36,050	36.7	41,425	37.3	5,375	14.9
rings	15,998	16.3	32,569	29.4	16,571	103.6
Non-metropolitan	46,227	47.0	36,903	33.3	– 9,324	–20.2
National population*	98,275	100.0	110,897	100.0	12,622	12.8
Population in all cities	66,919	68.1	84,260	76.0	17,341	25.9
Population in DID**	47,261	48.1	63,294	57.1	16,033	33.9

* Excluding Okinawa

** DID is the Densely Inhabited Districts (see note 4)

Table 13.3

Employment and employment change, 1965 to 1975

	Employment				Employment change	
	1965	% of total	1975	% of total	absolute change	relative change (%)
SMEAs	26,033	54.7	35,313	66.9	9,280	35.6
cores	20,031	42.1	24,007	45.5	3,976	19.8
rings	6,002	12.6	11,306	21.4	5,304	88.4
Non-metropolitan	21,577	45.3	17,448	33.1	–4,129	–19.1
Total employment	47,610	100.0	52,761	100.0	5,151	10.8

Table 13.4

Ratios of the population shares to employment shares by zones

	Urban cores	Metropolitan rings	Non-metropolitan areas
1965	0.87	1.29	1.04
1975	0.82	1.37	1.01

net importer of workers. The corresponding ratio for the rings has a value of more than one (1.37) in 1975, which means that the ring zone is a net exporter of workers. From the trends in these ratios given in Table 13.4, the decentralisation of population has clearly preceded that of employment, the ratios for cores having decreased considerably in the course of the decade. Conversely, the ratios of metropolitan rings – all above 1 – increased, reflecting a greater rate of increase in population than in employment. That shows that in spite of the recent decentralisation of jobs, the metropolitan rings had increasingly become net exporters of workers, and that the cores for their labour had become increasingly dependent on the rings. The trend led to increased commuting between the cores and the rings, giving rise to great pressure on the transport facilities in the urban system.

Change in the urban system

In 1975, the 104 SMEAs of Japan had a total population of 73,994,000, or an average of 711,489 each, which represents a steep rise from an average of 598,253 in 1965. But, as Table 13.5 shows, there are wide variations in scale, from Tokyo (23,076,000 in 1975) down to Iida, a newly emerged SMEA with 102,000 people. Tokyo is the prime city and a first-order central place, housing 30 per cent of all the people in metropolitan Japan, and 20 per cent of the national population. Osaka, another first-order central place, has a population of 10,685,000, about half as much as Tokyo. Seven other SMEAs with populations of more than one million in 1975, all second-order major regional centres, are in order of size: Nagoya (4,129,000) for Tokai, Kyoto (2,177,000) and Kobe (1,874,000) for Kinki, Sapporo (1,541,000) for Hokkaido, Fukuoka (1,503,000) and Kitakyushu (1,330,000) for Kyushu, and Hiroshima (1,172,000) for Chygoku. Sendai (899,000), the tenth biggest SMEA, is also a second-order regional centre for Tohoku. Together these ten areas accounted for 48,386,000 people, that is 65 per cent of Japan's metropolitan population. At the other extreme, 17 out of the 104 SMEAs accounted for less than 200,000 inhabitants each.

Another way to describe the urban system of a nation is by a rank-size graph. Figure 13.2 shows that the size distribution of SMEAs in Japan accord roughly with the rank-size rule, although there are some break points; especially significant is the break between the 9th and 11th rank order for both 1965 and 1975. In the figure, the rank-size graphs are almost parallel for both years, which suggests that urban

Table 13.5

Shift in size distribution of SMEAs (population: thousands)

1965 \ 1975	100–200	200–300	300–500	500–1,000	1,000–5,000	5,000	Disappeared	Total
100–200	20	13	2				2	37
200–300		10	16	1				27
300–500			4	9				13
500–1,000				1	3			4
1,000–5,000					4			4
5,000						2		2
new SMEAs	17	1	1					
Total	37	24	23	11	7	2		

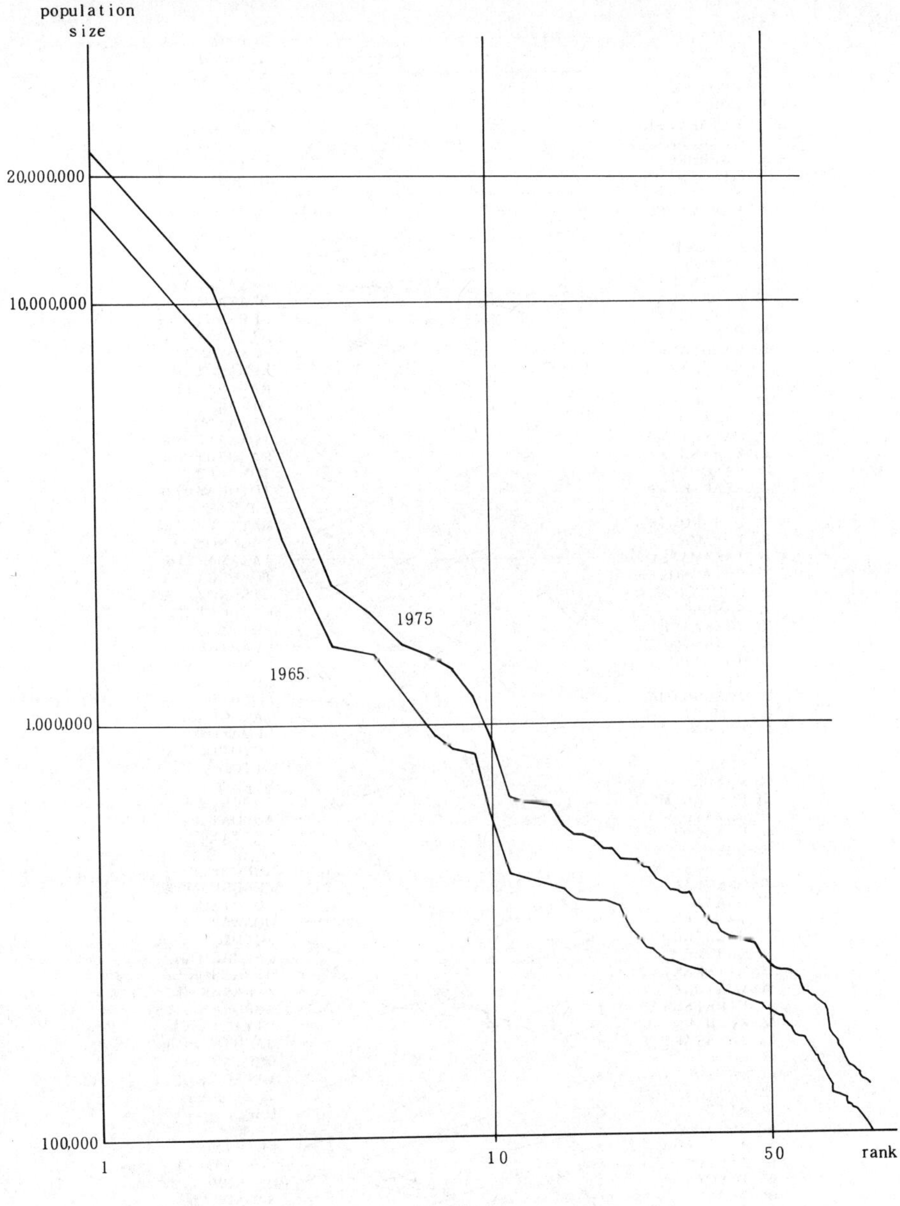

Figure 13.2 Rank size distribution of SMEA populations, 1965 and 1975

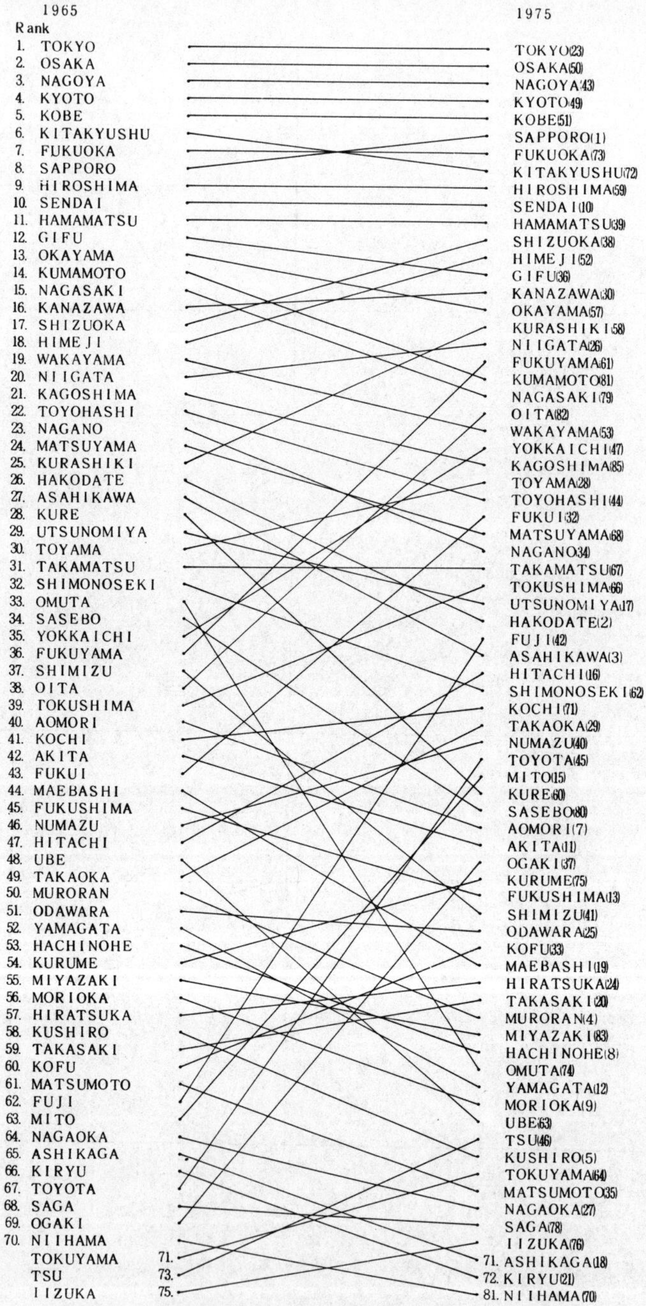

Figure 13.3 Change in population rank order of SMEAs (No. in parentheses is code number of SMEAs)

growth had been achieved in medium and small urban areas throughout the country as well as in the large metropolitan areas, although the growth of medium-sized SMEAs appears to have been most significant.

However, this graph does not reveal the changing fortunes of individual cities. Figure 13.3, comparing the rank orders of all SMEAs by their total population in 1965 and 1975, shows how dramatically the ranking of individual cities changed in the period. The top SMEAs are relatively stable in their ranks, but the remaining ones rarely maintain their positions, rather climbing up or dropping down the hierarchy. The cities which in this period rose significantly in rank, are mostly those that experienced rapid industrial development. Sometimes their growth was based on a newly developed manufacturing industry, such as the car industry of Toyota, the electronic industry of Hitachi, and the chemical industry of Yokkaichi. Another group of cities which grew remarkably in this period are the New Industrial Cities (NIC) or Special Districts for Industrialisation (SDI); the government encouraged the industrialisation of these growth poles, the most significant examples being Kurshiki, Fukuyama, Oita and Fuji.

Regional variations in urban change

For a more detailed view of the urban processes of the decade under consideration, the variation in central, intermediate and peripheral regions needs to be examined.

In the central region located on the Pacific coast of central Honshu – now often called the Tokaido Megalopolis, because it is one of the most urbanised regions of the world[5] – high concentrations of people and industry had developed in the previous decade. Table 13.6 shows the result: in 1965, 71.5 per cent of the regional population lived in the metropolitan areas, a proportion that rose fast to 81.4 in 1975. However, the distribution of population between metropolitan cores and rings had changed greatly: by 1975, the growth of the cores had almost stopped, those of Tokyo and Osaka even showing a marginal decline. Conversely, the rings gained more than thirteen million people in the decade under study, their share in the population increasing from 29.8 to 45.9 per cent, a larger share than that of the cores. Thus, by 1975, the central region had reached a high degree of metropolitan decentralisation.

In contrast, in the intermediate region only a small proportion of the population lived in metropolitan areas: in 1965, only 39.5 per cent, most of whom were living in the cores. But by 1975 that proportion

Table 13.6

Metropolitan and non-metropolitan population by regions (thousands)

	Population				Population change	
	1965	% of total	1975	% of total	absolute change	relative change
1 Central region						
SMEA	35,613	71.5	49,635	81.4	14,022	39.4
core	20,774	41.7	21,654	35.4	880	4.2
ring	14,839	29.8	27,981	45.9	13,142	88.6
Non-metropolitan	14,161	28.5	11,308	18.6	–2,853	–20.1
Total	49,774	100.0	60,943	100.0	11,169	22.4
2 Intermediate region						
SMEA	10,052	39.5	15,305	56.7	5,253	52.3
core	8,993	35.4	11,783	43.6	2,790	31.0
ring	1,059	4.1	3,522	13.0	2,463	232.6
Non-metropolitan	15,386	60.5	11,711	43.3	–3,675	–23.9
Total	25,438	100.0	27,016	100.0	1,578	6.2
3 Peripheral region						
SMEA	6,383	27.7	9,054	39.5	2,671	41.8
core	6,283	27.2	7,988	34.8	1,705	27.1
ring	100	0.4	1,066	4.6	966	966.0
Non-metropolitan	16,680	72.3	13,884	60.5	–2,796	–16.8
Total	23,063	100.0	22,938	100.0	– 125	–0.5

1 Central region: Coastal Kanto, Tokai, Kinki
2 Intermediate region: South Tohoku, Inland Kanto, Hokuriku, Sanyo (South Chugoku), North Kyushu (Fukuoka prefecture)
3 Peripheral region: Hokkaido, North Tohoku, Sanin (North Chugoku), Shikoku, South Kyushu

had jumped to 56.7 per cent, an increase due to growth of cores as well as rings, with a compensatory decline in non-metropolitan areas. In spite of a strong tendency towards centralisation – the share of cores having risen from 35.4 to 43.6 per cent – decentralisation also advanced in the intermediate region, for the rings, having grown much faster than the cores, by 1975 had acquired almost the same number of inhabitants.

In the peripheral region, the great majority of people lived in non-metropolitan areas in 1965, but by 1975 the proportion of the population living outside metropolitan areas had decreased from 72.3 to 60.5 per cent. The absolute population loss suffered in the non-metropolitan areas of the region during the decade was almost completely compensated by the gain in metropolitan areas, cores growing quite fast and suburbanisation having started in this region as well. So, the total population of this region decreased only slightly in the period. As a result, by 1975 the advance of urban development in the peripheral region had become very similar to that of the intermediate region in 1965.

In terms of employment, too, the decentralising trend was significant in the central region, as Table 13.7 shows. The share of the metropolitan rings had increased from 22.6 to 33.8 per cent – an increase of nearly four million jobs in absolute terms – while that of the cores had decreased from 50.5 to 48.5 per cent. However, the cores had still gained more than a million jobs, representing an 11 per cent increase, offsetting the loss of jobs in non-metropolitan areas. Evidently, the concentration of employment in urban cores was still continuing, though at a decreasing rate.

The same trend – concentration of employment in cores – is also observable in the intermediate and peripheral regions. In the period under study, the share of the cores in the total number of jobs increased by about 10 per cent in the intermediate region and by about 8 per cent in the peripheral region. The striking employment growth in the rings can be explained from the very low starting levels. In general, the employment trends in both regions are quite similar to the population trends.

Table 13.8 shows the distribution of the growth performance of SMEAs by region; the rates of population growth are classified into five types:

1 *Rapid* – growing faster than the SMEA average (42.2%+);
2 *Fast* – growing slower than the SMEA average but faster than the average for cities (25.9%–42.2%);
3 *Stable* – growing slower than the cities but faster than the whole nation (12.8–25.9%);
4 *Stagnant* – growing but slower than the whole nation (0–12.8%);
5 *Declining* – decreasing absolutely.

Table 13.7

Metropolitan and non-metropolitan employment by regions (thousands)

	Employment				Employment change	
	1965	% of total	1975	% of total	absolute change	relative change
1 Central region						
SMEA	18,004	73.2	23,363	81.8	5,359	29.8
core	12,435	50.5	13,845	48.5	1,410	11.3
ring	5,569	22.6	9,518	33.3	3,949	70.9
Non-metropolitan	6,598	26.8	5,186	18.2	–1,412	–21.4
Total	24,602	100.0	28,549	100.0	3,947	16.0
2 Intermediate region						
SMEA	5,024	40.4	7,604	57.0	2,580	51.4
core	4,627	37.2	6,230	46.7	1,603	34.6
ring	397	3.2	1,374	10.3	977	246.1
Non-metropolitan	7,402	59.6	5,738	43.0	–1,664	– 22.5
Total	12,426	100.0	13,342	100.0	916	7.4
3 Peripheral region						
SMEA	3,005	28.4	4,346	40.0	1,341	44.6
core	2,969	28.1	3,932	36.2	963	32.4
ring	36	0.3	414	3.8	378	1050.0
Non-metropolitan	7,577	71.6	6,524	60.0	–1,053	–13.9
Total	10,582	100.0	10,876	100.0	288	2.7

* For definitions of regions, see Table 13.6

Table 13.8

Growth performance of SMEAs by regions

	rapid (42.2%+)	fast (25.9–42.2%)	stable (12.8–25.9%)	stagnant (0–12.8%)	declining (<0%)
Central region	12	4	5	1	
Intermediate region	15	5	8	6	1
Peripheral region	5	6	14	3	
Total	32	15	27	10	1

This table reveals that out of the 85 SMEAs only one was declining, while 32 were growing rapidly, and that most of the rapidly growing SMEAs are located in the central and intermediate regions. Of the 12 SMEAs in the central region, 10 are in Tokai, 2 in Kinki and none in South Kanto. The 20 SMEAs of this type in the intermediate and peripheral regions are regional centres, such as Sapporo, Sendai, Kanazawa, Takamatsu, Hiroshima and Fukuoka, or prefectural capitals, such as Mito, Niigata, Toyama, Tokushima and Oita, or newly developed industrial cities, such as Hitachi, Kurashiki and Fukuyama. Sixty per cent of the SMEAs in the peripheral regions were stable or stagnant, which suggests that many urban areas in this region were still in the early stages of urban development.

Change within urban areas

The study of urban development on the aggregate national level has revealed a process of metropolitan decentralisation of population and employment, but the regional variance in urban change and the fortunes of individual cities suggest a considerable variation in urban development among individual cities. Therefore, the urban change in all SMEAs needs to be considered in more detail. To that end, let us examine the internal change within each metropolitan area. A simple way is to compare the relative rates of change in the constituent zones. Five patterns of change[6] can be identified among the SMEAs:

1 Absolute centralisation – core growing but metropolitan ring declining;
2 Relative centralisation – core growing faster than metropolitan ring;
3 Relative decentralisation – metropolitan ring growing faster than core;
4 Absolute decentralisation – core declining but metropolitan ring growing and SMEA growing;
5 Decentralisation during decline – SMEA declining with absolute or relative decentralisation.

Other patterns are possible: 'absolute centralisation during decline', which means a growing core but a declining metropolitan ring and a declining SMEA, and 'relative centralisation during decline', which means that the metropolitan ring is declining faster than the core. They have been omitted because no examples could be identified between 1965 and 1975.

As we can see from Table 13.9, a large number of SMEAs are classified under relative decentralisation; these have been sub-divided into four types (by the combinations of rates of change in population or employment in the core and in the SMEA as a whole) to permit examining the position of each SMEA in detail:

(i) Both core and SMEA growing fast;
(ii) Core stable, SMEA growing;
(iii) Core stagnating, SMEA growing;
(iv) Both core and SMEA stagnating;

The 16 SMEAs that have no ring (group 6) have also been classified in that way.

Table 13.9 reveals that in 1975, out of the 85 SMEAs only one (Omuta) was losing population, and that of the 69 SMEAs possessing metropolitan rings, only three were centralising their population: one relatively (Tokuyama), and two absolutely (Hiratsuka and Shimizu). The latter two SMEAs are considered not to be in the early stage of urban development but rather to be influenced by the growth of other metropolitan areas, which leaves 65 out of the 85 SMEAs in the decentralising category. Five of them were decentralising absolutely; they present a mixed list, including the largest SMEAs (Tokyo and Osaka) and smaller ones based on coalmining and old manufacturing. Out of the 60 relatively decentralising SMEAs, the ten fast-growing ones (3–i) comprise two groups, with regional or provincial centres such as Sapporo, Hiroshima, Fukuoka, Sendai, Utsunomiya and Mito in the one, and newly industrialised towns like Kurashiki, Toyota and Fukuyama in the other; Oita is considered to belong to both groups. Many provincial centres in which the central cities are prefectural capitals, belong to the 3–ii class, where cores are showing stable growth; most of these SMEAs are growing fast. The 3–iii class is a mixture of several groups; old large SMEAs (Kyoto, Kobe, Nagoya); old provincial centres (Hakodate, Fukui, Simonoseki, Tottori); and rapidly growing industrial cities (Hitachi, Ogaki, Yokkaichi). Most stagnating SMEAs (3–iv) are small industrial towns based on shipbuilding, coalmining and traditional textile industries.

Internal change in employment within each SMEA can be examined in the same way; Table 13.10 presents the results. In employment like in population, there is a general tendency to decentralise. Out of the 69 SMEAs, there was decentralisation of employment in 67, but only one (Kiryu), based on traditional textile industry, was decentralising absolutely, besides declining SMEA (Omuta) based on coalmining. Of the remaining 65, those with cores growing in terms of employment (belonging to the categories 3–i and 3–ii) numbered 44, compared with 35 in terms of population. The largest SMEAs, Tokyo

Table 13.9

Population shift by SMEA size (1975, thousands)

		Total	100–200	200–300	300–500	500–1000	1000–2000	2000–5000	5000
1	Absolute centralisation	2		2					
2	Relative centralisation	1	1						
3	Relative decentralisation								
3–i	Core fast growing SMEA fast growing	10		1	4	2	3		
3–ii	Core stable SMEA growing	25	4	4	9	8			
3–iii	Core stagnating SMEA growing	20	5	3	7	1	2	2	
3–iv	Core stagnating SMEA stagnating	5	2	3					
4	Absolute decentralisation	5	2	1					2
5	Decentralisation during decline	1		1					
6	Central city = SMEA								
6–i	Fast growing	3		2	1				
6–ii	Stable	9	2	6	1				
6–iii	Stagnating	4	4						
	Total	85	20	23	22	11	5	2	2

Table 13.10

Employment shift by SMEA size (1975, thousands)

		Total	100–200	200–300	300–500	500–1000	1000–2000	2000–5000	5000
1	Absolute centralisation	1		1					
2	Relative centralisation	1		1					
3	Relative decentralisation								
3–i	Core fast growing SMEA fast growing	15	1	2	7	2	3		
3–ii	Core stable SMEA growing	29	7	4	10	8			
3–iii	Core stagnating SMEA growing	19	4	5	3	1	2	2	2
3–iv	Core stagnating SMEA stagnating	2	1	1					
4	Absolute decentralisation	1	1						
5	Decentralisation during decline	1		1					
6	Central city = SMEA								
6–i	Fast growing	4		3	1				
6–ii	Stable	9	3	5	1				
6–iii	Stagnating	3	3						
	Total	85	20	23	22	11	5	2	2

and Osaka, though decentralising absolutely in population, were only relatively so in employment; their cores continued to grow employment-wise, if only slightly, the decrease in manufacturing employment having been offset by increases in service employment.

The matrix of Table 13.11 reveals the relation between the internal changes in population and employment, 45 out of 69 entries appearing on the diagonal and 29 in the lower corner. The tendency for entries to cluster either on the diagonal or immediately below to the left indicates that population showed more marked decentralisation than employment.

Table 13.11

Types of shift in population and employment

	Employment								
Population	1	2	3–i	3–ii	3–iii	3–iv	4	5	Total
1	1	1							2
2				1					1
3–i			11						10
3–ii			4	19	2				25
3–iii			1	8	11				20
3–iv					2	2	1		5
4				1	4				5
5								1	1
Total	1	1	15	29	19	2	1	1	69

Concluding remarks

In this chapter we have attempted to describe the change in the urban system in Japan from 1965 to 1975, though only in the broad terms of population and employment. The main finding is that during this decade decentralisation was predominant in terms of employment as well as population. Metropolitan decentralisation advanced in the larger SMEAs and started in many smaller ones. On the other hand, the dispersal of population and employment to the intermediate region was considerable and to the peripheral region recognisable. Although only one SMEA actually suffered urban decline, some SMEAs classified under absolute decentralisation and stagnating SMEAs possibly move towards urban decline.

What are the factors underlying these changes? One explanation of the recent trends may be found in the effect of government policy on employment decentralisation, for the national government has adopted a regional development policy to encourage the dispersal of industries. However, the working of market forces through land prices and other factors may also be very important. Our next task will be to analyse the effects of these factors on urban development.[7]

Notes

* I am deeply indebted to Kazuyuki Tokuoka for his great help. This chapter is based on the research which has been done in collaboration with him. The first draft of this was prepared for the OECD-Japan Seminar on Urban Growth Policies in the 1980s, Japan, 7–12 September 1981, and was written when I was a visiting fellow at Transport Studies Unit, Oxford University, 1981–82, and appeared in TSU's Working Paper (TSU ref. 195/wp). I extend thanks to Dr Phil B. Goodwin, the staff of TSU, and especially Peter Jones who kindly read my draft and corrected my English. I am also grateful to Professors Gordon C. Cameron, Richard M. Kirwan, Christine Whitehead at the Department of Land Economy, University of Cambridge, and Leo H. Klaassen, Jean Paelinck at Erasmus University of Rotterdam, for the opportunities to read my draft at their seminars and for their valuable comments and suggestions.

1 See Mills and Ohta (1976).
2 See Klaassen and Paelinck (1979) and Klaassen, Bourdrez and Volmuller (1981). As to the innter city problems in Japan, see Narita (1979).
3 Hall et al. (1973) and DOE (1975) should also be referred to.
4 The Densely Inhabited Districts, or DID, which have been used in the population census since 1960 are a set of contiguous enumeration districts, each having a population density of at least 4,000 people per square kilometre and a total population of at least 5,000.
5 See Nagashima (1981).
6 As to this classification, see Hall et al. (1973), DOE (1975), Drewett, Goddard and Spence (1976), Klaassen and Paelinck (1979) and Klaassen, Bourdrez and Volmuller (1981).
7 A part of this task has been performed in Yamada (1984).

References

Department of Environment (1975), British Cities: Urban Population and Employment Trend, 1951–1971, DOE Research Report 10, London.

Drewett, R., Goddard, J. and Spence, N. (1976), 'Urban Britain: Beyond Containment', in *Urbanization and Counterurbanization*, B.J.L. Berry (ed.), Sage Publications, Beverly Hills.

Glickman, N.J. (1979), *The Growth and Management of the Japanese Urban System*, Academic Press, New York.

Hall, P. et al. (1973), *The Containment of Urban England*, George Allen and Unwin, London.

Kawashima, T. (1981), 'Recent Urban Trends in Japan: Analysis of Functional Urban Regions', in *Human Settlement System: Spatial Patterns and Trends*, T. Kawashima and P. Korcelli (eds), International Institute of Applied Systems Analysis, Laxenburg, Austria, 1982.

Klaassen, L.H. and Paelinck, J.H.P. (1979), 'The Future of Large Towns', *Environment and Planning* A, vol. 11, no. 10.

Klaassen, L.H., Bourdrez, J.A. and Volmuller, J. (1981), *Transport and Reurbanization*, Gower, Hants.

Mills, E.S. and Ohta, K. (1976), 'Urbanization and Urban Problems' in *Asia's New Giant*, H. Patrick and H. Rosovsky (eds), The Brookings Institution, Washington D.C.

Mitsubishi Research Institute (1981), *Nippon no Toshiken* (The Urban Areas in Japan), National Institute for Research Advancement, Tokyo (in Japanese).

Nagashima, C. (1981), The Tokaido Megalopolis, *Ekistics*, vol. 48, no. 289.

Narita, K. (1979), 'Inner City Problem and Urban Policy in Japan', *Osaka City University Economic Review*, no. 15.

Yamanda, H. (1984), Urban Development and Regional Policy in Japan, *The Toshimondai Kenkyu (Journal of Municipal Problems)*, Oct. and Transport Studies Unit, Oxford University, *TSU* ref. 196/wp.

Appendix List of SMEAs (1975)

1 Hokkaido
- 1 Sapporo
- 2 Hakodate
- 3 Asahikawa
- 4 Muroran
- 5 Kushiro
- 6 Obihiro

2 North Tohoku
- 7 Aomori
- 8 Hachinohe
- 9 Morioka
- 11 Akita

3 South Tohoku
- 10 Sendai
- 12 Yamagata
- 13 Fukushima
- 14 Aizuwakamatsu
- 26 Niigata
- 27 Nagaoka

4 Inland Kanto
- 17 Utsunomiya
- 18 Ashikaga
- 19 Maebashi
- 20 Takasaki
- 21 Kiryu
- 33 Kofu
- 34 Nagano
- 35 Matsumoto

5 Coastal Kanto
- 15 Mito
- 16 Hitachi
- 22 Kumagaya
- 23 Tokyo
- 24 Hiratsuka
- 25 Odawara

6 Hokuriku
- 28 Toyama
- 29 Takaoka
- 30 Kanazawa
- 31 Komatsu
- 32 Fukui

7 Tokai
- 36 Gifu
- 37 Ogaki
- 38 Shizuoka
- 39 Hamamatsu
- 40 Numazu
- 41 Shimizu
- 42 Fuji
- 43 Nagoya
- 44 Toyohashi
- 45 Toyoda

7 Tokai (cont'd.)
- 46 Tsu
- 47 Yokaichi
- 48 Ise

8 Kinki
- 49 Kyoto
- 50 Osaka
- 51 Kobe
- 52 Himeji
- 53 Wakayama

9 Sanin
- 54 Tottori
- 55 Yonago
- 56 Matsue

10 Sanyo
- 57 Okayama
- 58 Kurashiki
- 59 Hiroshima
- 60 Kure
- 61 Fukuyama
- 62 Shimonoseki
- 63 Ube
- 64 Tokuyama
- 65 Iwakuni

11 Shikoku
- 66 Tokushima
- 67 Takamatsu
- 68 Matsuyama
- 69 Imabari
- 70 Niihama
- 71 Kochi

12 North Kyushu
- 72 Kitakyushu
- 73 Fukuoka
- 74 Omuta
- 75 Kurume
- 76 Iizuka
- 77 Tagawa

13 South Kyushu
- 78 Saga
- 79 Nagasaki
- 80 Sasebo
- 81 Kumamoto
- 82 Oita
- 83 Miyazaki
- 84 Nobeoka
- 85 Kagoshima

New SMEAs		(region)
101	Tomakomai	1
102	Ishinomaki	3
103	Koriyama	3
104	Iwaki	3
105	Tsuchiura	5
106	Sano	4
107	Koyama	4
108	Isezaki	4
109	Ota	4
110	Kimitsu	5
111	Joetsu	3
112	Ueda	4
113	Iida	4
114	Kariya	7
115	Matsusaka	7
116	Kuwana	7
117	Naogata	12
118	Yatsushiro	13
119	Miyakonojo	13

14 Australian urban dynamics

J. CONNER

Australian urban growth dynamics

Introduction

Australia is a land of contrasts – its large land mass and small population make it the most sparsely settled continent of the world – yet at the same time it must also rank as one of the most highly urbanised countries in the world, with 85 per cent of its population living in urban centres. The settlement pattern illustrates this point (see Figure 14.1) since it shows that nearly 80 per cent of the population live in Zone 1 adjacent to the eastern seaboard, within an almost continuous string of settlements. Zone 2 accommodates about 18 per cent of the population, with 60 per cent of these living in urban settlements. This zone also provides the major portion of the agriculturally productive land mass, which relies on a fairly low average annual rainfall pattern. Zone 3 is very sparsely populated containing only 2–3 per cent of the population, and is for the most part inhospitable to human settlement.

Six out of ten Australians live in their state capital cities of Sydney, Melbourne, Brisbane, Adelaide, Perth and Hobart. All are the economic, administrative, transportation and cultural hubs of their states.

Throughout Australia's history, there have been a number of phases of rapid population expansion due to migration. The most recent of these followed World War II and resulted in the population doubling from its 1947 base level of 7.5 million to nearly 15 million in 1981.

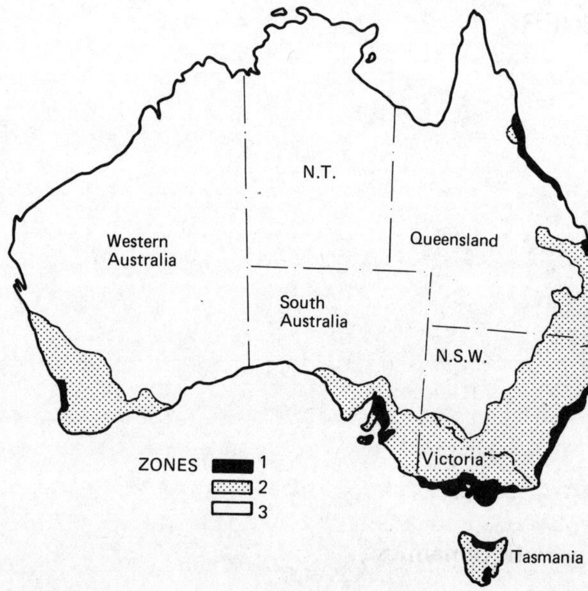

Figure 14.1 Settlement zones within Australia

Source: Australian Atlas of Resources (3rd series) (1980)
Scale: 1:52,500,000

Throughout this period about 40 per cent of total population growth was due to net migration (see Table 14.1). This reached a peak in the period 1966–71 when 48.4 per cent of population growth was due to net migration gains. The significance of net migration gains on population growth would be even more pronounced if births due to foreign-born parents could be identified separately. The First Report of the National Population Inquiry (1975) estimated that immigrants and their children were responsible for more than 50 per cent of Australia's growth during the postwar period. Since the net reproduction ratio has recently fallen below replacement level – zero population growth – further growth of the nation's population is even more dependent upon continued gains from immigration. In the past the federal government supported free migrant passages to Australia, but in the current economic recession, with unemployment figures increasing, this scheme has been abandoned. Despite this the government's annual intake target for 1982–83 was 130,000 (Birrell, 1982) which is quite high.

Table 14.1

Elements of population growth

Period	Pop. at end '000	Births '000	Deaths '000	Natural increase '000	Natural increase %	Net migration '000	Net migration %	Total increase '000	Total increase %
1947–54	8987	1336	552	784	55.72	623	44.3	1407	2.65
1954–61	10548	1544	601	943	60.41	618	39.6	1561	2.89
1961–66	11599	1152	482	670	63.75	381	36.3	1051	1.99
1966–71	12937	1232	541	691	51.64	647	48.4	1338	2.31
1971–76	14033	1242	557	685	62.50	411	37.5	1096	1.69
1976–81	14927	1131	545	586	65.55	308	34.5	894	1.27
Total				4359	59.33	2988	40.7	7347	

Source: References ABS Data; Australian Population and Immigration Council, *Population Report No. 4* (1980); Australian Atlas of Resources (1980)

In both federal and state politics, the rural sector has long held a disproportionate sway – and while this has been used to underwrite the continued development of the rural resources base of the economy (and some would say at the expenses of the city-dweller) it has not been a powerful force for regional development. As Stilwell (1974) has pointed out, this is because rural-based politicians are unable to reach agreement on a limited range of growth centres without jeopardising their own or the neighbouring electorate – so that regional policy becomes diffused to the point where it is ineffective. Regions then play no real role in the economic or urban development policies of the country.

Some researchers (Stilwell, 1974 and Rowland, 1979) have used regions as the basis for their research, but work in this field is severely hampered by the general lack of data at the regional level in any comparative time series. Regional boundaries were changed substantially at the 1971 census, and further data problems arose both in 1971 and 1976 due to under-enumeration of the censuses. These data bases have been revised and it is thus difficult to find consistent data sets. Per capita income figures are not available on a regional basis, nor are unemployment figures. The latter figures are available, but they are not published on anything other than a state or metropolitan basis. Any study of the dynamics of the Australian settlement pattern will thus inevitably focus on the urban system, rather than the regional one.

Outline of the study process followed

Because of the paucity of data on regional per capita income and unemployment, and the distinctive nature of the Australian urban system, in this chapter we have chosen a somewhat different approach to the problem of growth dynamics.

The study process adopted is as follows:

1 In the sub-section of 'Analysis of study results' (p.218) the elements of population growth are investigated on a state basis to show the importance of migration on the continued growth of the population.

2 Subsequently, the population growth data from 1947 onwards have been arranged into four structural components:

(a) *Functional Urban Regions (FURs)* being defined as those cities with a population in excess of 200,000.

(b) *Urban Municipalities (UMs)* being defined as those urban settlements with a population in excess of 10,000, but not exceeding 200,000.

(c) *Other Urban (OU)* being defined as urban settlements with a population falling within the range of more than 1,000 but less than 10,000.

(d) *The Rural Sector* which is the remainder.

This data is used in Table 14.2 to show the major structural changes which have taken place between these major categories.

Table 14.2

Percentage distribution of Australian population '000

Year	FUR	%	UMs	%	Other Urban	%	Rural	%	Australian Total
1947	3807	50.2	999	13.2	524	6.9	2250	29.7	7580
1954	4730	52.6	1352	15.0	1041	11.6	1863	20.7	8986
1961	6059	57.4	1550	14.7	1021	9.7	1918	18.2	10548
1966	6902	59.4	1793	15.5	933	8.0	1971	17.1	11599
1971	8487	65.6	1786	13.8	805	6.2	1859	14.4	12937
1976	9315	66.4	1827	13.0	944	6.7	1947	13.9	14033
1981	9838	65.9	2129	14.3	949	6.3	2011	13.5	14927

Source: ABS Statistics

3 Employment growth and change has then been examined as between workforce categories, and this is related to the growth that has taken place in the major categories of population aggregation (i.e. the FURs, UMs, etc.). This data shows that there has been a considerable change in the structural nature of the Australian workforce over the period of study, and that these changes can be related to emerging changes in the spatial population distribution pattern.

4 Data on both internal and overseas migration (available only since the 1971 census) is then used in conjunction with the major categories of population aggregation to develop a model of the structural interrelationships in the spatial settlement pattern. A preliminary analysis of foreign-born residents in the FURs is also used to suggest how the migrant population is concentrated here, and how these centres act as filters.

   This data is brought together in Figure 14.2 which shows how net population flows between the chief population aggregations have changed over time. The earlier attraction of the FURs seems to have been reversed and there is now an evident flow outwards from these to the Urban Municipalities.

5 In the final section, data is presented on the core and periphery growth within the FURs to suggest that most population growth within the metropolitan areas is now concentrated within the metropolitan periphery, as the cores continue to lose population. Some commentary is also offered on the growth of the UMs, but it is difficult to discern any particular pattern of growth or decline in these centres.

Some qualifications should be attached to the data used and the degree of accuracy which can be placed on the results. As mentioned earlier, both the 1971 and 1976 censuses were under-enumerated and this had led to various revisions of those data bases over time. Consistent and accurate data sets are not always available on a strictly comparable basis – a problem which is exacerbated by the usual boundary changes in statistical districts as these respond to growth pressures.

The model developed in the section 'Urban growth dynamics in the Australian urban system' deals only with net migration flows between the vital components of the urban settlement pattern. As Rowland (1979) has pointed out, net flows tend to mask the far greater volume of gross migration flows, and a study of both is needed to give a complete view of the situation. Rowland's thesis was that 'internal migration in contemporary Australia is concerned more with maintaining the settlement pattern than with modifying it'. The balancing effects of internal migration streams and counterstreams is a point well made in his description of the dynamic equilibrium of internal Australian migration flows. The chief interest in this chapter is however to identify the nodal points at which these countervailing streams cease to be in equilibrium, so that urban policy can adapt quickly and responsively. Given the fifteen year timespan of results to study (1966–81) the writer suggests that the results obtained from the use of net migration flows can in fact be indicative of incipient changes in the spatial settlement pattern.

Trends

The over-concentration of population in a limited number of important metropolitan areas has been the focus of attention in planning for some time in Australia, and has resulted in both decentralisation and growth centre policies being adopted by governments. Concentration of the population along the temperate seaboard of the continent is likely to continue indefinitely. While Canberra continues to grow as the only inland city of any size, its economic base is largely dependent upon the national government, and does not provide a model capable of being replicated throughout the nation.

Substantial population continues to be concentrated on the existing chief urban centres, but the results of this study suggest that for the first time, some trends are now evident. First, all five major metropolitan cities (Sydney, Melbourne, Brisbane, Perth and Adelaide) are now losing core population, and while still growing in absolute terms, this growth is now located on the urban periphery. This growth is increasingly costly to service and increasingly inaccessible to a wide variety of facilities. Diseconomies of scale and social inequality are now so apparent that it appears that other lifestyle and locational options are being sought and found by the more mobile element of the population. Other changes in the social, economic and technological fabric of society also support a greater variety in these locational choices.

This problem is more evident in the two larger cities of Sydney and Melbourne, while because of their smaller population bases, the other state capital cities are less affected. Sydney and Melbourne have been in recent times the primary reception centres for the immigrant population – since the jumbo-jet replaced the migrant ship – and this is evident in their growth rates and large numbers of foreign-born residents. While the absolute numbers are still small in comparison with both natural and migration growth, interstate migration patterns suggest that the northern state of Queensland is capturing a high percentage of interstate movements. One can perceive

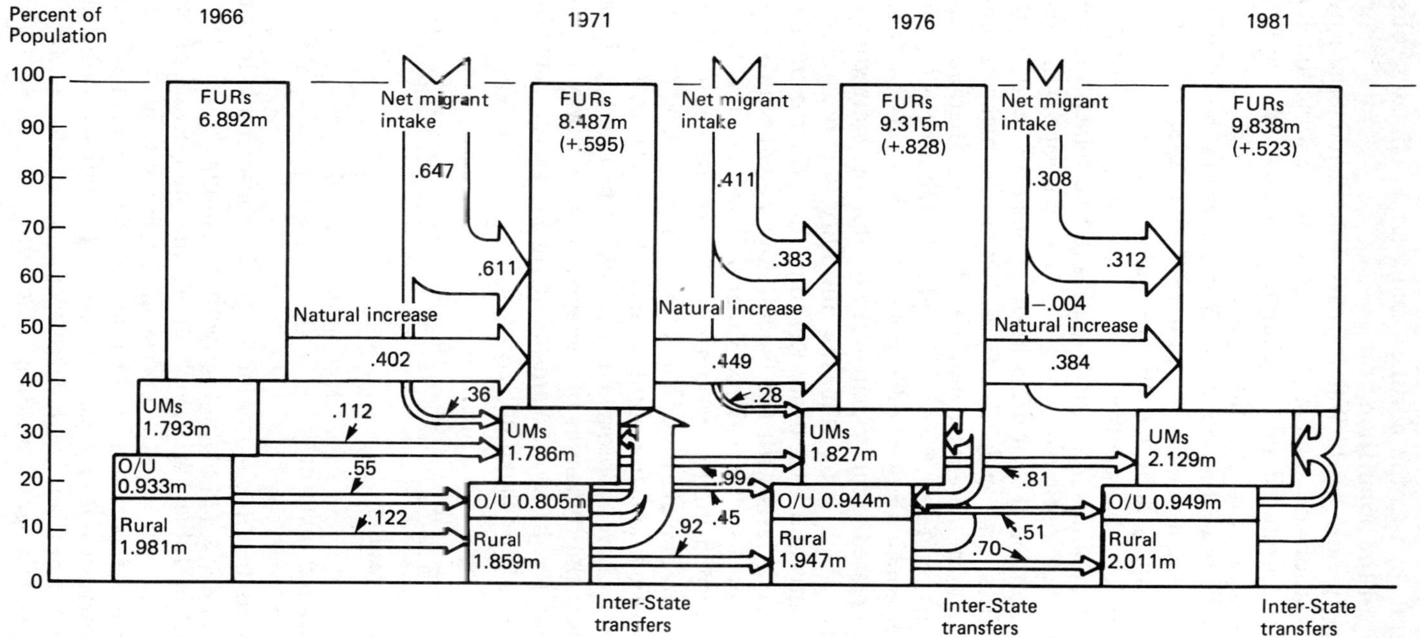

Figure 14.2 Australian urban growth dynamics

Source: Derived from Tables 14.8 tc 14.16

in this a general drift to the northern and warmer climates consistent with the ageing of the population.

While the early post World War II years were characterised by continued concentration of population in the prime functional urban regions, the data produced in this chapter indicates that the net flow now favours the smaller urban municipalities.

As Figure 14.2 shows, this trend was first evident in the 1976 figures, but is now confirmed in the more recent 1981 census figures. Structural change in the employment pattern also seems to support this new focus on the smaller urban centres.

The study also points out the significant role which immigration has played in the continued growth of the metropolitan areas. In 1976, 76 per cent of the overseas-born population lived in the six state capital cities, and again this figure would be higher if children born to foreign-born parents could be identified. Migrants have exhibited a strong preference for city life in their housing location decisions. The concentration of foreign-born residents in the inner city areas has created some social problems for the state government administrations which carry the responsibility for providing many services, i.e. health and education. Responsibility for the immigration programme as such rests with the federal government which in recent times, and except for the 1972–75 period, has steadfastly refused to accept any responsibility for metropolitan or urban growth issues.

In the final section of this chapter the policy implications of these trends are identified, and the point is made that as yet neither planners nor governments have approached national urban policy in a way which recognises the dynamics of the system, or in a way that allows monitoring and feedback mechanisms to make useful contributions or alterations to urban-related policy.

Analysis of study results

Elements of population growth

Earlier comments in this chapter indicated the considerable importance played in Australia's population growth by immigration. Details of this are set out in Table 14.1 which shows the inter-censal population growth due to natural growth (excess of births over deaths) and net migration. Over the period 1947–81 in fact 41 per cent of national population growth was due to net migration. The impact of this growth would be seen to be even greater if it were possible to identify separately births due to migrant mothers. The 1966–71 period shows that it was the period with the highest net migration intake – about 130,000 each year. The most recent period, 1976–81 shows the lowest net migration intake since World War II, (about 62,000 per year) and in fact in the last year of the preceding period (1975) Australia experienced its first net migrant loss in annual population terms.

With a net reproduction ratio now below zero population growth, continued growth of the Australian population is more dependent upon the continuation of the immigration programme. In order to develop some idea of the spatial implications of the immigration policy, census data for both natural and migration population increase has been derived for the various states and territories and this is shown in Table 14.3. Here the population for each state at the end of the period is known, as is the excess of births over deaths, so that by deduction, total migration gains can be calculated. These migrant gains – or losses – can be as a result of both interstate and overseas migration, and they represent net figures only, not total gross flows.

Since the 1971 census, data has been collected on internal migration, i.e. location of current residence as compared with location at the earlier census. This data has been used to determine the break-up between interstate and overseas migration gains for each state, as shown in Table 14.4. Total flows of interstate migrants are much higher than the net figures shown, and for a full description of this aspect the reader should consult Rowland (1979). Two aspects of importance flow from this table. Firstly, the most populous states of New South Wales (NSW) and Victoria – along with Tasmania and South Australia

Table 14.3

Growth components by states ('000)

	1966–71			1971–76			1976–81		
State	Nat.	Mig.	Total	Nat.	Mig.	Total	Nat.	Mig.	Total
NSW	216	223	439	230	30	260	192	90	282
Vic	204	96	300	176	114	290	147	–9	138
Q	101	106	207	115	96	211	94	159	253
SA	60	30	90	55	34	89	45	0	45
WA	65	130	195	70	65	135	63	58	121
Tas	24	–5	19	22	0	22	17	–2	15
ACT	13	40	53	12	65	77	18	3	21
NT	8	27	35	5	7	12	10	9	19
Total	691	647	1338	685	411	1096	586	308	894

Source: Neutze (1978) and ABS statistics

Table 14.4

State growth due to interstate & overseas migration ('000)

State	1966–71 Mig.	I/S	O/S	1971–76 Mig.	I/S	O/S	1976–81 Mig.	I/S	O/S
NSW	223	–20	243	30	–90	120	90	–36	126
Vic	96	–27	123	114	–31	145	–9	–57	48
Q	106	15	91	96	56	40	159	64	95
SA	30	–17	47	34	1	33	0	–13	13
WA	130	23	107	65	20	45	58	20	38
Tas	–5	–7	2	0	–2	2	–2	–1	–1
ACT	40	24	16	65	40	25	3	11	–8
NT	27	9	18	7	6	1	9	12	–3
Total	647	0	647	411	0	411	308	0	308

Source: Derived from Table 14.3 and Rowland (1979)

Notes:
Nat = natural growth (excess births over deaths)
I/S = Interstate migration gain
O/S = Overseas migration gain
Mig. = Migration gain (includes I/S and O/S)

(SA) to a lesser extent, have been consistently losing population to the other states for some time. While these net figures mask the size of the gross flows, the net impact on population distribution between the states is still small. Secondly, and more importantly, is the significant impact which net overseas migration flows have in comparison with both net interstate and natural growth figures. As the majority of overseas migrants elect to live in metropolitan areas the immigration programme is in effect a national policy for continued large scale metropolitan expansion.

Population growth by state and category

Table 14.5 shows the distribution of the population in the states in percentage terms across the population aggregation categories chosen for this study, i.e. FURs, UMs, OU and Rural. In the discussion that follows attention will be directed first to the Australian total figures shown at the foot of Table 14.5.

A number of interesting observations can be made here. Firstly, while Australia has almost doubled its population in the time span 1947–81, at the outset of the period, only about 50 per cent of the population was housed in the then FURs. By 1981, this percentage had risen to about 66 per cent. The FURs percentage figure appears

Table 14.5

Percentage distribution of population

State		1947	1954	1961	1966	1971	1976	1981
NSW	FUR	50	54	61	63	76	75	75
	UM	16	18	14	14	8	8	9
	OU	6	11	10	9	5	6	5
	Rural	28	17	15	14	11	11	11
Vic	FUR	61	63	64	65	72	76	69
	UM	7	9	10	11	10	3	12
	OU	7	10	11	10	6	8	7
	Rural	25	18	15	14	12	13	12
Q	FUR	36	38	45	47	47	47	47
	UM	19	20	22	24	23	24	25
	OU	6	16	9	5	9	10	10
	Rural	39	26	24	24	21	19	18
SA	FUR	59	61	68	70	72	73	73
	UM	2	3	5	6	7	7	7
	OU	9	11	6	6	6	5	5
	Rural	30	25	21	18	15	15	15
WA	FUR	54	55	61	66	67	70	71
	UM	4	5	8	7	9	9	9
	OU	7	12	4	3	5	5	5
	Rural	35	28	27	24	19	16	15
Tas	FUR	0	0	0	0	0	0	0
	UM	45	55	58	58	67	66	71
	OU	16	13	13	12	7	9	7
	Rural	39	32	29	30	26	25	22
ACT	FUR	0	0	0	0	0	99	99
	UM	94	93	95	96	98	0	0
	OU	0	0	0	0	0	0	0
	Rural	6	7	5	4	2	1	1
NT	FUR	0	0	0	0	0	0	0
	UM	0	0	27	35	51	56	61
	OU	27	69	51	19	15	9	7
	Rural	73	31	22	46	34	35	32
Aust	FUR	50	53	57	60	66	66	66
	UM	13	15	15	15	14	13	14
	OU	7	12	10	8	6	7	6
	Rural	30	20	18	17	14	14	14
Total		100	100	100	100	100	100	100

For definition of FUR, UM, OU and Rural, refer to text.
Source: ABS statistics
Raw data are shown in Table 14.21, Appendix 2

to have peaked in the 1976 period, although the fall off of about one-half per cent in the five year period might be too small to really indicate any major trend developing. The aggregation of the FUR population in these figures also tends to mask greater variation within individual cities.

The rural population has fallen significantly in terms of its percentage holding – from its high of about 30 per cent in 1947 to its current level of about 13 per cent. This is a dramatic shift, although the drop in absolute numbers has not been all that great. The UMs and Other Urban percentages have remained fairly static during this period, with the slight decrease accounted for by some upgrading of these centres over time into the next higher category. While these percentage figures give a good indication as to what has happened to the Australian urban and regional system since 1947, they tend to belie the significance of the absolute figures. The number of people now living in the FURs has increased by 6 million, from their 1947 base of 3.8 million – an increase of 258 per cent – or put another way, the FURs have captured about 80 per cent of total population increase. The UMs have more than doubled their holding in absolute numbers from 1 million in 1947 to their current holding of about 2.1 million. These centres have captured about 15 per cent of total population increase. Other Urban centres have just less than doubled their holding, and in fact have only captured about 5 per cent of total population increase.

Overall the significant change has been the increased dominance of the chief metropolitan centres – aided by the immigration policy – and the extremely high percentage of the population housed in urban centres. In the following section, brief comments will be made in respect of each of the six states and the two territories of the Commonwealth.

New South Wales (NSW) Whereas in 1947 NSW held 39 per cent of the total Australian population, by 1981 this holding had dropped to 35 per cent. National population had grown by 97 per cent between 1947–81 during which time NSW grew by only 75 per cent, capturing only 30 per cent of total population growth. In looking at regional growth rates over the 1947–81 period (see Table 14.22, Appendix 2) of the state's 12 regions, only four grew faster than the national growth rate (Sydney, Hunter, Illawarra and Richmond-Tweed). These four regions are all coastal.

The state started the period with an average holding of its population in its FUR, but by the end of the period it had the highest percentage holding of any state. NSW is also the most highly urbanised state, with 89 per cent of its population living in urban centres.

(Note: The ACT is in fact higher, but this is a special case to be discussed later.) This high percentage holding in urban centres is due to the two adjacent FURs to Sydney, Newcastle and Woolongong, which together make up an almost continuous conurbation extending along the eastern coastline for more than 200 km. No other state has yet achieved a subsidiary FUR in addition to its own state capital city.

Victoria Victoria started the period with 27 per cent of the nation's population and by 1981 this had dropped back by only one-half per cent. Its overall growth rate was 92 per cent compared with the Australian growth achieved of 97 per cent, although it did capture about 26 per cent of total growth which is consistent with its population holding. Three regions in the state achieved a higher than national average growth rate for the period. Region No. 19 (Loddon-Campaspie) was the only inland region, while the other two are coastal regions (Nos. 22 and 24).

Victoria started the period with the highest percentage holding in its FUR – Melbourne with 61 per cent – but it has slipped back below NSW in 1981. This state does however have a number of rapidly growing UMs of medium size. In overall terms, with 88 per cent of the state living in urban areas, it is highly urbanised. Its rural population has changed little since 1947 in absolute terms although in percentage terms it has fallen from 25 per cent of state population to only 12 per cent. Noticeable in both Victoria and NSW (both having the largest metropolitan cities) is that their FURs percentage holding peaked in 1971, five years earlier than the national figure.

Queensland Queensland improved its percentage holding of the total national population during this period from 14.6 per cent to 15.7 per cent, while in terms of state growth it grew by 112 per cent between 1947–81; faster than the 97 per cent figure achieved by the nation as a whole. Five out of its eleven regions grew faster than the national average growth rate and all five were coastal (see Table 14.22, Appendix 2). This state is somewhat atypical in comparison with the other states in that its FUR holding is still quite low, despite continued real growth within Brisbane, its capital city. What sets Queensland apart in the urban context is its highly developed set of secondary towns along its eastern coastline. This is borne out by the high percentage holding for the UMs – twenty-five per cent – and in combination with the FURs, this brings the state up to 82 per cent urbanised. The rural sector is also higher than the national average, and in percentage holding terms its FUR appears to have peaked in the 1971 period.

South Australia South Australia marginally improved its position, as its holding of the nation's population rose from its 1947 base of 8.5 per cent to 8.8 per cent in 1981. The only region in this state to grow at a rate faster than the national average was region No. 37 – Outer Adelaide itself (see Table 14.22, Appendix 2).

The state started the period with the second highest percentage holding in the FUR area, and it has retained this position in 1981. (Again discounting Canberra and the ACT as a special case.) The number in the rural area has stayed almost constant although in percentage terms it has halved. The state's FUR peaked in 1976, later than those of Victoria, NSW and Queensland.

Western Australia The most significant growth state during the study period was Western Australia. It improved its percentage holding of the nation's population from 6.6 per cent in 1947 to 8.7 per cent in 1981. State growth was 158 per cent for the period as compared with the equivalent national figure of 97 per cent. Two of its regions grew at a faster rate than the national average, and these were Perth itself and the remote northern Pilbara region. This region is a resource-rich region in terms of natural gas, iron-ore etc., and is currently under extensive development.

Perth, the state capital city, does not yet appear to have peaked in its percentage holding of the state's population. Like South Australia, this state has only a few UMs of any size.

Tasmania This state lost out badly in terms of its growth during the period. Its holding of the national population fell from 3.4 per cent to 2.8 per cent and as a state it achieved only 66 per cent growth for the period. Of its three regions, none grew consistently with national growth rates for the period 1947–81.

At the southern extremity of the continent and detached from the mainland, Tasmania is not well placed to attract population growth. Its capital city, Hobart, has not yet reached FUR status, and while it remains as the administrative centre for the island, its northern sister-city of Launceston rivals it for commercial and industrial growth. Tasmania also has a high percentage figure of its population still in the rural area, second only to the Northern Territory.

Australian Capital Territory Consistently the fastest growing territory of the nation, the ACT improved its percentage holding of the population from 0.22 per cent in 1947 to 2.8 per cent in 1981. The ACT is not a separate state, but Commonwealth-owned territory, and its prime function is to house the functions of the national capital. Canberra is the only large inland city of any size in Australia. Its performance as an inland growth centre has been unrivalled, but the formula for its constant growth is not one that lends itself to repeating throughout the nation. The ACT is also the most highly urbanised territory of Australia, with 99.6 per cent of its population living in the built-up urban area.

The Northern Territory This territory has also seen significant growth during the study period. At the base year it held only 0.14 per cent of the nation's population, but by 1981 this had increased to 0.82 per cent. The territory's capital city, Darwin, has now been rebuilt since cyclone 'Tracy' wiped it out a few years ago. The territory has a high proportion of its population still living in the rural sector, and with no FUR as yet, its two main towns of Darwin and Alice Springs account for its high percentage holding in the Urban Municipalities.

Summary During the 1947–81 period, three states lost ground in their holding of the nation's population. These were both NSW and Victoria, the two most industrialised states, and the third was Tasmania, perhaps the least industrialised. The other states and territories all increased their percentage holding of the national population. Few of the 56 regions achieved a growth rate in excess of the national average, and out of the 17 that did, 8 were metropolitan-based regions, and of the remaining 9, only 2 were inland regions.

The preceding commentary on the individual states and territories has shown some of the localised and individual characteristics of the urban pattern in each state which can tend to make broad generalisations somewhat difficult. Despite this, there are indications that the FURs have peaked at 66.45 per cent in the 1976 period.

A closer inspection of the individual FURs suggests that the three largest, Sydney, Melbourne and Brisbane, all peaked in percentage holding terms of total state population as early as 1971. The growth of the Urban Municipalities has been somewhat erratic, but this is largely due to Newcastle, Woolongong and Canberra all achieving FUR status during the study period. In percentage terms, both the Other Urban and Rural sectors are shrinking, although in absolute numbers they appear to be holding steady.

Australia started the post World War II period with 5 FURs and 37 UMs and by 1982 this had increased to include 8 FURs and 56 UMs, with a further 10 UMs being swallowed up by FURs in the growth process. Of major significance has been the doubling of the population – with 80 per cent of total population increase going to the metropolitan areas. Given this early metropolitan dominance and the continuation of the national immigration policy, this increase in metropolitan primacy is not surprising. The three largest cities, while still growing in absolute terms, are now showing signs that their peak percentage holding of their state's population has passed.

Industry–workforce analysis

*Workforce growth in categories and its distribution**

Between the period 1954–76 about 2.1 million new jobs were created in Australia. This represents about a 58 per cent growth in the workforce which is consistent with population growth for the same period (see Table 14.6). Referring to workforce categories however, it can be seen that the greatest part of this growth (73 per cent of it) occurred in only three categories – i.e. public administration (29 per cent), trade (22 per cent), and miscellaneous (22 per cent). These three categories were in fact the only ones to grow at a rate faster than the national average growth rate of 58 per cent for the period.

Also in this period there was a very slight increase in the number of jobs per thousand population (see Table 14.7). It rose from its 1954 level of 407 to the 1976 level of 412. It will be useful now to look at the absolute growth in jobs across the various workforce categories.

Farming The only sector which experienced an actual loss of jobs (100,000 in toto) and as might be expected, 78 per cent of this loss occurred in the Rural sector which holds 85 per cent of all farming jobs throughout the country. Jobs/thousand dropped from 55 to 28 over this study period.

Mining Only 10,000 new jobs were created in this category and the jobs/thousand figure fell from 7 to 5. All of the growth took place in the Metropolitan areas as both Other Urban and Rural areas lost mining jobs. This suggests that the new jobs created were more in the nature of administrative support for the industry rather than jobs on mining sites.

Manufacturing About 127,000 new jobs were created which represents a 12 per cent increase only. Of the 2.1 million new jobs created, manufacturing provided only 6 per cent of them. Clearly this is not an area of rapid expansion, as Australia moves out of the industrial age into the present. Most new jobs occurred in the Metropolitan areas, while Other Urban areas lost jobs in this category. The Rural sector gained some, so some decentralisation of industrial jobs did occur.

* This analysis covers the period 1954–76 only, since the results of the 1981 census cross-tabulations are as yet not available for inclusion.

Table 14.6

Australian workforce, 1954–76: growth and percentage change ('000)

	Metro				Urban				Rural				Australian Total			
	1954	1976	Differ	% change	1954	1976	Differ	% change	1954	1976	Differ	% change	1954	1976	Differ	% change
1 Farm	30	18	−12	−40	51	41	−10	−20	414	336	−78	−19	495	395	−100	−20
2 Mine	3	20	17	567	42	38	−4	−10	16	14	−2	−13	61	72	11	18
3 Manu	743	894	151	20	201	171	−30	−15	66	73	7	11	1010	1138	128	13
4 Serv	47	64	17	36	22	30	8	36	7	8	1	14	76	102	26	34
5 Cons	166	268	102	61	94	107	13	14	66	53	−13	−20	326	428	102	31
6 Tran	146	197	51	35	68	62	−6	−9	24	25	1	4	238	284	46	19
7 Comm	47	78	31	66	21	21	0	0	11	10	−1	−9	79	109	30	38
8 Fina	73	285	212	290	21	61	40	191	5	21	16	320	99	367	268	271
9 Trad	375	738	363	97	152	221	69	45	48	84	36	75	575	1043	468	81
10 PA	293	779	486	166	104	186	82	79	48	94	46	96	445	1059	614	138
11 Rec	131	185	54	41	63	68	5	8	29	28	−1	−3	223	281	58	26
12 Mis	18	303	285	1583	9	116	107	1189	8	82	74	925	35	501	466	1331
Total	2072	3829	1757	85	848	1122	274	32	742	828	86	12	3662	5779	2117	58
Population	4730	9315	4585	97	2393	2771	378	16	1863	1947	84	5	8986	14033	5047	56

Source: ABS statistics
Refer also to notes shown on Table 14.7 re Industrial categories etc.

Table 14.7

Australian workforce, 1954–76: jobs per 1000 over major categories

	Metro				Urban				Rural				Australian Totals			
	1954%	J/1000	1976%	J/1000	1954%	J/1000	1976%	J/1000	1954%	J/1000	1976%	J/1000	1954%	J/1000	1976%	J/1000
1 Farm	1.45	6	.47	2	6.01	21	3.65	15	55.80	222	40.58	173	13.52	55	13.52	28
2 Mine	.15	0.6	.52	2	4.95	18	3.39	14	2.16	9	1.69	7	1.67	7	1.67	5
3 Manu	35.85	157	23.35	96	23.70	84	15.24	62	8.89	35	8.82	37	27.58	112	27.58	81
4 Serv	2.27	10	1.67	7	2.59	9	2.67	11	.94	4	.97	4	2.08	8	2.08	7
5 Cons	8.01	35	7.00	29	11.08	39	9.54	39	8.89	35	6.40	27	8.90	36	8.90	31
6 Tran	7.05	31	5.14	21	8.02	28	5.53	23	3.23	13	3.02	13	6.50	26	6.50	20
7 Comm	2.28	10	2.04	8	2.48	9	1.87	8	1.48	6	1.21	5	2.15	9	2.15	8
8 Fina	3.52	15	7.44	31	2.48	9	5.44	22	.67	3	2.54	11	2.70	11	2.70	26
9 Trad	18.09	79	19.27	80	17.92	64	19.70	80	6.47	26	10.14	43	15.70	64	15.70	74
10 PA	14.14	62	20.34	84	12.27	43	16.58	67	6.47	26	11.35	48	12.15	50	12.15	75
11 Rec	6.32	28	4.83	20	7.44	26	6.06	25	3.91	16	3.38	15	6.09	25	6.09	20
12 Mis	.87	4	7.93	33	1.06	4	10.33	42	1.09	4	9.90	42	.96	4	.96	36
	100.00	438	100.00	411	100.00	354	100.00	405	100.00	398	100.00	425	100.00	408	100.00	412

Sources: ABS data.

Notes: Workforce categories above are as follows:- (1) Farming and agriculture; (2) Mining; (3) Manufacturing; (4) Services including electricity, gas, water, (5) Construction; (6) Transport; (7) Communication; (8) Finance; (9) Trade, wholesale and retail; (10) Public administration, defence and community services; (11) Recreation and entertainment; (12) Miscellaneous.

J/1000 = jobs per thousand population.

Workforce classification changed in 1971, but figures have been amalgamated to provide consistent data.

The real extent of the loss in this category is shown in the jobs/thousand figures which fell from 112 to only 81. Manufacturing industries maintained 27 per cent of all jobs in Australia in 1954, but by 1976 they captured only 20 per cent of the total workforce.

Services Very little structural change appears to have occurred in this category. In new jobs terms 26,000 were created for the period. Growth was distributed across the Metropolitan, Urban and Rural areas much as might be expected, except that the Urban category captured 30 per cent of them which is higher than straight population terms might suggest. A tentative conclusion here might be that as Other Urban areas expand, they require capitalisation and employment expansion in this sector.

Construction In this category 102,000 new jobs were created and most were in the metropolitan areas. The rural sector lost 13,000 jobs, while the Other Urban sector gained 13,000 jobs/thousand in this component fell from 36 to 30.

Transport Only 47,000 new jobs were created and the jobs/thousand rate fell from 26 to 20, a marginal change. The metropolitan areas gained 51,000 new jobs, Rural remained static so that what the Other Urban sector lost was the city's gain.

Communications Only 30,000 new jobs were created and the job/thousand fell marginally from 9 to 8. All new growth went into the Metropolitan areas, with the Urban and Rural sectors remaining static.

Finance This category is one of the real growth sectors, with 268,000 new jobs created, and the job/thousand rate climbing from 11 to 26. The jobs were distributed as follows: Metropolitan – 79 per cent; Urban – 15 per cent; and Rural – 6 per cent which is consistent with population distribution figures.

Trade The equal second major growth industry with 468,000 new jobs created and the job rate increasing from 64 to 74 per thousand population. The distribution of these was in accordance with population distribution, Metropolitan – 77 per cent; Urban – 15 per cent; and Rural – 7 per cent.

Public administration The major growth sector with 613,000 new jobs created and the job rate increasing from 50 to 76 per thousand. This category is now the second highest employer in Australia after Manufacturing. Distribution of jobs followed the standard population distribution pattern, i.e. Metropolitan – 79 per cent; Urban – 13 per cent; Rural – 7 per cent.

Recreation Only 59,000 new jobs were created here so that the job rate fell from 25 to 20 per thousand. The Metropolitan areas gained 91 per cent of this increase. Rural areas lost, and Urban gained by 8 per cent.

Miscellaneous This was a major growth category with 466,000 new jobs created. At first sight, one might infer that the absolute losses that occurred in other employment sectors is balanced by the growth in this sector, i.e. this growth represents in fact people adapting to new jobs following on the loss of old ones.

Structural change between the states

In the 1954–76 period three states achieved a growth rate in employment below the national average. These were Tasmania (42 per cent), NSW (44.9 per cent) and Victoria (52.4 per cent) – the national average being 57.76 per cent. Queensland performed close to the national average, while the other states were above (SA – 71.3 per cent; WA – 92.6 per cent; NT – 431 per cent and the ACT – 604 per cent). In every employment category, WA outperformed the national average growth rate. These same four states also performed well above the national average in population growth for the same period:

> SA, employment grew by 71 per cent; population grew by 60 per cent:
> WA, employment grew by 93 per cent; population grew by 84 per cent:
> NT, employment grew by 431 per cent; population grew by 550 per cent:
> ACT, employment grew by 604 per cent; population grew by 653 per cent:
> For comparative purposes in Tasmania, employment grew by 42 per cent, while population grew by 33 per cent.

Employment distribution and change between the metropolitan, urban and rural components of population

FURs – Metropolitan areas In terms of jobs per thousand population, from 1954–76 the metropolitan rate fell from 438 to 411, which is equal to the national average. Thus during this time, the metropolitan areas lost some of their job attractiveness, as compared with the other areas. Manufacturing is still the largest single employment category but in 1976 the differential had been decreased significantly. Five employment categories lifted their employment ratios in terms of jobs/thousand. They were trade (79 – 84); public administration (61 – 84); finance (15 – 31); miscellaneous (4 – 33) and mining (0.5 – 2). Significant factors then are as follows:

1 A loss in the importance of manufacturing.
2 Increasing importance of public administration, trade, finance and the miscellaneous workforce.
3 Decreasing importance of all other categories.

In metropolitan spatial terms, the employment growth sectors are not nearly as dependent upon spatial aggregation as was the manufacturing sector. Most central business districts have experienced a sizeable office building programme which still focuses jobs on the CBD, but office employment is now becoming more dispersed throughout the metropolitan area.

Urban areas During the study period jobs per thousand increased markedly in the other urban areas, from 354 to 405. Four workforce categories increased their importance considerably, and these were:

Trade, 64 to 80.
Public administration, 43 to 80.
Miscellaneous, 4 to 41.
Finance, 9 to 22.

Four categories lost in importance: manufacturing (84 to 62); transport (28 to 23); farming (21 to 15) and mining (17 to 14). The other four categories remained unchanged. Whereas in 1954, manufacturing was the largest single employer, by 1976 this has been displaced by both trade and public administration, with the miscellaneous category rising from last in 1954 to fourth in 1976. This result confirms the growth prospects for the other urban areas, since the expanding 'information' workforce can be decentralised with greater ease.

Rural areas Interestingly, jobs per thousand increased during the period from 398 to 424, well above the national average figure in 1976 of 411. While farming lost from 222 to 172 jobs/thousand it is still the largest single employment category. In 1954, the manufacturing and construction categories were second and third respectively; but by 1976, public administration, trade and miscellaneous had grown to second, third and fourth order of importance. Finance also grew from 3 to 11 jobs/thousand. The two categories to lose were farming and construction, while the remaining six remained static. Here too then a substantial change has taken place in the employment base, and it has become more diversified to reflect national trends.

Summary

The changeover from the industrial-manufacturing type of economy to the modern information processing and administrative type of economy occurred in Australia during 1954–76 – a brief 22 year period. The implications for the urban pattern are already apparent. The earlier necessary concentration of employment opportunities within the metropolitan areas, based on manufacturing and industrial economic growth, has now been superseded. Job opportunities in both the other urban and the rural areas have increased, thus reversing the earlier dominance of the metropolitan areas. While agriculture and farming will remain the dominant employment categories in the rural areas, the loosening-up of the 1954 employment structure has been to the advantage of the other urban areas, which now more than compete in job terms with their metropolitan counterparts.

These structural changes in the Australian economy have made it possible for alternative work and housing locations to the metropolitan areas to be sought and found by increasing numbers of the population.

Urban growth dynamics in the Australian urban system

Earlier sections of this chapter have made the following points:

1 Net gains from overseas migration have played a substantial role in Australia's continued population growth – particularly in the major metropolitan areas.
2 While gross inter-state migration flows are large, net figures are small. Yet over the period 1966–81, both NSW and Victoria have been consistent providers of population to the other states.
3 The FURs have captured nearly 80 per cent of all new population growth since 1947 and have retained and increased their dominance within the urban system. There are, however, indications that in 1971 growth in the three larger FURs may have peaked in percentage holding of state population terms. While growth in absolute numbers continued, more population growth is being located in the urban municipalities, particularly those located within the coastal zone.
4 The analysis of structural change that has occurred in the Australian economy supports the increasing diffusion of employment opportunities away from the major metropolitan areas.

All of these factors suggest that the national urban system, and the inter-relationship between its components, is undergoing gradual structural change.

In this section, an attempt is made to develop a model of the urban and rural system that will show up the dynamics of this change. The inputs are population growth, be this from natural growth, net inter-state and/or overseas migration. The population aggregate is broken down into its four constituent parts, i.e. FURs, UMs, O/U and Rural. The time periods chosen span from 1966 through to 1981 – since the first census data on inter-state migration was collected. Accurate census data is available for natural growth and net inter-state migration, as well as for gross population within each of the four population aggregation categories. There is also accurate data available for the net gains due to overseas migration. The model constructed then relates these inputs in a way to show the net flows of population between the four population aggregation categories over the inter-censal periods.

Calculations for the three time spans (1966–71; 1971–76; and 1976–81) are shown in the accompanying Tables 14.8 to 14.16 and the results have been shown graphically in Figure 14.2.

Some qualifications need to be placed on the accuracy of some of the data and the interpretations that can be drawn. Firstly, under-enumeration of both the 1971 and 1976 censuses and the necessary revisions of this data provides opportunity for conflicting data sets. Care has been taken to draw on consistent data wherever possible, but some adjustments have been necessary. Secondly, readily accessible census data does not differentiate between overseas and inter-state migration gains or losses, but shows these only as gains or losses due to 'migration'. A way of differentiating these two and distributing them between the four categories was required. To simplify the allocation procedure, net gains or losses due to overseas migration have been distributed only to the FURs and a few UMs in states that have no FURs; (i.e. Canberra in the ACT, Darwin in the Northern Territory and Hobart in Tasmania). Given the strong propensity for overseas migrants to live in urban areas [see Appendix 3 and Rowland (1979)] this is not an unreasonable assumption. Using this procedure then, and with the use of a computer based spreadsheet, the key population growth parameters were fed in and the allocations made to produce Tables 14.8 to 14.16 inclusive.

The resultant net internal migration flows between the FURs, UMs, O/U and Rural categories were then used to provide the data shown graphically in Figure 14.2. This diagram also shows the major population growth inputs into the system. This simplified flow model omits the gross flows involved in internal migration. (For example see

Table 14.8
Components of growth by category, 1966–71 ('000)

	FURs					UMs					Other Urban				Rural				Totals	
State	1966	Nat O	Seas I	Stat	1971	1966	Nat O	Seas I	Stat	1971	1966	Nat I	Stat	1971	1966	Nat I	Stat	1971	1966	1971
NSW	2681	137	243	271	3332	591	30	0	−75	546	390	20	−158	252	576	29	−74	531	4238	4661
Vic	2110	133	123	149	2515	339	21	0	1	361	309	19	−117	211	462	30	−59	433	3220	3520
Q	780	47	91	−27	891	413	25	0	−6	432	86	5	80	171	395	24	−32	387	1674	1881
SA	772	42	47	−18	843	65	4	0	19	88	66	4	2	72	192	10	−20	182	1095	1185
WA	559	43	107	−6	703	58	4	0	29	91	25	2	30	57	206	18	−32	192	848	1043
Tas					0	215	14	2	31	262	46	3	−21	28	110	7	−17	100	371	390
ACT					0	92	11	16	43	162	0	0	0	0	4	1	−2	3	96	165
NT					0	20	3	18	6	47	11	2	1	14	26	3	2	31	57	92
Total	6902	402	611	369	8284	1793	112	36	48	1989	933	55	−183	805	1971	122	−234	1859	11599	12937

Source: Derived from ABS data and Table 14.4 (refer to text for details)

Table 14.9

Australian growth components by type, 1966–71 ('000)

	FURs	UMs	O/U	Rural	Total
1966	6902	1793	933	1971	11599
%	59.51	15.46	8.044	16.99	100
Nat	402	112	55	122	691
%	58.18	16.21	7.959	17.66	100
O/S	611	36			647
%	94.44	5.564			100
I/S	369	48	– 183	–234	0
%					
1971	8284	1989	805	1859	12937
%	64.03	15.37	6.222	14.37	100

Table 14.10

Growth components by state, 1966–71 ('000)

NSW	Vic	Q	SA	WA	Tas	ACT	NT	Total	
4238	3220	1674	1095	848	371	96	57	11599	1966 Population
216	204	101	60	65	24	13	8	691	Natural Increase
* –36	–27	15	–17	23	– 7	* 41	9	0	Net I/S Increase
243	123	91	47	107	2	16	18	647	Net O/S Increase
4661	3520	1881	1185	1043	390	165	92	12937	1971 Population

* Note here that Queanbeyan within NSW is shown within the ACT in these figures.

Source of Tables: Derived from ABS data and Table 14.4 (refer to text for details)

Table 14.11

Components of growth by category, 1971–76 ('000)

State	FURs 1971	FURs Nat O	FURs Seas I	FURs Stat	FURs 1976	UMs 1971	UMs Nat O	UMs Seas I	UMs Stat	UMs 1976	Other Urban 1971	Other Urban Nat I	Other Urban Stat	Other Urban 1976	Rural 1971	Rural Nat I	Rural Stat	Rural 1976	Totals 1971	Totals 1976
NSW	3535	174	120	–146	3683	343	16	0	57	416	252	15	10	277	531	25	5	561	4661	4937
Vic	2515	127	145	–115	2672	361	17	0	20	398	211	11	61	283	433	21	3	457	3520	3810
Q	891	61	40	–6	986	432	27	0	27	486	171	8	36	215	387	19	–1	405	1881	2092
SA	843	40	33	8	924	88	4	0	2	94	72	3	–9	66	182	8	0	190	1185	1274
WA	703	47	45	31	826	91	6	0	5	102	57	5	–5	57	192	12	–11	193	1043	1178
Tas	:				0	262	15	2	–6	273	28	2	7	37	100	5	–3	102	390	412
ACT					0	162	11	25	26	224	0	0	0	0	3	1	–2	2	165	226
NT					0	47	3	1	7	58	14	1	–6	9	31	1	5	37	92	104
Total	8487	449	383	– 228	9091	1786	99	28	138	2051	805	45	94	944	1859	92	–4	1947	12937	14033

Source: Derived from ABS data and Table 14.4 (refer to text for details)

Table 14.12

Australian growth components by type, 1971–76 ('000)

	FURs	UMs	O/U	Rural	Total
1971	8487	1786	805	1859	12937
%	65.6	13.81	6.222	14.37	100
Natural	449	99	45	92	685
%	65.55	14.45	6.569	13.43	100
O/Seas	383	28			411
%	93.19	6.813			100
I/State	−228	138	94	−4	0
%					
1976	9091	2051	944	1947	14033
%	64.78	14.62	6.727	13.87	100

Table 14.13

Growth components by state, 1971–76 ('000)

NSW	Vic	Q	SA	WA	Tas	ACT	NT	Total	
4661	3520	1881	1185	1043	390	165	92	12937	1971 Population
230	176	115	55	70	22	12	5	685	Natural Increase
*–74	–31	56	1	20	–2	24*	6	0	Net I/State
120	145	40	33	45	2	25	1	411	Net O/Seas
4937	3810	2092	1274	1178	412	226	104	14033	1976 Population

* Note here that Queanbeyan within NSW is shown here within the ACT in these figures.

Source of Tables: Derived from ABS data and Table 14.4 (refer to text for details)

Table 14.14

Components of growth by category, 1976–81 ('000)

State	FURs					UMs					Other Urban				Rural				Totals	
	1976	Nat O	Seas I	Stat	1981	1976	Nat O	Seas I	Stat	1981	1976	Nat I	Stat	1981	1976	Nat I	Stat	1981	1976	1981
NSW	3683	125	126	−21	3913	416	26	0	47	489	277	12	−42	247	561	29	−20	570	4937	5219
Vic	2672	107	48	−105	2722	398	15	0	43	456	283	10	0	293	457	15	5	477	3810	3948
Q	986	55	95	−50	1086	486	20	0	91	597	215	15	0	230	405	4	23	432	2092	2345
SA	924	34	13	−18	953	94	3	0	−2	95	66	3	0	69	190	5	7	202	1247	1319
WA	826	45	38	9	918	102	5	0	8	115	57	4	10	71	193	9	−7	195	1178	1299
Tas					0	273	7	−1	23	302	37	5	−11	31	102	5	−13	94	412	427
ACT	224	18	−8	12	246	0	0	0	0	0	0	0	0	0	2	0	−1	1	226	247
NT					0	58	5	−3	15	75	9	2	−3	8	37	3	0	40	104	123
Total	9315	384	312	−173	9838	1827	81	−4	225	2129	944	51	−46	949	1947	70	−6	2011	14033	14927

Source: Dervied from ABS data and Table 14.4 (refer to text for details)

Table 14.15

Australian growth components by type, 1976–81 ('000)

	FURs	UMs	O/U	Rural	Total
1976	9315	1827	944	1947	14033
%	66.38	13.02	6.727	13.87	100
Natural	384	81	51	70	586
%	65.53	13.82	8.703	11.95	100
O/Seas	312	– 4			308
%	101.3	–1.3			100
I/State	–173	225	–46	–6	0
%					
1981	9838	2129	949	2011	14927
%	65.91	14.26	6.358	13.47	100

Table 14.16

Growth components by state, 1976–81 ('000)

NSW	Vic	Q	SA	WA	Tas	ACT	NT	Total	
4937	3810	2092	1274	1178	412	226	104	14033	1971 Population
192	147	94	45	63	17	18	10	586	Natural Increase
*–36	–57	64	–13	20	–1	*11	12	0	Net I/State
126	48	95	13	38	–1	–8	–3	308	Net O/Seas
5219	3948	2345	1319	1299	427	247	123	14927	1976 Population

* Note here that Queanbeyan within NSW is shown here with the ACT in these figures.

Source of Tables: Derived from ABS data and Table 14.4 (refer to text for details)

Rowland (1979) p.45 Figure 10). Its purpose however is to indicate the net product of these and other complex population flows, and to illustrate trends over time.

Figure 14.2 then shows the main structural components of the Australian urban system for the four census periods between 1966 and 1981. Each block of population is shown distributed between the four categories of FUR, UM, O/U and Rural. What is shown here is that between 1966 and 1971 the FURs increased their holding of the population from 60 per cent to 66 per cent and this later figure has stayed fairly static throughout the ensuing periods.

To the left of each population block, are shown the chief inputs of population growth, i.e. both natural increase and net gain from overseas migration. At the bottom right of each population block is shown the 'balancing' factor of net internal population movements between the four categories, as derived from Tables 14.8 to 14.16. The size of each population block is proportional to total population size, and to the left of the figure is shown a percentage scale (0 to 100) so that the distribution between the population categories can be observed.

In the 1971 period, it can be seen that net internal migration flows favoured both the FURs and the UMs, with the main contributors being the Other Urban and Rural sectors. Putting this another way, between 1966 and 1971, the drift of the Australian population was still towards the major urban areas and cities. By 1976 however, this drift was reversed and net internal migration flows favoured the UMs and Other Urban areas, at the expense of the FURs. This trend has been continued through into the 1976–81 period, with the FURs contributing population growth to the UMs.

Some caution is required in interpreting these flows. As the Supplementary Report to the National Population Inquiry (1978), pages 63–64 has pointed out, the decline in the growth rate of the larger FURs during these latter periods was probably due to a complex interplay of factors, the chief one being the marked down-turn in overseas migration gains. (In 1975 Australia experienced the first net loss in 30 years from all inward and outward movements. Immigration policies and Australian Population (1977) page 5.) Other factors possibly contributing to this decline in the growth rate are:

1 The decline in the rate of natural increase – the net reproduction ratio fell below 1.0 in 1976 (see Supplementary Report of the National Population Inquiry (1978) p.5).
2 The increasing flow of internal migration away from the FURs.
3 The changing workforce structure which yielded increased employment opportunities in locations away from the FURs.

The overseas immigration flow has since then increased rapidly, from its negative low point in 1975 up to over 100,000 a year net in 1981–82. The key policy area in this national programme is in the 'family reunion' component which accounts for almost 50 per cent of the migrant intake. Given the existing concentration of migrants within urban areas, this policy will only reinforce continued population growth within the chief metropolitan areas.

The net internal migration flows between the main sectors are small in comparison with gross flows. Rowland's thesis that internal migration supports the current urban structure has merit, but it does tend to see internal migration as being somewhat unrelated to overseas migration. If one does see the FURs as the repositories of the older, more diversified and cheaper housing stock – and if one accepts that overseas migrants may at least enter the country with a lower capital holding than their Australian counterparts, then it should not be surprising to see foreign-born migrants take up residence here – leaving their Australian-born cousins to move further out to the city's periphery, or even further afield. Put another way, while it is true to say that the immigration programme has provided the major growth vehicle for the FURs, it might also be encouraging internal migration away from those centres to smaller towns and cities in the coastal belt.

Despite these cautionary comments, and the need to recognise the complex inter-play of gross migration flows, this analysis has suggested that the key elements in the Australian urban system, the FURs, might now be poised to adapt to the growth forces in a somewhat different way than has been the case in the past. The situation within the FURs is explored further in the following section.

Analysis of core periphery growth

In their book, *The Dynamics of Urban Development*, Klaassen et al., have postulated a dynamic cyclical development of urban growth based on their research into European cities which consists of four phases, i.e. urbanisation, suburbanisation, desurbanisation and reurbanisation. This concept has been the chief motive for this preliminary study of the dynamics of the Australian urban system. The perspective taken focuses on two interrelated components of the urban system. First, the changing nature of the relationship between the metropolitan agglomeration as a whole and its surrounding hinterland. Second, a closer view of the internal relationships with the metropolitan agglomeration as between its core and peripheral components.

These aspects of the Australian urban system will be reviewed in the following sections.

While the Australian FUR system provides only a limited number of cities to study – there being only 8 FURs in 1981 – as has been identified earlier in this chapter, because these 8 cities house six out of every ten Australians, their future is of vital importance to the nation as a whole. The cities themselves are not large in population terms, the two largest, Sydney and Melbourne, are only 3.2 and 2.8 millions respectively. They would probably rank as say 30th and 40th in world city population size terms. Despite this, with their low density development of about 2000 persons per km^2, the cities do tend to be large in actual area. They are then in many ways similar to numerous cities on the west coast of the USA – which also grew up mostly coincident with the development of the private motor car. Because of the brief urban history in Australia, these cities do not exhibit a clearly defined urban core, in say the same way as their European counterparts sometimes do. Nonetheless, there is little difficulty in identifying an inner ring of suburbs, along with a middle and outer ring. The statistical units adopted for the purposes of describing the core areas of the Australian FURs is shown in detail in Appendix 1.

In referring to the Australian FURs as a group, it is important to underline the wide diversity that exists within this group. There are in fact probably three distinct sub-groups within the eight FURs. First, the two largest cities of Sydney and Melbourne can reasonably be grouped together; then comes a range of middle-order FURs such as Brisbane, Adelaide and Perth, each of which houses about 1 million people. Finally, a third order group exists consisting of Newcastle, Woolongong and Canberra, with each of these cities housing a population of less than 500,000 persons. The five largest cities are all state capital cities, while Canberra is the national capital and the largest inland city in Australia. Both Newcastle and Woolongong are in effect peripheral extensions of the Sydney metropolitan area. They are both coal and steel producing centres and when taken together with Sydney can be seen as the one conurbation of about 4 million people. A brief reference to the most populous lower-order urban municipalities also shows that Geelong and the Gold Coast are similarly metro-peripheral developments of both Melbourne and Brisbane respectively.

The high-order FURs are well-spaced out around the continental coastline – about 750 km distant from each other, although Perth in Western Australia is more than 3000 km distant from Sydney. With the exception of Canberra, all FURs are located on the coast with port facilities, so that in tracing their early growth pattern one can typically find a geographically constrained core at or near the port facilities, with successive rings of urban expansion fanning out both inland and along the coastline away from the core.

Table 14.17
Analysis of core-frame growth in FURs

(Population in 000)

	1947	1954	1961	1966	1971	1976	1981
FUR 101. Sydney							
Core	711.9	820.6	799.4	798	826.7	773.1	743
Frame	772.1	1042	1384	1649	2150	2321	2537
Total	1484	1863	2183	2447	2977	3094	3280
% Core	47.97	44.05	36.62	32.61	27.77	24.99	22.65
% Frame	52.03	55.95	63.38	67.39	72.23	75.01	77.35
FUR 201. Melbourne							
Core	814.5	776.9	755.3	764.6	765.7	670.7	604.8
Frame	411.5	755.1	1103	1345	1749	2001	2117
Total	1226	1570	1918	2160	2564	2816	2932
% Core	66.44	49.50	39.39	35.41	29.87	23.82	20.63
% Frame	33.56	50.50	60.61	64.59	70.13	76.18	79.37
FUR 301. Brisbane							
Core	145.3	134	126.3	123	113.8	100.7	95
Frame	256.7	368	567.7	657	777.2	885.3	991
Total	402	502	694	780	891	986	1086
% Core	36.14	26.69	18.20	15.77	12.77	10.21	8.748
% Frame	63.86	73.31	81.80	84.23	87.23	89.79	91.25
FUR 401. Adelaide							
Core	163.9	149.2	141	131.2	128.3	116.9	107.8
Frame	218.1	334.8	518	640.8	714.7	807.1	845.2
Total	382	484	659	772	843	924	953
% Core	42.91	30.83	21.40	16.99	15.22	12.65	11.31
% Frame	57.09	69.17	78.60	83.01	84.78	87.35	88.69
FUR 501. Perth							
Core	150.9	158.9	163.6	168.2	169.1	158.6	145.2
Frame	122.1	190.1	293.4	390.8	533.9	667.4	772.8
Total	273	349	457	559	703	826	918
% Core	55.27	45.53	35.80	30.09	24.05	19.20	15.82
% Frame	44.73	54.47	64.20	69.91	75.95	80.80	84.18
FUR 102. Newcastle							
Core	129	137	142	143	146	138	139
Frame	25	41	66	91	209	232	263
Total	154	178	208	234	355	370	402
% Core	83.77	76.97	68.27	61.11	41.13	37.30	34.58
% Frame	16.23	23.03	31.73	38.89	58.87	62.70	65.42
FUR 103. Woolongong							
Core	18	21	131	149	161	165	176
Frame	45	70	1	13	42	54	55
Total	63	91	132	162	203	219	231
% Core	28.57	23.08*	99.24	91.98	79.31	75.34	76.19
% Frame	71.43	76.92	7576	8.025	20.69	24.66	23.81

*Boundary changed

Source: ABS statistics (refer to Appendix 1 for definition of Core)

Details of the FUR Canberra are not included in this table.

In reviewing the internal growth dynamics of these metropolitan areas (see Table 14.17) it is clear that the high-order FURs have been losing core area population for some years. Indeed the loss of inner area population is not confined to the core areas, but as *Australian Atlas of Resources* (1980) shows, the extent of population loss in real terms is now extensive – covering almost 50 per cent of the total metropolitan areas. Here then is evidence that the Australian FURs are following the same dynamic growth pattern as their European counterparts.

All FURs are however still growing in absolute terms, so that in this sense they are still in the suburbanisation or second phase of cyclical growth, i.e. loss of population within the cores is offset by population gains within the metropolitan periphery. No FUR has entered the third, desurbanisation phase wherein population losses in the core area exceed population gains at the periphery. In the 1976–81 period, Melbourne was the FUR that perhaps came closest to this. Its core lost about 66,000 while its periphery gained only 116,000, so that in net terms, Melbourne's population grew by about 50,000.

What then are the primary forces shaping the core-periphery dynamics of these FURs? Of major significance is the national immigration policy. Not only has this programme contributed the chief part of net population gains for the FURs (i.e. in terms of an urban focus), but because of the propensity for migrants to settle in the inner areas of the cities, the social fabric of the city has changed to reflect their diverse cultural backgrounds.

During the boom years, see Daly (1982), which coincided with peak migration intake, many inner suburbs were transformed by medium-density redevelopment in the form of flats and home units, both for sale and rental. To some extent this higher-density form of redevelopment has amelioriated the otherwise more substantial population losses that might have occurred in these inner-city areas. They can also be seen as reflecting a more European higher-density style of living consistent with the origins of the majority of migrants. But they are as much the result of land and housing shortages, escalating land prices throughout the ever expanding metropolitan area, as they are a reflection on the different cultural backgrounds of their final consumers. Some of the earlier worst forms of this style of redevelopment have led to a situation in which local councils (the custodians of the greater part of planning and building development approvals in Australia) are reluctant to rezone land for medium-density redevelopment lest this should jeopardise the existing environmental quality of the area. Land then for medium-density redevelopment within the cities is frequently scarce.

Again, during the same rapid growth period, state and national governments foresaw the need to divert population growth away from the major cities by decentralisation and other growth centre policies. A number of inland growth centres and metro-peripheral centres were identified and planned – i.e. Albury-Wodonga, Bathurst-Orange, Monato, Geelong etc. With the change in national government in 1975 and with falling population projections, these policies are no longer being pursued.

Changes in the economic base have resulted in greater deployment of the workforce throughout the metropolitan area, although the CBDs, supported by the typical radial pattern of fixed-track public transport systems, still remain as the main employment centres for white-collar workers. As jobs have become diffused, greater reliance has had to be placed on private transport, so that the size of the public transport deficit escalates as its patronage declines.

In the current economic recession, land and building prices while not escalating, still remain high and out of reach for an increasing number of would-be home owners. New urban growth is focused on the periphery which is increasingly costly for governments to service adequately. The outward spread of the population calls for the relocation of existing central-area fixed overhead capital such as hospitals. Faced with these escalating costs, governments are now actively encouraging urban consolidation policies as a means of reducing the public sector financial burden. While government policy can have a significant impact on these forces, historically in Australia it has been the private sector market-forces which have taken the initiative, with governments following those leads almost irrespective of costs and equity issues.

These policy issues will be dealt with further in the next section of this chapter, but the present discussion has served to underline the dynamic nature of metropolitan relationships and the need for policy to anticipate change and help shape it, rather than to simply respond to it.

The Urban Municipalities

As part of the dynamic-cyclical urban growth pattern postulated by Klaassen et al., it was suggested that as the FURs enter their third phase of growth – desurbanisation – or actual loss of population within the FURs – new population growth is directed to smaller towns and cities in the surrounding region. In the earlier section on urban growth dynamics (p.217) attention was directed to the net flows of internal migration in Australia and the data provided suggested that since the 1976 census metropolitan concentration forces appear to have passed through a nodal point such that it is now the UMs that are the recipients of this population redistribution process. This section examines the 56 towns and cities in Australia which have populations ranging from more than 10,000 up to less than 200,000.

In 1947 there were 37 UMs accommodating nearly 1 million people, or 13 per cent of the total population. By 1981, there were 56 UMs accommodating 2.1 million people or 14 per cent of the total population (see Table 14.21). Of the 7.34 million additional people accommodated between 1947 and 1981, the FURs captured 82 per cent of that growth, while the UMs captured 15 per cent. The FURs then grew by 15 per cent, the UMs by 113 per cent, while Australia as a whole grew by 97 per cent. These figures give a holistic view of the role of the UMs throughout this period, but they do mask more subtle changes and some further explanation is required to draw these out.

Firstly, while the FURs captured 75 per cent of all new population growth in the 1971–76 period, by 1981 their inter-censal retention rate had fallen to only 58 per cent of new growth. In the corresponding period, the UMs on the other hand had retained 34 per cent of all new population growth, which is a substantial shift in their role. Secondly, during the 1966–76 period, both Woolongong and Canberra attained FUR status, and a further 8 UMs were swallowed up by metropolitan expansion. While the downturn in FUR growth rates was largely due to the downturn in gains from overseas migration, the substantial growth within the UMs has been as a result of internal migration of the Australian people, along with natural growth. As Table 14.19 shows, if one looks specifically at the growth rates of UMs between 1947 and 1981, they attained an overall growth rate of 188 per cent – or twice that of the national average for the same period. This growth is even all the more remarkable when one recognises that about 1 in 4

Table 14.18

Urban municipalities growth and categories

Type	No. Towns	1947 '000	population %	1981 '000	population %	1947–81 '000	growth %
Metro-Periph.	3	59	8	344	16	285	20
Coastal	27	360	48	1019	48	659	47
Inland	22	272	37	683	32	411	30
Outback	4	54	7	92	4	38	3
Total	56	745	100	2138	100	1393	100

of these centres (13 in toto) had a growth rate below that of the nation as a whole.

Is there any discernible pattern to the growth that has taken place in these centres? To assist in the following discussion, the towns have been classified under the following four categories: metro-periphery; coastal; inland and outback.

The data shown in Table 14.18 above indicates that those UMs which are located adjacent to FURs (i.e. Geelong, Gold Coast and Rockingham-Kwinana) have demonstrated a remarkable growth rate – moving from only 8 per cent of the 1947 UM population to 16 per cent of it in 1981 – and in the process capturing 20 per cent of all UM growth. The coastal towns have retained their 48 per cent holding from 1947 through to 1981 and have captured 47 per cent of all UM growth. Both inland and outback towns have lost position. Since the metro-periphery towns are also coastal, one can infer from this that 67 per cent of all UM growth went into the coastal regions.

Despite these broad generalisations – not insignificant in themselves – it is difficult to identify any other pattern in what is really a fairly uneven growth picture. Some coastal towns have grown slowly, while others have grown rapidly – and the same is true for both inland and outback towns. In summary then, this brief review of the UMs has show the following:

1 The UM growth rate between 1947–81 has been an outstanding one, given the considerable metropolitan primacy that exists in Australia and the fact that the FURs have captured over 80 per cent of all 1947–81 population growth. The 1976–81 figures show that the UMs captured 34 per cent of total growth, so the pattern is a changing one.
2 The metro-peripheral UMs out-performed all other UMs by capturing 20 per cent of all 1947–81 UM population growth.
3 While the coastal UMs retained their position over this period, inland and outback UMs tended to lose ground in their percentage holding of the UM population.
4 The coastal region captured 67 per cent of all UM population growth.

The population growth pattern of the UMs is an irregular one, reflecting the vast distances of the Australian continent and the small total population. For the most part, hostile terrain and climate rules out any chance of uniform closer settlement patterns developing. Despite this the data presented does suggest that in the future it is possible to envisage these centres accommodating a larger share of the population, with much of it focused on the coastal strip.

Table 14.19

Percentage growth rates in UMs 1947–81

No.	UM Population in '000	1947 Pop.	1981 Pop.	Annual av. growth rate	Type
105	Broken Hill	27	28	.11	O
107	Wagga Wagga	15	48	6.47*	I
108	Albury-Wodonga	14	72	12.18*	I
109	Tamworth	12	33	5.15	I
110	Orange	14	31	3.57	I
111	Goulburn	16	22	1.10	I
112	Lismore	15	35	3.92	C
113	Bathurst	12	23	2.70	I
114	Grafton	12	17	1.23	C
115	Dubbo	4	29	18.38*	I
116	Armidale	5	19	8.24*	I
117	Lithgow	14	19	1.05	I
119	Taree	5	32	15.88*	C
124	Coffs Harbour	5	34	17.06*	C
125	Griffith	6	13	3.43	I
126	Nowra	4	16	8.82*	C
127	Pt. Macquarie	3	18	14.71*	C
202	Geelong	44	164	8.02*	MP
203	Ballarat	40	77	2.72	I
204	Bendigo	31	65	3.23	I
205	Warnambool	10	21	3.24	C
206	Moe	2	17	22.06*	I
207	Morwell	3	26	22.55*	I
208	Shepparton	8	24	5.88*	I
209	Wangaratta	7	16	3.78	I
210	Traralgon	4	18	10.29*	I
211	Mildura	10	16	1.76	I
212	Horsham	6	12	2.94	I
302	Gold Coast	14	143	27.10*	MP
303	Townsville	34	97	5.45	C
304	Toowoomba	35	73	3.19	I
306	Rockhampton	35	55	1.68	C
307	Cairns	17	59	7.27*	C
308	Bundaberg	16	41	4.60	C
309	Maryborough	15	22	1.37	C
310	Mackay	13	46	7.47*	C
311	Mt. Isa	4	26	16.18*	O
312	Gympie	8	11	1.10	C
313	Warwick	7	9	.84	I
314	Gladstone	5	24	11.18*	C
402	Mt. Gambier	7	21	5.88*	I
403	Pt. Agusta	4	16	8.82*	C
404	Pt. Pierie	12	16	.98	C
405	Whyalla	8	31	8.46*	C
406	Pt. Lincon	4	11	5.15	C
502	Kalgoolie-Boulder	22	20	–.27	O

503	Geraldton	3	21	17.65*	C
504	Albany	2	15	19.12*	C
505	Rockingham-K	3	37	33.33*	MP
506	Bunbury	3	22	18.63*	C
601	Hobart	76	171	3.68	C
602	Launceston	40	87	3.46	C
603	Burnie	5	20	8.82*	C
604	Devenport	4	24	14.71*	C
801	Darwin	2	57	80.88*	C/O
802	Alice Springs	1	18	50.00*	O
	Total	744	2138	5.48	

* = UM with growth rate higher than national average
O = Outback; I = Inland; C = Coastal; MP = Metro-peripheral

Summary and policy implications

Introduction

This chapter has attempted to analyse the dynamics of the Australian urban system for two reasons. Firstly, to explore the cyclical urban pattern identified by Klaassen and other (1981) to see if the Australian growth pattern exhibits any of the same characteristics. Secondly, to explore the relationship between any system dynamics and the application and timeliness of government policy.

Summary

Because of Australia's initial remoteness in world geographic terms, its European settlement history goes back less than 200 years. Its unique geography with vast inland areas generally inhospitable to closer settlement has resulted in its settlement pattern largely following the temperate east and south-east coastline where adequate supplies of water are available. Given its relatively recent development history, its population is highly aggregated into a small number of large state capital cities. It offers the extremes of being, at the same time, the world's least densely populated continent, and also the most highly urbanised. It is against this background that the following conclusions on its urban system should be read.

During the 1947–81 period, Australia doubled its population base from 7.5 to 15 millions. A large portion of that growth (40 per cent plus) was due to net gains from immigration. While the late 1940s and early 1950s saw something of a 'baby boom' which resulted in high gains from natural increase, more recently, the net reproduction ratio has fallen below 1.0. Further significant expansion of the population base will be more reliant on continued net gains from immigration. Immigration policy is determined by the national government and while Australia registered its first net annual loss from overseas immigration for 30 years in 1975, current government policy has lifted the annual intake back up to its all-time high of 130,000 immigrants, despite the current depressed economy and rapidly escalating unemployment. The data already presented underlines the importance of net gains from overseas immigration and the fact that about 80 per cent of all new growth has been located within the main metropolitan areas. In 1947 the population was 70 per cent urbanised but by 1981 it was 86 per cent urbanised (see p.225).

To explore this phenomenon in greater depth, population distribution between the states and between the chief categories of settlement pattern were explored. This has shown that basically the number of the rural population has remained fairly static over the 1947–81 period – so that there was no real drift from the rural to urban Australia – it has been the significant migrant intake that has increased metropolitan primacy in Australia. Some states have grown at a faster rate than others – i.e., Queensland, Western Australia and South Australia – while the two territories also performed well. Net internal migration flows between the states were explored to show that the chief losers have been New South Wales, Victoria and Tasmania. Given the shift in immigrant transport mode to Australia – from ship to jumbo jet – Sydney and Melbourne have been the chief distribution centres for this incoming flow of immigrants. This in part would explain their continued loss of population to the other states.

For the most part, the examination of the major categories of the settlement pattern (i.e., FURs, UMs, OU and Rural) showed a steady increase in metropolitan primacy (i.e., in the FURs) across the states, but in both NSW and Victoria – the states with the largest capital cities of Sydney and Melbourne – there is some real evidence to show that a nodal point in their continued expansion had been reached. They are still growing in absolute terms, but their percentage holding of state population appears to have peaked (see p.225).

The employment workforce base and its distribution were examined next and considerable quantum changes have taken place in the relative importance of the various employment categories and their spatial distribution. The Australian economic base has responded quickly to changing world markets and trading needs. The early post World War II years were characterised by a heavy commitment to industrial development – steel, motor vehicles etc., together with the more traditional agricultural resource based extraction industries. In the brief 22 year period studied however, there has been a remarkable shift in the employment structure away from primary production and industry, to the white-collar 'information' processing and service areas of public administration, finance, trade and the miscellaneous sector. This last sector now ranks fourth highest in employment terms.

Alongside this structural change in the employment base, the distribution of jobs throughout the urban and rural system has also changed. As the white-collar and information-processing jobs grow in importance, the early industrial focus of jobs in the metropolitan areas has become less pronounced and it now appears that the new growth sectors of employment are capable of being more easily distributed throughout the whole of the urban system. So employment opportunities are now less concentrated on the main metropolitan areas and more jobs are available in the second order centres. The growth states in population terms (Queensland, South Australia and Western Australia) have also had higher than national average growth rates in employment opportunities, which supports the view that much internal migration is job-related (see p.232).

Further examination of net gains due to migration and internal migration were applied to the chief categories of the urban-rural system to show that these were consistent with the other trends identified. In the early post World War II years net internal migration flows favoured the major metropolitan areas while in more recent years, this flow has been reversed and now favours the smaller urban municipalities. While the flow of overseas migrants favours the continued growth of the metropolitan areas (particularly in the inner suburbs), this input might well be encouraging an outward migration of the Australian-born population to either metro-periphery or second order urban centres (see p.241).

The review of the internal dynamics of the FURs has shown that their cores are suffering from declining population, with new growth being directed to the metro-periphery. This redistribution of the population has been aided by the more diffused employment pattern, but outward urban expansion in both public sector and social costs are high, and in the two largest FURs, governments are now actively pursuing urban consolidation policies. No FURs are as yet declining in population terms, but if the current immigration policy were to be reversed quickly, then this might result (see p.245).

The urban municipalities (UMs) performed well in growth terms, particularly those on the metro-periphery. While the 1976–81 period saw these centres increase their capture rate of population increase to 34 per cent – this dramatic increase would be largely due to:

1 The 1976–81 downturn in net gains from overseas migration that has previously favoured the FURs;
2 The internal migration shift in emphasis which now seems to favour the UMs.

A clear preference in the growth pattern is demonstrated for coastal centres, over inland centres – but some inland regional service centres have also continued to attract employment and population (see p.247).

In summary then, can it be said that the dynamics of the Australian urban system is exhibiting the same cyclical growth pattern as evidenced by its European counterparts? The response is a qualified 'Yes'. Metropolitan cores are losing population, but the rate of loss is as yet not increasing, although it is to be regretted. The highest loss for the five largest FURs was in the 1971–76 period (all five cores lost a total of about 173,000, while their fringes grew by about 585,000). This coincided with a drop in the overseas migrant intake and a national government policy focus on growth centres and on inner-city rehabilitation. In the 1976–81 period, the same five cities lost only about 85,000 from their core areas while their peripheries grew by about 580,000, which partly reflects the policy change from growth centre to urban consolidation. All FURs are continuing to grow then in absolute terms, but there is evidence to suggest that they might now have attained their peak percentage holding capacity of total state population – so that from henceforth, more urban growth will be channelled into the urban municipalities, rather than into the FURs. Certainly, no FURs have as yet entered the third phase of desurbanisation as described by Klaassen et al.

The largest single issue which sets the Australian FURs apart from their European counterparts is their role in accommodating net gains from overseas migration. The Australian cities are the receptors for this growth sector, and their growth rates will be largely contingent upon variations in this national policy.

Also qualified are the results of the UM study component in that while a very few metro-peripheral UMs have captured a significant proportion of the FUR 'overspill' population, but when taken as a group their performance does not yet suggest any definite pattern emerging, except for a strong coastal location preference. In this context it seems likely that the Australian topography and climate work against the development of homogeneous regions and population distribution.

In overall terms then, while the Australian urban system dynamics does demonstrate some of the characteristics of the European model, there are significant 'local' factors in the Australian system that set it apart. What sort of dynamic picture is emerging then?

Further FUR growth as a result of continued high gains from the national government's immigration policy seem likely to exacerbate the existing social inequities and diseconomies in public sector costs in terms of these cities. If this is allowed to prevail over a substantial period of time, net internal migration flows will favour the metro-peripheral urban municipalities on the coast. Changes in the economic base and workforce will assist the dispersion of jobs and people. State and local governments, in this situation, are likely to be faced with increased social and public sector financial costs which they may be either unwilling or unable to meet. The net result seems likely to lead to an overall deterioration of the FUR environment – in deteriorating public sector services which can only in turn discourage private investment. This could be a gloomy forecast, and if taken to its extreme could lead to the scale of urban problems faced by some overseas cities in recent times (London, Manchester, Amsterdam etc.) and some extraordinary measures on the part of governments to overcome them.

Australia, for many complex and interrelated reasons has carried the concept of metropolitan primacy to perhaps its Western extreme, although it has by no means the problem cities like London, New York, Tokyo or Seoul to deal with. Is the 'glue' that held its population together for so long in so few large scale urban centres still available or indeed necessary? The earlier large scale European-based migration programme has strengthened the urban focus for their cultural background places greater emphasis on extended family life and the maintenance of cultural traditions in their new homeland. This has enriched the Australian social and cultural urban fabric enormously. But the rapid growth rates and spiralling land prices and overall deterioration in the government's ability to service the new peripheral growth areas adequately, is placing some question marks on the 'system's ability' to respond by providing acceptable urban life-styles.

Policy implications

In this final section, it will be useful to explore briefly the relationship between government policy and the dynamics of the urban system as they have been demonstrated in this chapter. It has been shown that the federal government's immigration policy has had direct consequences for the main urban areas – the FURs. While the scope of this policy might have initially included economic growth, national defence, humanitarian reasons etc., it has resulted in a de facto policy for on-going large scale metropolitan growth. Significant in this context is the fact that with the exception of the 1972–75 Whitlam administration, the national government which has overall responsibility for immigration policy, has declined any responsibility for urban affairs. This situation prevails today, even though a joint-house Parliamentary Committee of Inquiry (Australian Government, 1978b) clearly identified the direction relationship between the immigration policy and continued metropolitan growth. The federal government is then pursuing a policy which has direct consequences for state governments, yet no policy coordination or consultation mechanisms exist.

Faced with rapidly growing metropolitan areas, the Whitlam 1972–75 administration was quick to encourage 'growth centre' policies and seek collaborative joint-partnership agreements with the states on these, including financial assistance. At the termination of this administration, net gains from immigration were approaching zero, and the National Population Inquiry report identified falling birth rates, and produced reduced population estimates. The incoming Fraser administration dismantled the urban and growth centre programmes and has, over the intervening years, again increased the annual immigration intake, so that growth rates in the major metropolitan areas are again increasing.

For their part, the state government administrations have been slow to react to this policy reversal. In the two largest cities of Sydney and Melbourne, where peripheral urban expansion is burgeoning, as a means of reducing public sector costs, both government and planning agencies are attempting to win support for 'urban consolidation' policies.

This chapter has shown that while the FURs will continue to grow in response to net immigration gains, there is already evident a spread effect in operation, as increasing numbers now seek alternative lifestyles in the nearby urban municipalities, away from the congested and more costly cities. To date, there is no evidence in Australian urban policy that the spread effect – the dynamics of the flow – is understood or appreciated. Urban consolidation policies are seen almost as an alternative to what is perceived to be the more expensive 'growth centre' policies, which without federal financial support, are simply not acceptable.

This study has attempted to explicate, in a preliminary way, the nature of the Australian urban system when viewed as a dynamic process. It is not as yet an area well researched in Australia, yet if the linkage can be made between system inputs, policy outputs and urban system response, there may be scope for establishing not only consistent inter-government policy, but also coordination and control mechanisms more finely attuned to the dynamic nature of the urban system itself.

Appendix 1

Definition of FUR cores statistical units

The following information shows the various local government areas (statistical units) which have been included in the definition of 'core' areas of functional urban regions (FURs). This was used to determine the data shown in Table 14.20.

FUR 101: Sydney Leichardt, Marrickville, Randwick, South Sydney, Sydney, Waverley, Woollahra, Ashfield, Drummoyne, Botany, Hunter's Hill, Lane Cove, Mosman, North Sydney, Willoughby.

FUR 201: Melbourne Melbourne, Caufield, Brunswick, Collingwood, Essendon, Footscray, Fitzroy, Kew, Hawthorn, Malvern, Northcote, Pharhan, Port Melbourne, St. Kilda, South Melbourne, Richmond, Williamstown.

FUR 301: Brisbane Brisbane changed its census boundaries in 1961–66 but the approximate areas included are as follows: Albion, Bowen Hills, Bulimba, City, Cutton Park, East Brisbane, Fortitude Valley, Hawthorn, Higate Hill, Herston, Kangaroo Point, Hamilton, Morningside, Milton, Norman Park, Kelvin Grove, Newstead, New Farm, Windsor, Wilston, Woolloongabba, West End, South Brisbane.

FUR 401: Adelaide Adelaide, Prospect, Walkerville, St. Peters, Kensington-Norwood, Unley, The Barton, Hindmarsh.

FUR 501: Perth Perth, South Perth, Subiaco, Nedlands.

Table 14.20

Functional urban regions (FURs) and urban municipalities (UMs) (showing population in census years – '000)

No.	Name	1947	1954	1961	1966	1971	1976	1981	
*101	Sydney	1484	1863	2183	2447	2977	3094	3280	
102	Newcastle	154	178	208	234	355	370	402	
103	Woolongong	63	91	132	162	203	219	231	
104	Gosford	15	17	26	43	*	*	*	Inc. in 101
105	Broken Hill	27	31	31	30	31	29	28	
106	Blue Mountains	21	23	27	31	*	*	*	Inc. in 101
107	Wagga Wagga	15	19	22	26	30	44	48	
108	Albury-Wodonga	14	19	26	32	38	45	72	
109	Tamworth	12	16	19	22	27	30	33	
110	Orange	14	18	19	21	24	30	31	
111	Goulburn	16	19	21	21	22	23	22	
112	Lismore	15	18	19	19	21	23	35	
113	Bathurst	12	16	17	17	18	19	23	
114	Grafton	12	15	16	16	17	17	17	
115	Dubbo	(4)	12	14	16	18	24	29	
116	Armidale	(5)	10	13	15	19	19	19	
117	Lithgow	14	15	14	13	13	19	19	
118	Queanbeyan	(5)	(7)	(9)	13	*	*	*	Inc. in 701
119	Taree	(5)	(7)	10	11	12	27	32	
120	Cesnock	37	38	35	35	*	*	*	Inc. in 102
121	Maitland	24	26	27	28	*	*	*	Inc. in 102
122	Shellharbour	(3)	(6)	13	*	*	*	*	Inc. in 103
123	Penrith	12	18	32	*	*	*	*	Inc. in 101
124	Coffs Harbour	(5)	(6)	(7)	(8)	19	26	34	
125	Griffith	(6)	(7)	(8)	10	11	12	13	
126	Nowra	(4)	(6)	(6)	10	13	15	16	
127	Pt. Macquarie	(3)	(4)	(6)	(7)	10	14	18	
*201	Melbourne	1226	1532	1858	2110	2515	2672	2722	
202	Geelong	44	73	88	105	123	136	164	
203	Ballarrat	40	48	54	58	59	70	77	
204	Bendigo	31	37	39	49	52	57	65	
205	Warnambool	10	13	16	17	19	21	21	
206	Moe	(2)	12	23	23	16	16	17	
207	Morewell	(3)	(9)	15	17	17	17	26	
208	Shepparton	(8)	11	14	17	19	21	24	
209	Wangaratta	(7)	11	14	15	16	17	16	
210	Traralgon	(4)	(9)	12	14	15	16	18	
211	Mildura	10	11	12	13	14	15	16	
212	Horsham	(6)	(8)	(9)	11	11	12	12	
213	Newtown	10	12	12	*	*	*	*	Inc. in 202
*301	Brisbane	402	502	694	780	891	986	1086	
302	Gold Coast	14	20	34	53	79	106	143	Inc. NSW
303	Townsville	34	41	52	60	75	82	97	
304	Toowoomba	35	43	50	56	62	69	73	
305	Ipswich	32	39	49	55	*	*	*	Inc. in 301

Table 14.20 continued

No.	Name	1947	1954	1961	1966	1971	1976	1981
306	Rockhampton	35	41	44	46	51	53	55
307	Cairns	17	21	24	27	31	34	59
308	Bundaberg	16	20	23	25	28	31	41
309	Maryborough	15	18	19	21	21	22	22
310	Mackay	13	15	17	19	20	21	46
311	Mt. Isa	(4)	(8)	14	18	27	27	26
312	Gympie	(8)	10	11	11	11	11	11
313	Warwick	(7)	(9)	(9)	10	10	10	(9)
314	Gladstone	(5)	(7)	(7)	12	17	20	24
*401	Adelaide	382	484	659	772	843	924	953
402	Mt. Gambier	(7)	10	15	17	18	20	21
403	Pt. Augusta	(4)	(7)	10	10	12	15	16
404	Pt. Pierie	12	14	14	16	16	15	16
405	Whyalla	(8)	(9)	14	22	32	34	31
406	Pt. Lincon	(4)	(6)	(8)	(9)	10	10	11
*501	Perth	273	349	475	559	703	826	918
502	Kalgoolie-B'dr.	22	23	22	20	21	20	20
503	Geraldton	(3)	(8)	11	12	15	18	21
504	Albany	(2)	(8)	11	11	13	13	15
505	Rockingham-K.	–	(2)	(5)	(8)	24	31	37
506	Bunbury	(3)	11	13	15	18	20	22
601	Hobart	76	95	115	119	143	151	171
602	Launceston	40	49	57	60	79	82	87
603	Burnie	(5)	14	17	19	20	19	20
604	Devenport	(4)	12	14	17	20	21	24
*701	Canberra	16	28	56	92	162*	224*	246*Inc. 118
801	Darwin	(2)	(8)	12	20	36	44	57
802	Alice Springs	(1)	(5)	(5)	(6)	11	14	18

* = FUR (for definition of FUR and UMs refer to text)

Source: ABS data.

Table 14.21

Population distribution by state and category – '000

		1947	1954	1961	1966	1971	1976	1981
FURs	NSW	1484	1863	2391	2681	3535	3683	3913
	VIC	1266	1532	1858	2110	2515	2672	2722
	Q	402	502	694	780	891	986	1086
	SA	382	484	659	772	843	924	953
	WA	273	349	457	559	703	826	918
	ACT	0	0	0	0	0	224	246
	Total	3807	4730	6059	6902	8487	9315	9838
UMs	NSW	477	600	533	591	343	416	489
	VIC	145	228	299	339	361	398	456
	Q	211	268	337	413	432	486	597
	SA	12	24	53	65	88	94	95
	WA	22	34	57	58	91	102	115
	Tas	116	170	203	215	262	273	302
	NT	0	0	12	20	47	58	75
	ACT	16	28	56	92	162	0	0
	Total	999	1352	1550	1793	1786	1827	2129
Urban	NSW	189	366	410	390	252	277	247
	VIC	140	251	328	309	211	283	293
	Q	62	206	129	86	171	215	230
	SA	56	88	54	66	72	66	69
	WA	33	78	33	25	57	57	71
	Tas	41	41	44	46	28	37	31
	NT	3	11	23	11	14	9	8
	Total	524	1041	1021	933	805	944	949
Rural	NSW	835	595	583	576	531	561	570
	VIC	504	441	445	462	433	457	477
	Q	431	342	368	395	387	405	432
	SA	196	201	206	192	182	190	202
	WA	175	179	200	206	192	193	195
	Tas	100	98	103	110	100	102	94
	ACT	1	2	3	4	3	2	1
	NT	8	5	10	26	31	37	40
	Total	2250	1863	1918	1971	1859	1947	2011
Total	NSW	2985	3424	3917	4238	4661	4937	5219
	VIC	2055	2452	2930	3220	3520	3810	3948
	Q	1106	1318	1528	1674	1881	2092	2345
	SA	646	797	972	1095	1185	1274	1319
	WA	503	640	747	848	1043	1178	1299
	Tas	257	309	350	371	390	412	427
	ACT	17	30	59	96	165	226	247
	NT	11	16	45	57	92	104	123
	Total	7580	8986	10548	11599	12937	14033	14927

For definition of FUR, UMs, etc., refer to text.

Source: ABS data.

Table 14.22

Regional growth rates – Australia, 1971–81

No.	Region	Population '000 1971	1976	1981	Annual average percentage increase 1971–76	1976–81	
	NSW						
1	Sydney	2935	3143	3280	1.42	0.87	M/R
2	Hunter	405	441	473	1.78	1.45 *	M/R
3	Illawarra	247	283	305	2.91	1.55 *	M/R
4	Richmond-Tweed	99	108	133	1.82	4.63 *	
5	M-N. Coast	128	144	176	2.50	4.44 *	
6	Northern	168	174	178	0.71	0.46	
7	North-West	101	103	109	0.39	1.17	
8	Central West	155	162	165	0.90	0.37	
9	South East	121	131	139	1.65	1.22	
10	Murrumbidgee	135	140	144	0.74	0.57	
11	Murray	88	95	101	1.59	1.26	
12	Far West	35	33	33	– 1.10	0	
	Total NSW	4679	4960	5237	1.20	1.12	
	Victoria						
13	Melbourne	2514	2723	2803	1.66	0.58	M/R
14	Barwon	167	190	200	2.75	1.05	
15	Sth. West	97	100	101	0.61	0.20	
16	Cen. Highlands	105	115	120	1.90	0.87	
17	Wimmera	55	56	55	0.34	–0.36	
18	Nth. Mallee	68	71	73	0.88	0.56	
19	Lod-Campaspie	127	141	152	2.20	1.56 *	
20	Goulburn	118	126	134	1.36	1.27	
21	Nth. East	67	74	78	2.09	1.08	
22	East Gippsland	49	54	58	2.04	1.48 *	
23	Cent Gippsland	119	124	134	0.84	1.61	
24	East Central	30	36	41	4.00	2.78 *	
	Total Victoria	3520	3801	3948	1.60	0.77	
	Queensland						
25	Brisbane	891	986	1086	2.13	2.03 *	M/R
26	Moreton	169	223	315	6.39	8.25 *	M/R
27	Wide Bay	143	158	154	2.10	–0.51	
28	Darling Downs	154	163	169	1.17	0.74	
29	Sth. West	32	29	28	–1.90	–0.69	
30	Fitzroy	119	132	147	2.18	2.27 *	
31	Cent. West	16	14	14	–2.50	0	
32	Mackay	68	81	91	3.82	2.47 *	
33	Northern	131	150	157	2.90	0.93	
34	Far North	113	129	142	2.83	2.02 *	
35	North West	41	42	41	0.48	–0.48	
	Total Queensland	1881	2111	2345	2.45	2.22	

Table 14.22 continued

No.	Region	Population '000 1971	1976	1981	Annual average percentage increase 1971–76	1976–81	
	South Australia						
36	Adelaide	850	900	932	1.18	0.71	M/R
37	Outer Adelaide	53	59	67	2.26	2.71 *	M/R
38	York	40	39	40	–0.50	0.51	
39	Murray	57	59	61	0.70	0.67	
40	Sth. East	56	57	59	0.35	0.70	
41	Eyre	31	32	35	0.64	1.88	
42	Northern	95	95	92	0	–0.63	
	Total SA	1185	1241	1286	0.94	0.72	
	West Australia						
43	Perth	712	806	899	2.64	2.31 *	M/R
44	Sth. West	78	82	98	1.03	3.90	
45	Low GS	39	39	42	0	1.54	
46	Upper GS	24	23	23	–0.83	0	
47	Midlands	53	48	50	–1.90	0.83	
48	Sth. East	41	40	43	–0.49	1.50	
49	Central	45	48	52	1.33	1.67	
50	Pilbara	33	39	47	3.64	4.10 *	
51	Kimberley	15	15	19	0	5.33	
	Total WA	1040	1140	1273	1.92	2.33 *	
	Tasmania						
52	Hobart & Sth.	193	193	198	0	0.51	
53	Northern	111	110	118	–0.18	1.45	
54	Mersey	103	101	108	–0.39	1.39	
	Total Tasmania	407	404	424	–0.15	0.99	
	ACT						
55	Canberra	142	198	246	7.89	4.85 *	M/R
	Total ACT	158	220	246	7.85	2.36	
	Northern Territory						
56	Darwin	36	44	61	4.44	7.73 *	
	Total NT	86	97	123	2.56	5.36	
	Total Australia	12956	13974	14882	1.57	1.30	

* = region with above national average growth rate for the two inter-censal periods covered.
M/R = metropolitan region

Source: ABS statistics

Appendix 3

Notes on the distribution of foreign born population

In 1976, 66 per cent of the Australian born population lived in FURs, whereas in the same year, 79 per cent of foreign born Australians lived in the FURs. Other comparative figures for the same year are as follows:

> 14 per cent of the Australian born lived in the UMs, and
> 15 per cent of the foreign born lived in the UMs.
>
> 20 per cent of the Australian born lived elsewhere, while
> 6 per cent of the foreign born lived elsewhere.

These figures show that the foreign born tend to live in the FURs and the UMs, i.e. about 94 per cent in toto.

An analysis of the Sydney statistical division for the 1971–76 period shows the following:

	Core '000	%	Frame '000	%	Total '000	City %
1971 Total	827	28	2150	72	2977	100
Australian born	547	25	1672	75	2219	75
Foreign born	280	37	478	63	758	25
1976 Total	773	25	2321	75	3094	100
Australian born	467	20	1825	80	2292	74
Foreign born	306	38	496	62	802	26

Between 1971–76, nearly 60 per cent of the foreign born metropolitan increase went into the core of the city

The above figures indicate the important role which foreign born migrants play in maintaining the core population of the Sydney metropolitan area – the inner city has become a staging area for immigrants.

References

Australian Government (1975), *First Report of the National Population Inquiry. Population in Australia. Volume 1*, AGPS, Canberra.

Australian Government (1978a), *Supplementary Report of the National Population Inquiry. Population in Australia*, AGPS, Canberra.

Australian Government (1978b), Report from the House of Representatives Standing Committee on the Environment and Conservation (The Hodges' Report), *The Commonwealth Government and the Urban Environment*, (Formulation and Co-ordination of Policies) May, AGPS, Canberra.

Australian Government (1981), *Review of Australia's Demographic Trends*, AGPS, Canberra.

Australian Population and Immigration Council (1977), *Population Report No. 1*, November, AGPS, Canberra.

Australian Population and Immigration Council (1977), *Immigration Policies and Australian Population*, A Green Paper, AGPS, Canberra.

Australian Population and Immigration Council (1980), *Population Report No. 4*, September, AGPS, Canberra.

Australian Institute of Urban Studies (1971), *First Report of the Task Force on New Cities for Australia*, AIUS, Canberra.

Australian Institute of Urban Studies (1978), *Towards Urban Strategies for Australia*, AIUS Publication No. 77, Canberra.

Birrell, R. (1982), 'How Many Migrants' in *Australian Society*, vol. 1, no. 2.

Burnley, I.H. (ed.) (1974), *Urbanisation in Australia*, Cambridge University Press, London.

Burnley, I.H. (1980), *The Australian Urban System*, Longman Cheshire, Sydney.

Cities' Commission (1975), 'Studies in Internal Migration' (1966–1971) *Occasional Paper No. 2*, Canberra.

Daly, M.T. (1982), *Sydney Boom, Sydney Bust*, George Allen and Unwin, Sydney.

Department of Immigration and Ethnic Affairs (1978), 'Australian Immigration', *Quarterly Statistical Summary*, vol. 3, no. 36, June 1977, AGPS, Canberra.

Department of Immigration and Ethnic Affairs (1980), *Australian Immigration*, Consolidated Statistics no. 11, 1979, AGPS, Canberra.

Division of National Mapping (1980), *Australian Atlas of Resources, (3rd Series)*, vol. 2, Population, Canberra.

Klaassen, L.H., Molle, W.T.M. and Paelinck, J.H.P. (1981), *Dynamics of Urban Development*, Gower Press, Aldershot, Hants.

Logan, M.I., Maher, C.A., McKay, J. and Humphreys, J.S. (1975), *Urban and Regional Australia*, Sorrett Publishers, Melbourne.

Logan, M.I., Whitelaw, J.S. and McKay, J. (1981), *Urbanisation: The Australian Experience*, Shillington House, Melbourne.
Manning, I. (1978), *The Journey to Work*, George Allen and Unwin, Sydney.
Neutze, M. (1977), *Urban Development in Australia*, George Allen and Unwin, Sydney.
Neutze, M. (1978), *Australian Urban Policy*, George Allen and Unwin, Sydney.
Rowland, D.T. (1979), *Internal Migration in Australia*, Census Monograph Series, Australian Bureau of Statistics, Canberra.
Stilwell, F.J.B. (1974), *Australian Urban & Regional Development*, Australian and New Zealand Book Company, Sydney.

PART IV
TOURISM AND TRANSPORTATION

15 Recreation and regional development

A. J. HENDRIKS*

Introduction: increasing attention

Now that so many branches of activity are stagnating, governments are showing increased attention to leisure activities. People get more leisure time; the distance to be covered for holidays abroad is getting more and more of an obstacle; do not investments in leisure time provisions offer good prospects?

In the face of unemployment, regional authorities are looking at the potential leisure time provisions in their own regions: the expansion of leisure activities and tourism might yield a number of job opportunities.

This chapter will discuss the prospects of facilities for leisure time activities in the open air, both those intended for daytime activities only and those also offering accommodation for a prolonged stay, although some of the activities in the latter may take place inside. Daytime leisure activities are those which people join in from home or from the holiday accommodation. Holiday accommodation and daytime leisure activities influence each other. Facilities for daytime leisure make a region more attractive to holidaymakers, who in turn are valuable potential customers of daytime leisure facilities. Of course, finer distinctions are possible and useful: among the daytime provisions

* The author would like to thank the Instituut voor Arbeidsvraagstukken of Tilburg Economic University and the Netherlands Research Institute for Tourism, Breda, for permission to quote Tables 15.2 and 15.3 appearing in this chapter.

there are one-day attractions and areas of natural beauty; holiday provisions may be hotels, guesthouses, summer bungalows or camp sites. One-day attractions need capital and must be run economically; areas of natural beauty are mostly collective property and rather call for limitation of the number of visitors. As to holiday accommodation, people staying in large camp sites offering many facilities appear to be less in need of outside attractions as those in small camp sites. Holidaymakers staying at hotels and guesthouses go out more than those staying on camp sites. Such differences are relevant, among other things, for the relation between leisure activities and the natural environment.

In this chapter little distinction will be made between leisure time activities and tourism. One difference is that tourism, unlike leisure time activities, cannot be exercised at home. Another is that tourism much more than leisure time activities can be linked to business: purchase tours, congresses. Open-air leisure activities share with tourism the need to bridge distances.

The positive attitude regional authorities take with respect to the development of leisure time activities and tourism has been encouraged by the central government. In *A Note on Tourism* issued in 1979, the Ministry of Economic Affairs indicated the following policy principles:

1 To maintain and promote the potential of tourist attractions;
2 To guard and improve tourist attractions offered to citizens at home and abroad.

One argument is the fast growth of demand for leisure time facilities, due not only to increased prosperity, but also to the changed structure of the total time budget. In a year, a person has 8760 hours to spend. If the way all persons spend their time could be assessed, a national time budget could be computed. Clawson (1974) has estimated such a budget for the United States with respect to the years 1900, 1950 and 2000; it shows the enormous increase of total leisure time in the course of the century, namely, from 177 in 1900 to 453 in 1950 and 1,113 in 2000 (in milliards of hours).

No such figures are available for the Netherlands, but figures of the Central Bureau for Statistics referring to the years 1971–81 do indicate a similar development as in the United States. In that period, the total number of vacation days rose from 123 to 179 million. The Scientific Council for Government Policy (1977) expects for the period 1975–2000 a rise in the annual number of vacation days per person from 19 to 35.

From such figures, the central government assumes a continued growth of leisure time activity and tourism. The minister of economic affairs is prepared to accord subsidies for feasibility studies of new projects, provided they are regionally stimulating as well as nationally relevant. The minister will also give financial support towards the improvement of the tourist infrastructure (for instance the construction of car parks), the modernisation of existing daily attractions and the cost of promotion abroad.

Against that background, several provincial governments have had a so-called Tourist Recreative Overall Plan (TROP) drawn up for their provinces. The first TROP was the one developed for South Limburg, a peripheral part of the Netherlands. Ever since the 1960s, South Limburg has been confronted with serious regional unemployment caused by the closing down of the coal mines. In the South Limburg TROP, the demand for and supply of leisure time and tourist services in the region are dealt with in the next section.

The TROP

The area covered by the TROP planning is the provincial territory. Areas beyond the provincial border are considered home regions of potential holidaymakers. Development plans of leisure time projects outside the province are left out of consideration; indeed that is one element of the TROP structure that is much criticised.

The philosophy behind TROP is that good development prospects demand a consistent packet of measures and the adjustment of tourist attractions to changing market conditions. To that end, two basic concepts are introduced: spear points and stage points. Spear points are concentrated impulses given to develop tourism. They are oriented to a specific object group in the tourist market and contribute to a level of provisions that is attractive also outside the season. They should act as dynamic motors for the tourist and leisure time development. Examples are: a centre for water sports, a large scale daily attraction, a complex of sites for stationary caravans.

Stage points are complementary attractions and tourist provisions, supporting visits to spear points and generally promoting holiday visits to the province; examples are: catering provisions, information centres and intelligence services.

In the case of the province of Limburg, the TROP envisages spearpoints in the fields of watersports, day-trip provisions and holiday accommodation. For each spearpoint, the effects on the development of employment, both primary and indirect, have been estimated.

Criticism with respect to TROP

The interest shown in spearpoints in the leisure time industry in regions suffering from very serious unemployment is understandable. Of the 15 initiatives for new day-trip attractions listed by the Netherlands Research Institute for Leisure-time Activity and Tourism (NRIT, 1983), 11 refer to areas well known for their retarded employment growth and as such involved in the regional-economic policy of the central government.

Drawing up a concrete scheme for a region's leisure time development is a complicated proposition, however. One objection to leisure time development schemes like the TROP is that the purposeful exploitation of regional prospects for holidaymaking and tourism carries the danger of transgressing certain borderlines; these borderlines are associated with the quality of the area. Large concentrations of holidaymakers are marked by various harmful phenomena, such as traffic congestion, noise, disharmony between different categories of holidaymakers. For example, the municipality of Valkenburg in South Limbburg, a well known holiday resort, has problems every season because of tensions among groups of holidaymakers (Anderson and Hendriks, 1982). Moreover, too many holidaymakers in one spot tend to spoil the natural environment, the quality of which is often an important attraction of the area in question. When too many people come too frequently, the stock of flora and fauna may deteriorate visibly. On that score, holiday camps with many provisions within their territory do less harm than accommodation in hotels and guesthouses. Too much commercial exploitation, moreover, can violate the 'recreational' quality of leisure time activity.

What do we understand by 'recreation'? Though often motivated by one's daily work, recreation is in essence a way of experiencing one's leisure time. It is a way to spend one's leisure time, and the functions of leisure distinguished by sociologists apply to it. A very useful function division of leisure time has been given by J. Dumazedier: leisure time is needed for relaxation, amusement and personal development. The three functions are interrelated and occur in changing combinations. Socio-economic conditions, normative opinions as to the spending of leisure time, and personal characteristics such as age, disposition and education, all play a role.

Next to its intrinsic significance, recreation also has social relevance: it can be programmed with a view to relations with other people; think of the family holiday in summer or the annual social evening of the firm one works for. The family cycle is an important factor with respect to recreation. If recreation means relaxation, amusement or personal development, perhaps too much commercial exploitation is not, in the long run, in the interest of the region involved.

Distance

The importance of distance was pointed out in 1968 by L.H. Klaassen in *Social Amenities in Area Economic Growth* (OECD, Paris, 1968) in which the author commented on an investigation in which nature parks in California had been classified by type of scenery. For each type, the number of visitors was related to the distance from Los Angeles. Los Angeles is richly endowed with facilities for seaside and desert recreation relatively close by and its inhabitants will not be prepared to travel far to visit such attractions. That was confirmed by Klaassen's analysis. Such treatment of distance in leisure time travel was elaborated further in Klaassen, Verster and Wagenaar, 1983. Applying gravitation analysis to leisure time behaviour, the authors take distance to be inversely proportional to the leisure time flow between two areas. The size and quality of recreation areas are taken into consideration by the assumption that a leisure time flow to a region is larger as the regional recreation provisions are larger and better. The interest for a given recreation area has thus been made dependent on the position of the area involved among the set of qualifying alternatives available to the population, the distance from the residential areas to each alternative limiting their development prospects. As distance weighs more heavily for those seeking recreation and weighing up their preferences, close-to-home recreation areas stand a better chance.

That theory is as plausible as it is current. In the holiday season 1983, preferences have been found to shift from destinations abroad to destinations nearer home. Given the general drop in prosperity, the weight of costs of bridging distances is likely to increase in the future, and thus the leisure time facilities around large urban residential areas will become more attractive at the expense of more remote recreation areas.

The TROP for South Limburg does not concern itself with distances or with the consequences of future societal change.

The influence of societal developments

The structure of leisure time activity in terms of distance, time and money changes constantly under the impact of societal factors. That has been especially true in the last few years, and will probably remain so in the near future. The following changes are relevant: the ageing population, the increasing number of working married women, unemployment, worktime contraction, the higher level of education, smaller households and the general decline of prosperity. We shall briefly comment on each factor on the basis of future developments as estimated by the Scientific Council for Government Policy.

As in many countries of the west, demographic development in the Netherlands is marked by an ageing population and a rising level of education. If we take the age of 35 as the borderline between young and older people it is expected that the number below 35 will be 6.2 million in 2000 against 7.8 at present, and 7.9 million older people against 5.9 at present (WRR, 1977). As regards the level of education the expectation is that by 2000, 29 per cent of the 50–60 year olds will have a secondary or higher education as against 22 per cent now. Age and level of education are important variables for the structure of leisure time activity, besides such exogenous ones as unemployment and worktime contraction.

In view of the economic technological development, the influence of unemployment might increase. The manner and degree of worktime contraction will also have an impact on the demand for leisure time activities. Worktime contraction can be achieved by the day, the working week or year, or in respect to one's whole working life; another relevant question is to what extent will wages decline in proportion to the shorter hours worked. According to calculations made by the Socio-Cultural Planning Bureau (SCPB, 1982), the disposable income of a family with two children and a modal income will decrease by 6.7 per cent if the working hours are cut by 10 per cent, and by 20 per cent for a worktime contraction of 13.8 per cent. So, the disposal time will increase as the disposable income decreases. In the circumstances, a rise in the demand for leisure time activities is highly doubtful; a shift in its composition is more plausible.

Even without the income effects of shorter working time, the growth of the incomes of employed people is stagnating, while the costs of recreation, consisting of travel costs and sometimes entrance fees, are rising. By contrast, in the past decades, when incomes were generally rising, many of the cheaper categories of consumption were replaced with more expensive ones. Better housing, more comfortable transportation, and more expensive forms of leisure time spending. The current societal developments will presumably entail inverse substitutions; more modest housing, cheaper transportation, less expensive holidays.

The professional participation of married women is on the increase. From about 22 per cent in 1960 their share in the active population rose to 27 per cent in 1975 and to 30 per cent in 1980, a continued rise being expected for 1990. A large proportion of the additional income is spent on leisure time activities and holidays.

The number of households has increased from about 3.2 million in 1960 to 4.9 million in 1980, and will probably rise to about 5.6 million in 1990. The size of households diminished accordingly from 3.5 in 1960 to 2.8 in 1980 and is expected to shrink to 2.5 in 1990. In 1990, one in five will presumably be a one-person household. How the smaller size of households will work out in leisure time expenditure in terms of space, time and money is uncertain as long as we do not know whether the increase in the number of small households is due to youngsters setting up house earlier than they used to, or to the increasing number of divorces. The assumption is that the impact corresponds with that of the phenomenon of working married women. The effects of the societal factors mentioned on the structure of leisure time activity in terms of distance, time and money are summarised in Table 15.1.

Table 15.1

Increase of the claim of leisure time activities on:

Exogenous factor	Distance	Time	Money
Ageing population	–	+	–
Higher level of education	+	–	+
More unemployed	–	+	–
Worktime contraction	–	+	–
Declining prosperity	–	–	–
Working women	+	–	+
Smaller families	+	–	+

In this table, distance is interpreted in the sense of action radius around the place of residence. From the table, societal developments appear to move on balance towards the kind of leisure time activity that takes more time but is less expensive and at a shorter distance. Given the spatial concentration of people in certain parts of the country, that implies a shift in the prospects of recreation areas in function of their distance to large residential areas and their level of costs.

The need for vertical coordination

In the Netherlands, the use to which land is put is normally decided in physical plans. To achieve a project, one needs a building or construction licence from the municipal authorities, who will not issue a licence for a construction if the intended use of it is in conflict with the 'plan'. The completion (or periodical revision) of a plan is preceded by a period of investigation and of weighing up various societal interests as well as guidelines of higher and local authorities. The societal interests come into play in particular when activities are mutually intolerant, for instance industry and living, and also leisure time activity and environmental protection. One objection against the TROP is that this plan, coming from a higher authority (the province) does not incorporate the process of careful weighing by the relevant lower authorities indispensable for justified spatial planning. Natural surroundings figure in the TROP exclusively as an attraction factor in interregional recreation traffic; the relation between the number of holidaymakers and the consequences for nature, as captured in the concept of 'capacity to tolerate' does not enter into the discussion. Another matter that goes unheeded is the necessity to investigate the spatial consequences of the spearpoints proposed. Thus, for Central Limburg the plan proposes giving the lakes along the Maas over to watersports, yacht harbours and related accommodation supposedly acting as stimulants for local and regional employment. However, on looking deeper into the development of watersports (Onderwater and Hendriks, 1983), one finds that zoning is necessary to keep conflicting forms of watersports and use of the riversides from harassing each other and especially to keep motorboats and sailing yachts from pushing out small sailing boats, surfers and canoes. Now zoning reduces the exploitation prospects of yacht harbours. The contrasts within the very sector of recreation activities require careful and detailed weighing of interests as spatial plans are prepared, planners having to go down to the small scale level. The obviously indispensable vertical coordination among the various government levels is lacking in the TROP, as is a study of the relations among sectors, for instance between leisure time spending and nature control, which is of utmost importance for good horizontal coordination.

SPAMO

The SPAMO model, developed by L.H. Klaassen, deals in general terms with employment in a sector of a region's economy; one of its sub-systems, called SPAMOI, is the spatial model of industrial location. In SPAMO, the development prospects of the regional production level depend on demand potentials, supply potentials, investments, secondary location factors, and the environment. Dependent on the development of labour productivity, a rising production level results in a growing number of job opportunities. Although SPAMO was designed primarily to analyse industrial developments, its approach can largely be applied also to a region's leisure time provisions. On the analogy of the definition of the industrial demand potential, the demand potential of a region's leisure time provisions can be understood as the indicators of the development of demand for leisure time activity, summed over all regions and weighted with the costs of communication. In respect of leisure time provisions, communication costs refer to information as well as the bridging of distances. Indeed, marketing and accessibility are highly relevant to the leisure time sector, next to the spatial dispersion and composition of the population.

The notion of supply potential refers to intermediary supplies by other sectors of activity; it may vary for different branches of leisure time services. Thus, hotels and restaurants may be expected to buy more in their own region than, for instance, yacht harbours. Because leisure time provisions are strongly oriented to final demand, the general assumption is warranted that supply potentials are less important than demand potentials for leisure time developments in a region. Let us now look somewhat closer at the leisure time prospects.

Leisure time behaviour

Given the evolution of society, a region's potential for leisure time developments depends greatly on the relatively strong and weak aspects of the projects to be realised. What is 'strong' and what is 'weak' will appear from the holidaymakers' and daytrippers' behaviour.

Leisure time behaviour is the result of the holidaymakers' comparison of leisure time alternatives available to him. The set of alternatives selected by a given group of holidaymakers, constitutes that group's behavioural pattern. Age, sex, phase in the family cycle, education, and other personal characteristics affect that pattern (Oppedijk van Veen, 1983). The individual holidaymaker's option for a particular leisure time activity from the set of attractive alternatives open to him will also be affected by his specific situation at the moment, for instance a new job, a turn in the weather, a house move or some unexpected high bills to be paid. Such circumstances may alter planned leisure time activities at very short notice. The influence of such more or less random factors is very hard to assess. Central to research into leisure time behaviour is the question which general and personal factors influence the set of alternatives attractive to the holidaymaker. Differences among holidaymakers expressed in different leisure time behaviour permit market segmentation, the total leisure time market being split into sub-markets (for instance holidays and daytrips), which can be studied for various groups of consumers. Such a segmentation of the holiday market has been attempted by the Institute for Labour-Market Problems IVA in Tilburg. The segmentation was carried through on the basis of a survey among 1,020 individuals in the period 1980–81. The intention was to trace groups of holidaymakers showing as much as possible the same kind of holiday behaviour within the group but wide differences among the groups. Seven kinds of holiday were distinguished (see Table 15.2). For two of them, namely beach holidays and holidays in the Netherlands, no difference could be perceived as to personal, household and property characteristics.

Table 15.2

Types of holidays and personal and household characteristics

Type of holiday	Holiday behaviour	Characteristics
1 All-in holiday	Transportation: bus, train, aeroplane Accommodation: hotel, apartment, etc. Transport and accommodation reserved	Own tent, caravan Over 50 years old Small family Own car
2 Beach holiday	Seaside holiday, beach, dunes	No specific characteristics
3 Holiday in the Netherlands	Holidays in the Netherlands; woods or heather; summer house, bungalow or stationary caravan	No specific characteristics
4 Holiday with children	One or more children Party of 3 or more Summer holidays	Families with children up to 12 years old Housewives under 40 Large families Professional main breadwinner
5 One or two person holiday	Without children Not in summer	Solitary people Households, age 34 No children, age 18 Older housewives, age 50 Small families Main breadwinner not (no longer) professionally active

6 Long camping holidays	More than a fortnight With tent or caravan With children	Own tent, caravan Young respondents (age 30) Large families (3) Own car
7 Short holidays	Less than a fortnight Without children Not with tent or caravan	Own tent/caravan Older respondents (age 50) Small families Own car

The volumes of the market segments were found to be stable, but as holidaymakers pass through the phases of the life and family cycles, they may in the long run pass to other segments as to their holiday behaviour.

Such a market segmentation may help regional authorities to decide what new holiday accommodation to create in a region and what marketing strategy to follow. Apart from orienting to the patterns of holiday behaviour, regions may of course seek to improve their market position in other ways. Hotels cooperating in hotel chains, and tourist information services cooperating with foreign tour operators are examples. Public authorities may stimulate such developments by using financial instruments. Local governments can use their own or subsidised agencies to stimulate vigorously the use of hotel accommodation for conferences, courses, fairs, exhibitions, etc.

Daytrip attractions and regional employment

Apart from the development of holiday accommodation, regional authorities look upon the creation of attractions for daytrippers as an instrument of employment policy. The Netherlands Research Institute for Leisure-time Activity and Tourism (NRIT) has carried out calculations on the employment effects on the basis of a survey among all attractions for daytrippers in the Netherlands. A distinction was made between direct and indirect effects of leisure time expenditures. The direct employment created consists of the job opportunities in the attraction points themselves; the indirect employment effects refer to the employment due to the deliveries made to the exploiting firms by other companies. By relating, in SPAMOI terminology (p.274), labour productivity to turnover, calculated from collected data, NRIT has been able to express the developments in job opportunities. Labour productivity (i.e. production by man year) being relatively low with daytrip attractions, the resulting employment coefficient was relatively high, but the indirect employment effects did not add any striking cumulating effects; see Table 15.3.

Table 15.3

Comparison of employment effects of daytrip attractions with those of other service sectors

Branch of activity	Coefficient of direct employment effects	Coefficient of direct plus indirect employment effects
Catering	11.67	19.39
Repairs	14.25	21.25
Transport and communication	8.72	14.98
Business services	5.43	11.27
Attractions	13.48	21.03

Source: NRIT, 1983

While these employment effects are not particularly striking, the distance visitors are willing to travel to visit attractions certainly is. From an investigation by the Central Bureau of Statistics (CBS, 1979), visitors to daytrip attractions appear to be prepared to spend considerably more on travelling than visitors to areas of natural beauty or sporting events (Dfl. 5.50 a person as against Dfl. 2.60 and Dfl. 2.10, respectively, in 1979). More than half the visitors come from places 50km or more removed from the attraction spot. That visitors of attractions pay so little heed to the travel costs involved opens perspectives for regional authorities desiring to promote employment in leisure time activities in their regions. On the other hand, their customers' large radius causes the proprietors of attraction spots to be highly mutually dependent in the sense that they experience the effects of one another's marketing actions, and share the effects of newly created attractions. In that light one understands why the plans for a large scale attraction spot for daytrippers in Limburg as a spearpoint for regional development, as announced in the TROP, has created much anxiety among the operators of existing attractions, and why they are trying to defend themselves by highlighting the disadvantages to existing daytrip provisions. Their oligopolist market situation increases the danger that a declining turnover spells a general loss of profitability. In that way, an expansion of the daytrip capacity in one region may entail loss of employment elsewhere because of declining numbers of visitors.

Conclusion

Because of the relations between leisure time activities and tourism and other sectors as well as among regions, a strong case can be made for planning tourist and leisure time provisions on a higher level of abstraction than that of individual regions and individual projects. The dynamics of societal development support that case.

References

Anderson, P. and Hendriks, A.J. (1982), *Valkenburg in Zuid-Limburg; de ontwikkeling van een toeristisch-recreatief complex* (Valkenburg in the region of South Limburg: the development of a tourist and leisure-time complex), Internal report, Erasmus University, Rotterdam.

CBS (1979), *Enquête vakantie en uitgaan* (Survey holidays and going out), The Hague, 1979.

Clawson, M. (1974), 'How Much Leisure Now and in the Future?' in C.S. van Doren, J.E. Lewis and G.B. Priddle (eds), *Land and Leisure: Concepts and Methods in Outdoor Recreation*, Maaroufa Press, Chicago.

Klaassen, L.H., Verster, A.C.P. and Wagenaar, Sj. (1983), *Ruimtelijke Interactie* (Spatial interaction), Netherlands Economic Institute, Rotterdam.

NRIT (1983), *De toeristische en economische betekenis van dagattractiepunten in Nederland* (The importance of attraction points for daytrippers in the Netherlands for tourism and economy), Breda.

Onderwater, D. and Hendriks, A.J. (1983), *De inrichtingsproblemen van het ontgrindingsgebied van de gemeente Heel/Panheel* (Planning problems of the gravel-winning area of the municipality of Heel/ Panheel), EIT, Tilburg.

Oppedijk van Veen, W.M. (1983), *Consumentenonderzoek als basis voor strategie-ontwikkeling in de recreatiesector* (Consumer survey as a basis for the development of strategies in the leisure-time sector), IVA, Tilburg, p.5.

Wetenschappelijke Raad voor het Regeringsbeleid (1977), *De komende 25 jaar. Een toekomstverkenning* (The coming 25 years. An exploration of the future), The Hague.

Wetenschappelijke Raad voor het Regeringsbeleid (1982), *Sociaal Cultureel Rapport* (Socio-cultural Report), The Hague.

16 Tourism and regional economic development

N. VANHOVE

Introduction

Regional economic policy includes all public interventions intended to improve the geographical distribution of economic activities. In reality, regional policy tries to correct certain spatial consequences of the free market economy in order to achieve two interrelated objectives: economic growth and a better income distribution. Regional policy favours some regions and might discriminate against others.

Like any other policy, regional economic policy has three main facets: (a) objectives, (b) strategies and (c) instruments. The objectives of regional policy are largely determined by the prevailing problems: they are also influenced by an amalgam of political, social and economic pressures. Originally, regional policy was regarded as a rescue operation for certain areas. In the late 1950s and early 1960s the interdependence of regional and national policies was recognised; in that period economic rather than social motivations for regional policy came to the fore. The criterion of growth was introduced into the regional policy of almost all European countries, and there was a renewed emphasis on the rational uses of resources. In the late 1960s

* The author would like to thank the Longman Group Limited, Harlow and London, and the Wales Tourist Board, Cardiff for kind permission to quote from the *Annals of Tourism Research*, Wisconsin (1975: p.132), from 'Tourism: Economic, physical and social impacts' (by A. Mathieson and G. Wall, 1982), and from 'Tourism in Gwynedd – An Economic Study' (by B. Archer, S. Shea and R. Vane (1974), respectively.

a closer link was formed between regional policy and physical planning goals.

Instruments are indispensable to implement the objectives; they are very often identified with financial incentives, but there are other kinds. Indeed, we can distinguish several categories of instruments: infrastructural aids, financial incentives, disincentives, decentralisation of government offices, regional allocations of public investment and public orders and, finally, regional development agencies.

Regional economic policy is usually presented under the headings of objectives and instruments. A third, equally important aspect, however, is the strategy of regional development, that is, the path that should be followed to realise the objectives with the support of the available instruments.

There are several aspects to a strategy of regional development (Vanhove and Klaassen, 1980, p.284):

1 The preparation of regional development plans;
2 The role of regional development authorities;
3 The choice of the regions to be assisted;
4 The option of concentrated or non-concentrated efforts within the designated areas;
5 The choice of the centres to be developed;
6 The option with respect to the deconcentration of congested areas;
7 The decentralisation of power to the regions;
8 The economic activities which must be given priority.

This last point is of particular interest for our topic. Practically all studies, when giving an answer to the question 'what kind of activities should be attracted?' lay the emphasis on industrial activities. In fact, the whole conception of regional economic policy is based on industry, little or no attention is paid to agriculture, tourism or other tertiary activities. Not so much the practice but rather the theory of regional economic policy has neglected tourism as a strategic element of regional development.

Tourism as a strategic activity of regional development

Peripheral regions, free utilities and tourism

In a national context, many underdeveloped regions are peripheral and rich in natural resources such as the sea, forests, mountains or natural beauty. There are numerous examples in Europe: many regions in Ireland; Scotland and Wales in the United Kingdom; Groningen, Friesland and Drenthe in the Netherlands; Schleswig-Holstein and North-Niedersachsen in Germany (Federal Republic); Bretagne, Aquitaine, Midi-Pyrénées, Languedoc-Roussillon, Auvergne and Corsica in France; Campania, Marche, Calabria, Sicily and Sardinia in Italy; Andalucia in Spain, etc. They all possess 'an attraction' as the essential element of a tourist product; indeed such attractions are what motivates a man or woman to leave their place of residence for a recreational activity.

All above mentioned regions have one comparative advantage, which we emphasised a few years ago in a contribution with respect to a number of countries of the Mediterranean zone (Vanhove, 1977, p.264):

> The first point to be emphasised concerns the tourist attractions of the Mediterranean area. They are the reason why people undertake a journey to a tourist region. Without such attractions – natural, cultural, etc. – there would be no basis for tourism at all. From that point of view the Mediterranean area offers undoubtedly highly attractive and varied products for tourism. One might also say that in terms of tourist attractions they possess comparative advantages. We will mention two factors that at the same time are related to the balance of payments. First, tourist attractions are as it were raw materials which can be upgraded quite a number of times at low cost, and which can hardly or not at all be exhausted.[1]

We find the same idea with R. Mossé (1973):

> Besides, the host country may have been endowed by nature with an abundance of readily marketable assets for whose enjoyment tourists are willing to pay: sandy beaches, picturesque sites (mountains and forests), a sunny climate, and the remnants of ancient civilizations. Out of the 20 dollars, the tourist may well have spent 5–6 dollars to enjoy these 'free utilities', as Bastiat would have called them, on whose supply the host country did not have to spend a penny, either in local or in foreign currency.

This section must not give the impression that the above mentioned regions do not value their tourism vocation; some of them demonstrate a well developed tourism sector, but there is a tremendous gap between regional economic theory and economic reality.

'Tourism consumption' may take different forms, such as daytripping (excursionism), short and/or weekend holidays and the holidays proper (four or more nights away from home for leisure time purposes). Proper holidays are the main category. Net holiday participation (the number of holidaymakers per 100 inhabitants) and gross holiday participation (the number of holidays per 100 inhabitants) give a good idea of the importance of tourism to the behaviour of the average individual. Hereafter we mention the results of the latest holiday surveys in a number of European countries; the ratio's mentioned in Table 16.1 are not fully comparable.

Table 16.1
Holiday participation in countries of Western Europe

Country	Year	Net holiday participation	Gross holiday participation	Share of holidays abroad	Statistical universe
Belgium	1982	48	64	62	Total population
The Netherlands	1982	67	102	50	Total population
Germany (FRG)	1982	55	67	61	14 years and more
United Kingdom	1982	58	87	27	15 years and more
France	1982	58	105	15	Total population
Italy	1980	46	66	13	14 years and more
Denmark	1980	56	87	42	16 years and more
Ireland	1981	49	59	35	16 years and more
Switzerland	1980	76	162	47	up to 75 years
Sweden	1982	83	180	33	15 to 65 years
Norway	1979	76	126	33	15 to 75 years
Austria	1981	47	80	45	14 years and more
Spain	1981	48	n.a.	7	16 to 65 years

Sources: Various (e.g. publications of the National Statistical Offices).

Each year, 50 to 70 per cent (in some countries 80 per cent) of the population are involved in tourism, which, by definition, means a stay away from home. Every year millions of Europeans move from their own region to another, from the conurbation areas, where holiday participation is highest, to the countryside and/or peripheral regions. In many cases such a move implies a stay in another country. The total tourism expenditures of the people of the above mentioned countries make up four to six per cent of national private consumption; there are not many economic activities which achieve such a high share in private consumption, characterised by a transfer from one region to another region, domestic or abroad. The total amount of tourism expenditures represents several times the annual regional incentives paid by national and international agencies. Nevertheless, most regional scientists do not consider tourism a strategic activity in the regional development.

Basic and non-basic activities and tourism

In regional economic theory much emphasis is laid on the basic/non-basic approach, a distinction being made between basic and non-basic activities. A non-basic activity is defined as an activity that for economic reasons needs to be performed within the areas considered (e.g. shops, primary schools); a basic activity is one that, although performed within the boundaries of the area, need not be located there (e.g. an industrial plant, a university). It follows from this definition that non-basic activities are not exported to other areas; as the same holds for the other areas neither are there imports of those activities: by definition therefore, there is no interregional trade of services or goods produced by non-basic industries (Klaassen and Van Wickeren, 1969, p.245). It should be emphasised that a basic industry (mark the choice of the word industry) is not necessarily an importing industry; it may export its products just as the area might import its products. In terms of a region's (nation's) balance of payments, a basic industry will reduce imports or contribute to exports (or both). It follows that basic activities generate initial income in the region. This income will be spent partly in the region and the relationship to non-basic activities is quite evident. A subdivision of all activities into basic and non-basic activities enables us to derive an average demand multiplier.

However, the concept of non-basic activity is more complex than is usually presented. So far, non-basic activity is linked to basic activities through the spending of consumers' income earned in basic activities, but there are also non-basic activities that originate in spending by the basic industries themselves. If basic industries purchase goods or services (e.g. transportation services) though part of these services may have to be performed within the area, they certainly are not non-basic in the sense used so far. These goods are produced, or these services are rendered, only because the basic industry is located in and producing within the region (Klaassen and Van Wickeren, 1969, p.247); their production is induced as a secondary production (see below). Secondary effects should be called non-basic in so far as they must be produced within the region and basic in so far as they need not. With the introduction of the secondary effects the distinction between basic and non-basic becomes vaguer, a distinction between multipliers for different industries becomes necessary.

Surprisingly, in regional economics agriculture and industry are mostly classified in the group of basic activities, and tertiary activity is considered the non-basic group. The very term 'basic industries' illustrates that general idea; it is, of course, too rough a classification. Not all agriculture and industrial activities are basic and not all services rendered are non-basic; tourism is an excellent example of the latter, all the services rendered by the tourism sector of a region being exports to other regions. Its contribution to the balance of payments of the region is by definition positive, and tourism generates initial income in the region, as Figure 16.1 indicates (Archer, Shea and de Vane, 1974). Tourist activity is also a good illustration of an activity that by its own spending supports other activities: when the tourist sector purchases goods (for instance, a hotel buying bread) or services (for instance, transportation) these may be produced in the region but cannot be compared with the non-basic activities in the strict sense.

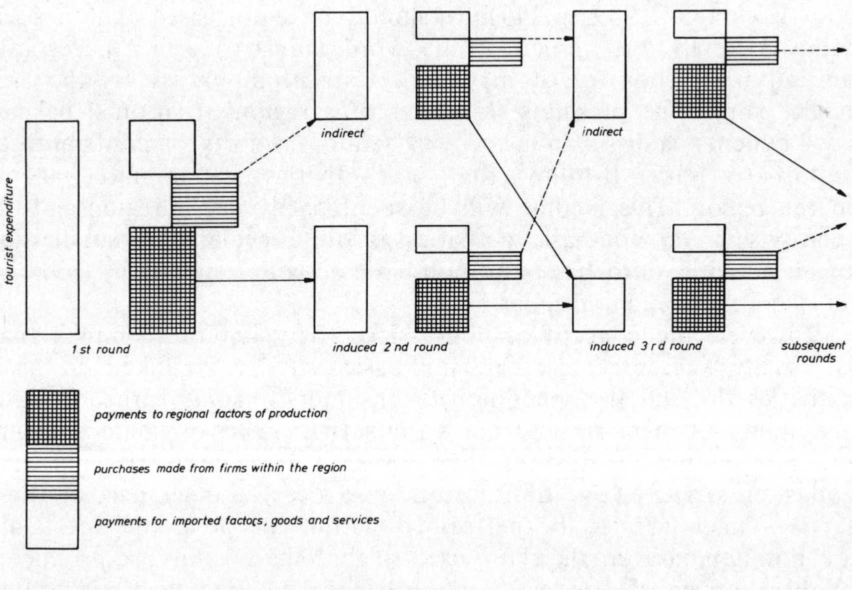

Figure 16.1 Direct, indirect and induced income generation of tourism

In Figure 16.1 the left-hand unshaded block represents the initial volume of tourist expenditures as revenues for hotels, shopkeepers and others; it is a turnover for firms within the region. This turnover should not be confused with income generated. The firms that are in direct contact with the tourist are, in fact, importing, and must pay taxes to the central government; furthermore, some profits from these firms may accrue to people outside the region, representing 'leaks' out of the region. In Figure 16.1 the leakage of money is represented by the dotted upper segment, the middle segment representing the purchase of goods and services from firms within the region. Payments to local government also belong to this group. The heavily shaded segment represents payments to regional factors of production (wages and salaries to local employees, payment of rent to local property owners, and profits retained in the region). The further mechanism is as follows (Archer, 1978):

> As the initial round of spending seeps its way through the regional economy, the general turnover of the area rises, employment opportunities increase and personal incomes rise. The rest of figure 1 shows how these flows occur. On the upper line, labelled indirect, the business firms within the region which receive the extra orders from hoteliers, shopkeepers and others, in turn re-spend their money. Some is spent outside the region, some is spent in other establishments within the region and some is paid out as additional rent and wages and salaries, or is retained as extra profits. The degree of magnitude of these so-called indirect effects is governed by the extent of the intraregional linkages, i.e. the extent to which the firms within the region supply each other with goods and services. In general, the smaller the region the fewer are the linkages between firms and the greater is the likelihood that replacement orders and purchases of new machinery etc., will be given to firms outside the region.
>
> As wages and salaries within the region rise, so local consumption increases and this may give further impetus to the region's income. Along the lower line of figure 1 the effect of these so-called induced effects can be seen. Some of the money is re-spent outside the region and forms a direct leakage, and some is spent within the region forming an additional source of revenue to local business establishments. These induced effects can be quite considerable.

Tourism and growth pole theory

A theory which played an essential role in regional economic policy of the postwar period is undoubtedly growth pole theory. It is not only an essential part of location theory but should also be considered a very helpful conception to elaborate a strategy of regional development.

What is a growth pole? There are many definitions; we limit ourselves to just two of them. The first is from Davin, Degeer and Paelinck, belonging to the French school of Perroux and Boudeville.

> A growth pole is formed when an industry, through the flow of goods and incomes which it is able to provoke, stimulates the development and growth of the industries that are technically related to it (technical polarization), determines the prosperity of the tertiary sector by means of the incomes which it promotes (income polarization), or stimulates an increase of the regional income by causing a progressive concentration of new activities, attracted to a given place by the prospect of finding there certain factors or production facilities (psychological and geographical polarization). (Davin, Degeer and Paelinck, 1959, p.96)

It is a functional interpretation of the growth pole concept; a more general interpretation (functional and geographical polarisation) is given by Vanneste.

> A growth pole can be defined as a set of economic elements concentrated in a geographical space, among which certain links exist which sustain growth. (Vanneste, 1971, p.21)

The growth pole notion acquires a more precise content with the definition of the 'propulsive unit' of a growth pole. Originally, 'propulsive unit' meant a propulsive industry, but later on a broader context was created: a propulsive unit might be an industrial sector, a firm, or even an element of infrastructure. Hansen attaches three main characteristics to a propulsive unit (Hansen, 1967, p.717):

(a) it must be relatively large to ensure that it will generate sufficient direct and potential direct effects to have a significant impact on the economy;
(b) it must be a relatively fast growing sector;
(c) the quantity and intensity of its interrelations with other sectors must be important so that a large number of induced effects will indeed be transmitted.

To our knowledge, in the vast number of publications about the subject, tourism has never been mentioned as a propulsive unit. Nevertheless, tourism incorporates the three main characteristics of Hansen: relatively large (see the complex Languedoc-Rousillon), a fast growing sector, interrelated with other sectors (see Figure 16.1). In a tourists' area we have technical polarisation, income polarisation and psychological polarisation. At the same time it illustrates very well the above mentioned definition of Vanneste.

The preceding sections prove the potentials of the tourism sector as a strategic element of regional development. In the next section we pay attention to a number of characteristics of the sector.

Some economic characteristics of the sector and the tourist product

A holidaymaker in fact purchases a tourist product. In contrast to the productions of other sectors, the tourist product is first of all typically composite, an amalgam of attractions, transport, accommodation and entertainment. Each component is supplied by the individual hotel company, airline, or other suppliers, and offered by them directly to the tourist. From the individual consumers' point of view, there is an infinite number of ways in which these individual tourist products can be combined. The real tourist product is a composite product, either sold as a package or assembled by the tourist himself or his travel agent. The large number of forces at play within an economy make the full measurement of economic impacts a highly complex undertaking.

The fact that many firms participate in tourism brings us to a second characteristic: the sector is dominated by small and medium sized companies. The larger firms operating in the sector are exceptions, and do not properly belong to the tourist regions: they are the carriers (airlines, shipping companies, tour operators etc.).

Thirdly, tourism is an invisible export industry. There is no tangible product which is carried from one place to another. It is one of the few industries in which the consumer actually collects the service personally from the place where it is produced.

Fourthly, the demand pattern of tourism varies much with the seasons. Many tourist regions attract tourists only during a short period of the year, there are but few areas (mountains, for example) that offer more than one season. This leads to market fluctuations in levels of activity in the sector.

Fifthly, tourism demand is highly unstable. There are not only the seasonal fluctuations, but the demand is subject to changes from unpredictable external influences such as political unrest (Spain, Portugal and Greece in the 1970s), changes in international currency exchange rates, energy shortages, unusual climatic events.

Sixthly, tourism demand is price- and income-elastic. Tourist decisions are greatly influenced by small changes in price. Too long, the price-elasticity of tourism demand has been underestimated. Although the annual holiday is a must in the developed generating countries, tourism demand is subject to changes of income and more particularly to discretionary income. When the latter decreases, holidays are taken less far from home, the average stay becomes shorter and self-catering accommodation more popular.

Lastly, we have already mentioned the importance of 'the attraction' as the basic element of a tourist product. Attractions can be defined as those elements in the tourist product which determine the choice of the tourist to visit one destination rather than another. Most tourist attractions are site attractions. Site attractions more than event attractions are sensitive to ecological factors (see Mathieson and Wall, chapter 4; tourism and environment in conflict) such as urbanisation, leisure pressures, some industrial activities, water quality, air quality, etc. The waters of the Mediterranean zone are an asset to the tourist industries of many countries, but the Mediterranean is also a dumping-area for municipal and industrial waste, oil spills from tankers and pesticides brought down by the rivers flowing into the sea.

The fact that tourism is very often in conflict with the environment, makes it difficult to combine the tourist industry with many other economic activities. This leads very often to mono-structures, or one-sided regions.

The above enumeration of characteristics is not exhaustive; there are so many and so typical features that they should be considered in any conception of regional development. Some of them should lead to a particular content of a regional development plan, others are a mortgage on the success of the regional development. More than for any other sector, for tourism comprehensive regional planning is a *conditio sine qua non*.

Advantages of tourism with respect to regional development

The development of tourism in a developing country gives rise to benefits and costs in many fields. That is not the subject of this contribution, but the assertion holds for some backward regions of developed countries as well, though the advantages may be different (foreign exchange, for example).

According to Mathieson and Wall (1982, p.52) the magnitude of the benefits is governed by a multitude of factors; they mention some of the more pertinent ones:

1 The nature of the main facility and its attractiveness to tourists;
2 The volume and intensity of tourist expenditures in the destination;

3 The level of economic development of the destination area;
4 The size of the economic base of the destination area;
5 The degree to which tourist expenditures recirculate within the destination;
6 The degree to which the destination has adjusted to the seasonality of tourist demand.

With respect to regional development five major benefits might result from the development of tourism:

1 income generation;
2 employment generation;
3 improvement of economic structures;
4 encouragement of entrepreneurial activity;
5 improvement of population distribution.

A first advantage of tourism is the income-generating effect. This brings us immediately to the notion of the income multiplier. For a good understanding of the tourist income multiplier we have to refer to Figure 16.1 in which we made a distinction between direct, indirect and induced effects. The tourist income multiplier (or the 'orthodox' multiplier) is the ratio of the total income generated (primary, indirect and induced) to the direct income created by the primary expenditure. Sometimes the multiplier is defined as the ratio of the total income generated to the initial expenditure. This is known as the 'unorthodox' tourist multiplier, not to be confused with other types of tourism multipliers such as the sales or transactions multiplier (i.e. the increase in business turnover created by tourist expenditure), the output multiplier, and the employment multiplier (see below).

There is of course no single 'tourism income multiplier'; it differs from country to country and from region to region. Regional multipliers are usually lower than those calculated for countries. The magnitude of the multiplier is highly influenced by import leakages. During the 1970s several British authors made an effort to calculate tourist multipliers (see Archer, Owen and Sadler, 1973; Archer, Shea and de Vane, 1974; Henderson and Cousins, 1975; Vaughan, 1977 etc.).

Not only the tourist multiplier of the region is significant, but also the multipliers by type of accommodation; the results of Archer, Shea and de Vane (1974) in their Gwynedd study are relevant in that respect. In the Gwynedd case (see Table 16.2) a tourist expenditure of £1 generates a primary and secondary income equal to 37 pence; the magnitude as such is not important, but the following aspects are:

1 The income generation is much lower than the original expenditure.
2 The indirect and induced effects represent one-third of total

income generation. Evidently the share of the direct component decreases progressively with the increase in the size of the region envisaged. In the Henderson and Cousins study the tourist multiplier for the Greater Tayside region equals 0.32 but becomes 0.46 on the Scottish level.

3 The total effects of £1 expenditure differ markedly by the type of accommodation: £0.63 for bed and breakfast arrangements to £0.21 for caravans.

Table 16.2

Tourist multipliers in Gwynedd, 1973

Type of accommodation used	Direct income (1)	Direct, indirect and induced income (2)	'Orthodox' income multiplier [(2) : (1)] (3)	'Unorthodox' income multiplier (4)
1 Hotels and guest-houses	0.2265	0.3237	1.43	0.3237
2 Bed and breakfast	0.5775	0.6351	1.10	0.6351
3 Furnished accommodation	0.3389	0.4012	1.18	0.4012
4 Caravans	0.1407	0.2097	1.49	0.2097
5 Holiday cottages	0.1786	0.2682	1.50	0.2682
6 Tents	0.1937	0.2845	1.47	0.2845
7 Friends and relatives	0.1767	0.2836	1.60	0.2836
8 Day trippers	0.2113	0.3032	1.43	0.3032
Composite multiplier	–	–	1.34	0.3682

Source: Archer, Shea and de Vane, 1974, p.42

Mark that the 'orthodox' income multiplier is of little importance as it reflects intraregional production and consumption relationships.

In the framework of regional development the potential tourist multipliers should be compared with the potential multipliers for other sectors. For the same demand, it is plausible that the tourist multiplier exceeds the multipliers of other sectors (Marquand, 1980, p.63); in other sectors the intraregional linkages are low or negligible. However, we agree that in the final sectoral choice the multiplier is only one of many aspects to be taken into consideration.

Parallel to income generation, there is high employment generation. Three types of employment are generated: (a) direct, (b) indirect and (c) induced employment. In the Vaughan study (1977) 19 jobs (standardised jobs) are created for every £100,000 spent by tourists in the Lothian area. Henderson and Cousins (1975) obtain a similar result for the Greater Tayside area, of which 13 are direct employment, 2 indirect and 4 induced. The same calculations on the Scottish level reveal the creation of 25 jobs of which 13 are direct employment, 6 indirect and 6 induced. Archer (1973, p.76) asserts that the employment creation of tourist expenditure is much higher than the employment created by general spending.

The effects on employment are also influenced by the type of accommodation. In the Vaughan study an expenditure of £100,000 creates 21 jobs in serviced accommodation and only 14 in unserviced accommodation. Two drawbacks should be mentioned. Tourism requires large numbers of workers with minimal skills; but few jobs are created at the managerial and professional level, these being often brought in from other regions (Mathieson and Wall, 1982, p.80). A second restriction concerns the highly seasonal character of the employment.

A third effect of tourism development is the generation of entrepreneurial activity (Mathieson and Wall, pp.82–4). In terms of technical polarisation one can notice backward linkages: when a number of big hotels are located in a region, there is an immediate demand for large volumes of agricultural products and services, which local suppliers are often unable to meet in quantity and quality. After a number of years, however, the imported supplies might decrease and the local supplies increase, much depending on the capacity of local suppliers to meet the new demands. Entrepreneurial activity may be further stimulated by the external economies created. Tourism development improves the transportation networks, the sanitation facilities, the telecommunication network, the water supply, the access to other regions (airport); the new activities lead to a changed economic structure (see Krippendorf, Messerli and Hänni, 1982).

A further effect of tourism development is its contribution to a better population distribution. Outward migration to conurbation areas will decrease and inward migration increase. This is important, given the low population density of tourist regions. The indirect impact on population cannot fulfil all the national distribution objectives. Nevertheless, the creation in a region of 100,000 beds can create 10,000 to 15,000 jobs. A regional growth pole, based on industry, must be quite successful to reach that level of new employment.

Disadvantages and costs with respect to tourism development

When one decides in favour of tourism development, a number of disadvantages and costs should be envisaged. A first cost is the public cost of supporting the tourist facilities by a new transportation network, an airport, water supply, improvement of telecommunication, training facilities, rubbish disposal, sanitation facilities, maintenance cost of tourist attractions, etc. In a micro cost-benefit approach these costs are not considered by the individual company, but they do have a real weight in a macro cost-benefit analysis. The development of Languedoc-Roussillon, in Southern France, in the 1960s is an excellent illustration of the large public costs involved in the development of a new tourist region.

Another disadvantage concerns the labour market. Tourism demand is in most cases highly seasonal and tourism establishments attract a high percentage of low-skilled female labour force.

Tourism is a growth industry and the total volume of tourist demand is likely to increase in the medium and long term (increase of net and gross holiday participation). Nevertheless one has to be aware that most tourist regions are mono-structured and thus highly dependent on tourism: it makes them highly susceptible to changes within the sector (e.g. price changes and changing fashions) and outside it (e.g. political situations, currency restrictions, etc.). Another often mentioned drawback of tourism development in the destination area is the inflation it induces.

> Rich tourists can afford to buy items at high prices. Retailers, recognizing that their profit margins can be greatly increased by catering to tourists, increase their prices on existing products and provide more expensive goods and services . . . inflation within destination areas is also caused by increasing land values (Mathieson and Wall, 1982, p.88).

Conditions for regional development based on tourism

When a government decides in favour of tourism development, it must be aware that tourism will flourish only under appropriate conditions.

A first condition is that the efforts concentrate on a limited number of regions with valuable tourist attractions and a suitable location with respect to markets. These concentrated efforts must be maintained during a long period of time. A region of tourist resorts must have a minimum size to make significant regional impact. A minimum size is also a necessity to achieve economies of scale and to appeal to the potential demand. The practice is most often in the opposite direction. Insufficient financial resources are spread across too many regions, some of them with less potential.

A second condition is the preparation of a comprehensive regional development plan. Planning a series of tourist resorts is more than the construction of thousands of beds. Economic and social overheads and complementary tourist infrastructure are essential parts of a plan. The implementation should be gradual, respect the environment, and aim at creating a warm atmosphere.

Thirdly, considering the characteristics of the tourist sector one should avoid a hundred per cent mono-structure. The development of the region should parallel that of other activities. Not all industrial activities are incompatible with tourism development, and coherent physical planning will contribute to an ideal mixture of tourism and other propulsive units of the new growth pole.

One characteristic of tourism is the predominance of small and medium sized undertakings. They are linked by common interests, so that the tourist region should be regarded as one very large company. The latter cannot function in an adequate way without a regional development and marketing agency. A fourth requisite is that the tourist region has to be built up and promoted step by step and effective economies of scale can be achieved by cooperation between public and private sectors rather than by individual efforts.

Final considerations

Regional tourism development is probably one of the best possible application fields of both the programme approach, and attempts to exploit the indigenous development potentials of a region as advocated by the European Commission with respect to the Regional Development Fund. Indeed, the European Commission has the intention to replace gradually the system of financing individual investments with a system of financing programmes, which may concern both infrastructure and national aid systems to industrial, handicraft and service activities, including tourism. The Commission will broaden the field of aid to include the financing of operations designed to promote the local development potential of regions. The programme approach already exists within the non-quota section of the former ERDF. Under the enlargement measures, Community assistance has been granted to the special programmes for the Mezzogiorno and South-West France (Aquitaine, Midi-Pyrénées and Languedoc-Roussillon). These two programmes are designed to encourage economic activities with a view to correcting the unfavourable effects of Community enlargement. They comprise measures to help small and medium sized companies and craft industries, promote innovation and boost rural tourism (see Council Regulation no. 2615/80 of 7 October 1980).

Tourism is emphasised even more in the Council Regulation (no. 2619/80 of 7 October 1980) instituting a specific regional development measure to improve the economic and social situation of the border areas of Ireland and Northern Ireland. This measure is designed to promote tourism and the development of craft industries in the border areas. Aid is provided to tourist accommodation, services to promote tourism, the provision of amenities and infrastructure directly linked to the development of tourism, the improvement of communications giving access to tourist areas, development of transport activities facilitating access for tourists.

These two regulations are in line with the objective of the EC to exploit the indigenous development potentials of the regions. In this new strategy, tourism is considered of vital importance to some peripheral regions.

International tourism is likely to become more costly. Therefore EC countries should pay more attention to the development of tourist regions with sufficient attractions. In that way tourism can be a strategic element in regional development. The long term trend for tourism demand is positive; holiday participation will progress. Many site attractions are not yet valued and the tourism sector has all the characteristics of a basic sector and of a propulsive unit (unité motrice) as described in regional development theory. In some peripheral regions of the EC, tourism development is likely to be the best and the only way. Here we quote the OECD report 'La politique régionale et le secteur des services' (1978, p.42).

> It is an important tertiary activity, helping in many a country to improve the balance of payments and local employment. Many regions best suited to national and international tourism are situated in the countryside, in the mountains or at the seaside, where new employment needs to be created. The management of the natural beauties in these regions with a view to creating tourist and leisure centres for the urban population is an instrument of regional policy.[2]

This quotation aptly summarises the basic idea of this contribution; tourism might be a strategic element of regional development.

Notes

1. Der erste Punkt, den wir betonen, betrifft die touristischen Anziehungskräfte des Mittelmeerraumes. Sie bilden das "Warum" einer Reise in eine Fremdenverkehrsregion. Ohne solche Attraktionen – natürliche, kulturelle usw. – gäbe es überhaupt keine Grundlage für Tourismus. Von hier gesehen, besteht kein Zweifel, dass der Mittel-

meerraum sehr attraktive und mannigfaltige Produkte für den Fremdenverkehr anbietet. Man kann auch sagen, dass unter dem Gesichtspunkt der Sehenswürdigkeiten hier ein komparativer Vorteil besteht. Wir nennen zwei Momente, die zugleich einen Bezug zur Zahlungsbilanz haben. Einmal sind touristische Attraktionen sozusagen Rohstoffe, die man ziemlich häufig zu einem geringen Preis valorisieren kann und bei denen die Gefahr der Erschöpfung sehr begrenzt oder gar nicht vorhanden ist.

2. C'est une activité tertiaire importante qui contribue dans maints pays à améliorer la balance des paiements et l'emploi local. Nombre des régions qui se prêtent le mieux au tourisme national et international sont situées à la campagne, à la montagne ou en bordure de mer, où il faut créer de nouveaux emplois. L'aménagement des beautés naturelles de ces régions en vue de créer des centres de tourisme et de loisirs pour les populations urbaines est un instrument de la politique régionale.

References

Archer, B. (1973), *The Impact of Domestic Tourism*, Bangor occasional papers in Economics.

Archer, B. (1978), Domestic tourism: a development factor, *Annals of Tourism Research*, no. 1, pp.126–41.

Archer, B. Shea, S. and de Vane, R. (1974), *Tourism in Gwynedd: An Economic Study*, Wales Tourist Board, Cardiff.

Bellwald, A., Zurschmitten, K., Pfammatter, T. and Zurbriggen, R., (1981), *L'apport économique du tourisme valaisan.*

Bryden, J. (1973), *Tourism and Development*, Cambridge University Press, Cambridge.

Davin, L.E., Degeer, L. and Paelinck, J.H.P. (1959), *Dynamique Economique de la Région Liégeoise*, PUF, Paris.

Defert, P. (1966), Le tourisme: facteur de valorisation régionale, *Recherche Sociale*, no. 3.

Ghali, M. (ed.) (1982), *Tourism and Regional Growth*, Martinus Nijhoff, Social Sciences Division, Leyden.

Gold, S. (1982), *Recreation Planning and Design*, McGraw Hill Book Company, Hamburg.

Hansen, H. (1967), Development Pole Theory in a Regional Context, *Kyklos*, no. 3.

Henderson, D.M. and Cousins, R.L. (1975), *The Economic Impact of Tourism: A Case Study in Greater Tayside*, University of Edinburgh.

Klaassen, L.H. and van Wickeren, A.C. (1975), Interindustry relations; an attraction model, in H.C. Bos (ed.), *Towards Balanced International Growth*, North Holland Publishing Company.

Krippendorf, J., Messerli, P. and Hänni, H. (eds) (1982), *Tourismus und Regionale Entwicklung*, Verlag Rüegger, Diessenhofen.

Loukissas, Ph.J. (1982), Tourism's Regional Development Impacts: A comparative Analysis of the Greek Islands, *Annals of Tourism Research*, no. 4, pp.523–41.

Maiboroda, J. and de Lanfranchi, A. (1983), *Le Tourisme en Corse, Bilan et Propositions.*

Marquand, J. (1980), *Le Rôle des Activités Tertiaires dans la Politique Régionale*, Série Politique Régionale, no. 19.

Mathieson, A. and Wall, G. (1982), *Tourism: Economic, Physical and Social Impacts*, Longman, London.

Meinke, H. (1968), *Tourismus und Wirtschaftliche Entwicklung*, Weltwirtschaftliche Studien, Göttingen, no. 13.

Mesplier, J. (1976), Un indicateur d'apport du tourisme côtier à la production régionale: l'exemple des fruits et légumes, *Revue Economique du Sud-Ouest*, no. 2.

Moser, C.R. (1972), *Tourismus und Entwicklungspolitik*, Verlag Weltarchiv, Hamburg, 1972.

Mossé, R. (1973), *Tourism and the Balance of Payments*, IUOTO, Geneva.

NRIT (1983), *Aan het werk met toerisme – Een studie naar huidige en mogelijke toekomstige werkgelegenheidseffekten van het toerisme in Drenthe* (At work with tourism – a study of present and possible future employment effects of tourism in the province of Drenthe), Breda.

OECD (1978), *La Politique Régionale et le Secteur des Services*, Paris.

Spinrad, B.K. (1982), *Economic Impact of Tourism in St. Lucia*, Caribbean Tourism Research and Development Centre.

Vanhove, N. (1977), Fremdenverkehr und Zahlungsbilanz der EG-Länder und der Mittelmeerländer, in R. Regul (ed.), *Die Europäischen Gemeinschaften und die Mittelmeerländer*, Baden-Baden, pp.225–72.

Vanhove, N. and Klaassen, L.H. (1980), *Regional Policy. A European Approach*, Gower, Aldershot.

Vanhove, N. (1981), Tourism and employment, *International Journal of Tourism Management*, September, pp.162–75.

Vanneste, O. (1971), *The Growth Pole Concept and the Regional Economic Policy*, De Tempel, Bruges.

Vaughan, R. (1977), *The Economic Impact of Tourism in Edinburgh and the Lothian Region*, Scottish Tourist Board, Edinburgh.

17 Transportation facilities and dispersion

E. H. VAN DE POLL

Introduction

The spread of people and economic activities across geographical space cannot be envisaged without traffic and transportation facilities, for they make it possible to bridge the distances caused by the spread. Thus, they enable people to make full use of the possibilities offered by geographical space, and to do so efficiently. It is necessary to overcome distances anyway for the simple reason that it is physically impossible to concentrate all persons and activities in one single spot.

However, there are other good reasons for the dispersion of individuals and economic activities and thus for creating traffic and transport provisions. First, the function of traffic and transport, and more especially of passenger and goods transport, will be examined, and next the transportation factors causing the spread of persons and activities. The ideas to be developed, which are borrowed from existing theories of location, represent an attempt at emphasising the principles of location, principles that apply to goods and passenger transport alike.

Passenger transport and goods transport

Traffic and transport facilities make movement of persons and goods possible. The first question to be raised with respect to passenger transport is, of course, why people travel from one spot to another. The simple answer is that people tend to perform activities such as living, working, spending their leisure, consumption, at different places. At home there are already different spots for different activities, such as sitting, working, cooking, sleeping, and even there traffic and transport call for provisions; but individuals also leave their homes to go to places outside: their jobs, shops, places of leisure, the doctor, the social services cultural institutions, the sports field, etc. The provisions needed for traffic and transport outside the home are the ones that are most in the limelight when there is a question of the dispersal of persons; the moves to bridge distances out-of-doors do not differ essentially, however, from those indoors.

Out-of-doors, people go from one place to another for productive purposes (for instance to obtain an income), and for consumptive purposes.

The situation in goods transport is comparable to that in passenger transport. Goods, too, have to be conveyed from one spot to another because different things have to be done to them at those different places. Sometimes great distances are covered from the acquisition of raw materials to final consumers. During this journey goods are processed, stored, kept etc., at many different places in specialised establishments: industrial companies, distribution centres, storage establishments, cold storage, etc. As people move *indoors*, thus goods (and persons as well) are moved *within* establishments, undergoing specialised treatment in specialised departments. Further processing of the goods will take place outside the establishment, that is to say, after they have been transported to another establishment.

Factors causing dispersion of people and activities

With respect to traffic and transport outside homes and establishments the question arises naturally why the places served are dispersed across geographical space, and why in a particular way. The answer to that question is essential to understanding the volume and manner of goods and passenger transport, and why certain traffic and transport provisions are necessary. Dispersion is due not only to the physical impossibility of everything and everybody settling in one place but to other causes as well.

To keep the cost of producing and distributing goods as low as possible, economic activities tend to be carried on in separate units at certain places offering so-called scale and specialisation economies. On the other hand, large or specialised industries producing at one place to profit from such economies have to serve from that place customers spread across a large geographical area, which involves transportation. Moreover, they often have to recruit specialised staff from a large area and fetch some of their raw and auxiliary materials from far away, because neither the staff nor the raw materials are available in sufficient quantities close by. The same holds for many non-industrial companies, such as distributing firms. Entrepreneurs want to maximise their profits not only by keeping their costs low but also by selling as much as possible, and a larger turnover implies more transport.

Similarly, persons or families settle at places where they do not find all they need, which means they must have access to other places. They go away to their work, cafés, shops, football fields, theatres, holiday resorts, areas to spend their leisure time, etc. These, in turn, also tend to specialise. Certain activities require a minimum volume of clients to be profitable so they are concentrated in one place, and they, too, have to rely on their customers coming distances. This also applies, for that matter, to doctors, social services, theatres, football clubs, etc.

Traffic and transport, and location

The connection between transport and settlements of persons and activities thus being recognised, let us go into the considerations which cause people and industries to locate at a certain place, in particular, considerations of traffic and transport. Indeed, conditions of traffic and transport appear to be of vital significance for locational choices.

The first thing to be observed is that in themselves, traffic and transport have no value at all for settling persons and companies; indeed, the opposite is true: traffic and transport are felt to be an obstacle. The term 'traffic and transport resistance' neatly expresses the need for people to overcome an obstacle before participating in traffic and transport. The same feeling appears from the slogan that the best form of transport is no transport! Recongising transport and traffic as an obstacle rather than an asset, one understands that the reasons to move or travel must be found in outside circumstances. Those reasons must not only explain the phenomenon and its volume, but also justify the sacrifices to be made for it. Their main justification is that thanks to traffic and transport provisions, both production and consumption can profit from economies of scale and specialisation and thus be cheaper than they would be otherwise. So long as the sacrifices for traffic and transport are compensated by the advantage obtained in production and consumption, traffic and transport contribute to efficient production and consumption, and are therefore justified.

However, there are limits to efficiency and specialisation; this is true also with respect to traffic and transport. Over a certain size or degree of specialisation, the economies of even larger or more specialised production or consumption no longer weigh up against new sacrifices for traffic and transport. On the one hand, traffic and transport make large scale production and specialisation possible, on the other hand they set limits to them. Low transport resistance stimulates large scale production and specialisation and a wide-meshed location pattern; a higher resistance achieves the opposite. Thus, traffic and transport provisions strongly influence the location pattern. For instance, rising energy prices and hence rising transportation costs will cause a tendency to settle closer together; dropping transportation costs will have the opposite result.

A second point to consider is that, traffic and transport as such being a disadvantage or a resistance, any person or company choosing a location will try to minimise the traffic and transport sacrifice. In other words, they will try and get a good overall view of the future traffic problems to be encountered from the alternative locations, and tend to choose the location presumably involving the least traffic sacrifices. To envisage future sacrifices, any future changes in the infrastructural or other traffic conditions will also have to be taken into consideration. Such changes are as it were anticipated in choosing a location.

Individuals or families choosing a new residence will try and minimise the sacrifice to be made for the entire packet of traffic flows in which they may get involved: from home to work, from home to places of leisure activity, to the theatre, to spots of natural beauty, to relatives, to the social service, etc. Virtually the same is true of manufacturing industries and distributing or consumption establishments; they, too, have to consider the expected traffic flows, such as supply and dispatch flows of goods and persons (working at the establishment or visiting it for business reasons). To overcome the disadvantage of traffic and transport and maximise their competitive capacity, entrepreneurs will try and choose their location so as to minimise the problem of transport services. They will shop around until they have found a location which offers the best transportation facilities to serve their customers as cheaply as possible and maximise profit. In other words, they will try and minimise the sacrifices they or their customers will have to make for transportation.

Naturally, the circumstances of individuals or families and companies vary; they will be different, for example, for working and non-working persons. To working persons, resistance to home-to-work travelling will weigh more heavily than resistance to travelling to lesiure time activities etc.; for non-working persons, commuter distances play no role at all. Grandma, when choosing a place to live, will give no thought to transport sacrifices to be made to reach a workplace, for she has no work to go to, but she will consider the sacrifices to be made when she wants to visit her grandchildren. A lover of nature will prefer to live as near as possible to areas of natural beauty, a lover of 'pubs' to live in the city centre where 'the action is', a housewife close to shopping centres, and so on. In choosing a residence they will take such preferences into account.

Companies, too, choose their locations on different considerations. To an oil company, the sacrifices to be made to acquire and dispatch goods will probably be paramount, because they represent a large proportion of the costs of the final product, and have to be considered if the company is to be competitive. The transportation of persons to and from oil refineries mostly plays a minor role, because an oil refinery needs relatively few people to run it and most business traffic is oriented to other establishments, such as selling points, which have locational considerations of their own. So, oil refineries tend to be established either in ports, where crude oil can be shipped at low cost, or in large selling areas, where the refined product can be transported cheaply to the consumers.

Entirely different considerations prevail in the case of a bank: good transportation hardly plays a role, but passenger transportation is most important. For competitive reasons, the bank's customers should experience as little transport resistance as possible, and banks will choose their location accordingly. Similar arguments apply to a supermarket or shop.

Other establishments have yet another transport problem to consider. If qualified labour is essential to them, they will want to settle where qualified workers live. Industries that process raw materials will settle where the raw materials are won, etc. Moreover, all companies when choosing a location, will consider other establishments in the vicinity, existing ones and those that will presumably settle there in the future. Account is taken of mutual transport resistance, and attempts to keep them as small as possible may lead, for instance, to pool formation. The many and manifold transport conditions of individuals and companies have resulted in varied location and transport patterns.

To conclude, choosing a location is a micro decision. Each company has its own specific traffic conditions, with regard to persons as well as goods, and has to choose a location that fits its specific transport pattern, of course, within the existing possibilities. If the government restricts the choice of location in a certain direction by prohibiting settlement in certain places, the minimisation of transport resistance may not function properly. Neither does it function properly if the government subsidises location in, say, peripheral areas. Often the subsidy compensates for the greater transport costs, so that companies locate at places they would not have chosen otherwise. Which is, indeed, what the subsidising government intended in the first place.

Traffic and transport conditions essential to location

We have tried to show that individuals and companies choose their location in accordance with their specific transport expectations; more precisely, they will at least take into account the expected transport resistances which they *expect to experience themselves*. That should be kept in mind in analysing and explaining locational behaviour. For indeed, certain results of transportation ensuing from settlement will be experienced not by the settlers but by others. Thus, the construction of infrastructural or other transport facilities may be induced in part by the location of certain industries without the costs being charged to them. But settlers will not reckon with consequences of their location with which they are not confronted, and perhaps choose locations which are societally harmful – the government or third parties having to foot the bill – locations they would not have chosen had they been confronted with the disadvantageous outcomes themselves.

The tendency towards establishing more specialised or larger scale establishments will also be stronger the less the harmful results of transport can be assigned to the settlers, their transport resistances being thus diminished. The inverse is also true: should the government rule that expenses to prevent environmental nuisance or insecurity be obligatory (special provisions to motor vehicles, for example), then the tendency to establish specialised or large scale establishments would decline.

To complete the picture we must add that companies, when choosing a location, tend to consider the transportation consequences of locating at a certain place or at certain places, in the sense that they look at the total costs of the final product including transportation cost. Relatively expensive transport may indeed be warranted if its use decreases other expenses. Road transport may be relatively expensive, but it makes the frequent supply and dispatch of small parcels possible and thus considerable savings on storage. Individuals, weighing the transport disadvantages of certain residences, will consider not only the expenses of transport, but also the time needed for it, because they assign a certain value to time saved, which can be used for extra work or extra leisure. Often they will, therefore, prefer relatively expensive but fast transport, and consider the relevant possibilities when deciding about their future residence. Comfort may play a role, too.

The influence of changes in traffic and transport conditions on the location pattern

We have argued above that companies as well as individuals and families choose their location on the basis of expected future individual transport conditions, and therefore on the basis of expected traffic provisions. However, the expectations may later prove to have been unfounded.

Traffic conditions may be better or worse, or equal to, expectations. If they are better, an individual or family will experience more advantages from transport than they had expected. If the same applies to many, the area they live in will also become more attractive to others, and attract more residents, than had been expected. The same holds for companies. If the circumstances turn out better than expected, entrepreneurs may consider expanding their existing establishments. Moreover, the area will become more attractive to people and industries. Sometimes the government plays along, for instance, by constructing new infrastructure in certain areas to stimulate activity there and open up the region.

The opposite happens if traffic conditions in a certain area deteriorate for certain people or companies. Fewer persons and companies will be attracted to the area, and the hopes of those already settled there will be frustrated. An individual or company may find that their expectations as to traffic provisions being maintained and regularly modernised to keep up with developments, are not fulfilled. The government may not keep the infrastructure abreast of developments, with traffic queues and congestion as a result, or they may be unprepared to give support to modernisation, refusing, for example to make a larger entrance to a port or build locks suitable for shipping or construct a motorway. In such a case those already settled in an area may feel drawn towards areas with better conditions, but the effect will not be immediate in view of the consequences. The move will be undertaken only if it is considered worthwhile and if frictions can be overcome.

Of course, certain provisions may be beneficial to some companies and/or persons but harmful to others. Suppose a new motor road is built from A to B so that it is no longer necessary to drive the longer way through C. The new connection, which may not have been foreseen by settlers, changes the location climate in A as well as in B. Transportation has become cheaper because the trip from A to B claims less time of staff and vehicle. If the new connection between A and B is moreover faster than the old one also in a relative sense, the cost of transportation is additionally reduced. An entrepreneur whose transportation packet is favourably influenced by the change, will be inclined to locate in A, but others may be affected negatively, however; a potentially strong company in A which previously could not serve B because the roundabout route caused high transport resistance, may be eminently able to do so now that the resistance has diminished. Consequently, the company in B which used to serve B may be threatened, and the new connection is not an advantage to the company in B. The pattern of expectations on which the company in B had decided to locate there, is broken, and in retrospect the choice appears to have been the wrong one. The new development makes the location pattern wider-meshed, which may imply the growth of some companies at the expense of others. New establishments in B meant to serve only the area of B become less viable when A already houses potential suppliers to B, and certain companies in B may even disappear. Governments trying to make certain regions more attractive to industry by constructing new transport provisions, should take into account the negative influence which new establishments may have on the location climate, particularly in the economically weaker regions.

To give another example: the sudden closing of a city centre to certain kinds of traffic and transport may shatter the expectation pattern of companies located in that city centre. To some companies who were strongly based on that kind of traffic, the situation deteriorates; they will be inclined to move their establishment. To other kinds of companies the situation may improve; companies dependent on pedestrian traffic will welcome a prohibition of motor traffic. Indeed, a zone may become much more attractive to pedestrians when cars are kept outside, and cafés, boutiques and other such establishments will profit. Similar reasonings apply to individuals. A person living in the city centre who is used to or dependent on his car for transport, will find himself living in the wrong place when the city centre is closed to car traffic; to others, on the contrary, living in the city centre becomes more attractive when it is free of motor traffic.

Conclusions

The conclusion from the above is that individuals and companies try to get an overall survey of the traffic conditions before settling, and will choose the place least beset, on the whole, with transport disadvantages, considering, however, only the disadvantages which they experience themselves. The conditions with respect to transport vary considerably among persons and companies, and what is a favourable location to one, need not be favourable to others. Choosing a location is typically an individual decision; models setting out to explain the location pattern need to take that into serious account. Attempts will have to be made to examine the individual factors better than they have been so far, to make a more knowledgeable forecasting of the location consequences of certain traffic and transport measures or of changes in traffic and transport provisions possible. More knowledge in that field will also enable the government, which has a strong influence on the arrangement of traffic and transport provisions that comes available, to envisage the locational implications of its transport policy better.

References

Klaassen, L.H., van de Poll, E.H. and Volmuller, J. (1983), Praeadvies Nederlands Wegencongres (preliminary advisory note for the Dutch Road Congress), Utrecht.

Poll, E.H. van de (1983), *Enige beschouwingen over vervoer en vestigingsplaatskeuze* (Some considerations on transport and locational choice), University of Antwerp.

Volmuller, J. (1976), *Welzijn is afhankelijk van mobiliteit* (Well-being depends on mobility), Stichting Weg, The Hague.

18 Tele-information, demand for transport services and vehicle traffic

J. VOLMULLER

Introduction

With the recent upswing in the development of electronic aids to telecommunications and tele-information, its influence on the future demand for transport services, and thus on the volume of vehicle traffic, has become a much discussed topic. The main object of discussion has been how far face-to-face confrontation between persons can be replaced with electronically aided long-distance communication, so that the geographical distance separating those who want to communicate directly and orally, need no longer be bridged physically. Generally the outcome of studies of the subject has been that some substitution, and hence a corresponding decrease in the demand for transport services and thus in the volume of vehicle traffic can be expected; quantification of that expected substitution, however, is hardly possible as yet (ECMT, 1983).

Much less attention has been given to the question, whether a spectacular evolution in telecommunication and tele-information techniques could have other effects on the demand for transport and on vehicle traffic than partial substitution. Indeed, the impact of that evolution might even *generate* demand for transport services and *increase* the volume of vehicle traffic; some authors indeed expect such a neutralising effect, basing their 'guess' mainly on the fact that earlier 'jumps' in telecommunication and tele-information techniques – telegraph, telephone, telex, television, teletext, etc. – have never had a measurable effect on overall vehicle-traffic volumes.

In this chapter, we will analyse the various manners in which the expected advanced telecommunication and tele-information techniques may affect traffic volumes and the demand for transport services; the discussion will be limited to the conveyance of persons.

The ideal telecommunication and tele-information system

In recent years, successful attempts have been made to integrate computer installations, computerised databanks and telecommunication systems in one system; experimental forms of such integrated systems are already in use at research institutes, banks, tourist offices, manufacturing plants, etc., and before long they will be available to the general public; any subscriber could then enter the system at any point at any moment, or at least at a great number of stations, and communicate directly with any other subscriber, orally, in writing, or in pictures. In addition he would be able to draw any information he requires from one of the linked databanks, and have this information grouped, analysed and commented on by any of the computer installations of the system.

To the author's knowledge there does not exist such a public tele-information system anywhere at present; its availability to the public, at least in industrialised countries, seems only a question of time, however.

Let us assume that such a public telecommunication and tele-information system is indeed available, and concentrate the discussion on its expected impact on the transport system, the demand for transport services, and consequently on the volume of passenger traffic.

The need for information for the operation of the transport system

In any region, the transport system is composed of a number of sub-systems – modes of transport – which operate in competition and/or are complementary to one another. Each mode has solved in its own way the problem of combining the three elements: carrying vehicles, physical infrastructure and operational management; as a result, basically different modal sub-systems have evolved, characterised by the vehicles they use: pedestrian, bicycle, motorcar, public bus, tram, train, canoe, passenger liner, aeroplane, etc. (Volmuller, 1981). Their common factor is that they all provide transport services at the moment there is a demand for them.

The physical infrastructure

A region's traffic volume – that is, the number of vehicles en route at a given moment – and the corresponding capacity of its physical infrastructure are functions of the temporal and geographical distribution of the demand for transport in that region. The physical infrastructure of a modal sub-system tends to be slow in adapting its capacity and geographical layout to changes in the demand for transport services; adaptation involves planning, designing and building many works of civil engineering, which in most cases have to be financed out of the public budget. The impact of such works on their surroundings and their political implications are often considerable. Much information on present and future demand for transport services, geographical and geological conditions, the costs of material and labour, and many other issues is needed for the plans to be prepared properly, but because the whole process is inherently slow, at no stage is there an urgent need of sophisticated means of telecommunication and tele-information. Technologically advanced telecommunication and tele-information will no doubt be applied, but hardly influence either the structure or the speed of the adaptation process.

Operation of the vehicle fleet

That conclusion by no means applies to the vehicle fleet of each mode. Indeed, fleet operators need instantaneous (tele-) information about the ever changing pattern of demand for transport services, about the whereabouts of their vehicle(s), and about the condition of that part of the physical infrastructure that is important to them at that particular moment. A fair assumption seems to be that the advanced techniques of telecommunication and tele-information will find wide application, greatly improving the operational quality of any mode as perceived by the would-be traveller, and decreasing the generalised cost of travel for the consumer. A change in modal split and an overall increase of the demand for travel may ensue. The subject seems worth pursuing further; however, in the next section the author wishes to draw attention to the impact of advanced tele-information on the demand for transport services as such.

Substituting telecommunication and tele-information for transport services

People do not want to move and use the transportation system just for the sake of moving; the purpose of any journey is to let the traveller reach a destination, there to perform the activity of his desire. The effort of travelling comes on top of that of performing the activity; could the same activity be performed as well without travelling, then the would-be traveller would save on expenses, time, and physical and mental effort. Whether telecommunication or tele-information can replace physical travel will depend on the type of activity to be performed at the point of destination.

Telecommunication or tele-information are excluded as a substitute for travel in all cases where emotions among people, or between people and concrete objects, play a role, such as meeting one's friends, visiting a museum, or enjoying the scenery; where the activity requires that goods accompany the traveller, as with shopping; or where the activity requires manual action on the part of one or more persons participating, for instance visiting a physician, signing a document, or operating a machine. Telecommunication and tele-information could indeed replace travelling, however:

1 If the purpose is oral face-to-face communication with others about matters of business, and the functional rather than the emotional personality of the participants is relevant; trip purposes like 'business' and 'private business' come under that heading;
2 If the purpose is to perform non-manual work, including computer analysis and computations on numerical and written data, that is, activities coming under the trip motive of (home-to-)work.

Substitution of travelling for the above mentioned motives has been the principal subject in most studies of the impact of new electronic aids in telecommunication and tele-information on the demand for transportation services.

Professional journeys

Most authors expect the present proportions of communication by telecommunication, mail, and face-to-face meetings requiring travel, to shift in favour of the first as far as business meetings are concerned; the estimation is that the total number of business trips will presumably decrease by a percentage between 10 and 20 (ECMT, 1983). Attempts to develop numerical models describing the substitution have failed so far; intensive research would be required in a field of the human sciences as yet hardly explored. Indeed, business trips, although functionally very important from a societal point of view, are numerically modest, constituting as a rule less than one in 25 of all personal journeys made in a region on a workday, including trips on foot of over ten minutes (COVW, 1972). What proportion of business trips are made for the single purpose of meeting other persons face-to-face for oral communication is unknown; anyhow a substitution of telecommunication for trips serving the single purpose of communication would have no more than a marginal effect on the total demand for transport services and hardly any on the overall volume of traffic.

In meetings arranged for reasons of private business, more often than not the meeting partner is an institution (townhall, solicitor's office, bank, etc.) equipped to receive large numbers of visitors. For identification, locating the relevant documents, etc., a face-to-face confrontation with representatives of the institution is often necessary, which might discourage the use of telecommunication or tele-information. Even so, substitution of telecommunication for some face-to-face encounters for motives of personal business seems possible, but, as the total number of trips for such motives amounts to no more than some 6 per cent of the total number made by persons on a working day (COVW, 1972), even a substantial substitution will cause only a marginal decrease in traffic volumes.

Home-to-work journeys

In terms of transport and traffic planning, the possibility of substituting telecommunication and tele-information from home-to-work journeys seems more important. The total number of journeys for motives of work form a substantial portion of the total number of journeys made on a workday, namely between 25 and 30 per cent (COVW, 1972), return journeys from work to home and all trips on foot taking more than ten minutes included.

There has been much speculation, particularly in the popular press, about how many workers would be able or allowed to work at home if connected with their employer's office by telecommunication and tele-information. Recent studies (ECMT, 1983) seem to indicate that the development of relevant means of telecommunications and tele-information might in the far future achieve a 10–20 per cent reduction of commuting. Because commuting, mostly concentrated in the conventional peak hours of traffic, accounts for between 40 and 60 per cent of peak hour traffic volumes (the latter figure applying to the larger conurbations), such a reduction might relieve traffic and transport problems in and around the larger cities and conurbations a great deal. For that reason, authorities responsible for urban planning and urban transport should further, by all means available to them and with high priority, the substitution of telecommunication and tele-information for work journeys.

Shopping journeys

The purpose of shopping journeys is to select and purchase goods; usually the customer carries the purchased articles home with him. Mail order companies have made an inroad on the number of shopping trips, their customers responding to pictorial and written information; that more advanced techniques of tele-information will increase that type of shopping considerably, seems unlikely.

Other trips

The purpose of journeys other than for business, work or shopping is mainly to meet other persons or enjoy certain physical or social surroundings or objects; the visit is appreciated because of the personalities of the people met – rather than their social functions – or because of the emotions aroused by the perception of the surroundings or objects. That such face-to-face contacts could to an appreciable extent be replaced with any form of telecommunication or tele-information is unlikely. Videophone contact could perhaps play an important role in courting, but face-to-face contact remains indispensable; visiting a sick relative or watching one's own football club play can hardly be replaced by telecommunication, for if the factual information is important, often the emotional ambience is an even more valuable part of the encounter.

In all these cases of social contact, the availability of advanced telecommunication and tele-information techniques may be expected to increase the number of visual-oral contacts between parties without reducing the number of face-to-face contacts involving travel.

The argument has often been heard that television keeps people at home at the expense of social contact involving travel, but there seem to be reasons to doubt that argument. The large scale introduction of television into the homes of industrialised countries coincided with a substantial shortening of working hours and the introduction of many labour-saving devices into the households. Indeed, the more than three hours the average adult spends watching television (Vidaković, 1970), seem to have come available from decreased worktime rather than from cutting down on social activities. An exception should be made for households moving to a housing area unknown to them; the instant availability of the already familiar television programmes may effectively kill the urge to seek non-obligatory social contacts in their new neighbourhood. The findings of a survey on social journeys in old and new parts of Amsterdam confirm that expectation (Vidaković, 1980); in a sense telecommunication replaces social contacts and thus trips from social motives by changing the structure of the temporal activity pattern of the persons involved. The phenomenon might have a substantial negative influence on the average number of journeys per person from social motives, particularly in the evening hours, but its effect on the capacity of the physical infrastructure and the vehicle fleet required will still be marginal.

The effect of telecommunication and tele-information on conventional journeys

The decision process to be completed by the would-be traveller

A journey will be undertaken after the traveller has passed through a sequence of decisions; the following steps can be distinguished:

1 Choose from all possible activities the one to undertake once the current activity is completed (sleep, work, sport, visiting friends, etc.);
2 Decide on the geographical location of the new activity if it can be performed at various locations;
3 Decide on the time of arrival at the selected location;
4 Decide on the mode of transport to be used;
5 Decide on the time of departure from the present location.

The sequence of 3, 4 and 5 can be reversed.

In the above sequence of the decision process one recognises the sequence of the models used in conventional transport-forecasting techniques; actually the process is simultaneous. Relevant information obtained from possible decision variants later in the sequence is used to formulate the decisions in the earlier stages, and vice versa; for instance, estimates of cost and travel time pertaining to a certain mode of transport will be applied to decide what activity to choose next and at what location. The development, in the last decade, of so-called simultaneous models to forecast travel and traffic volumes, can be seen as an effort to simulate the actual decision process more closely (Klaassen, 1983).

To make the proper decision about what activity to undertake next, a person needs to know

1 That he is able to perform that activity: borrowing a book from a library serves no purpose if one cannot read, nor does visiting

a friend if illness makes one unable to enjoy social contacts;

2 The criterion by which he wishes to choose one among possible activities; in general it will be the financial, professional, religious, social-emotional and/or personal-emotional satisfaction he expects from performing the activity – that is, the benefit he will achieve – weighed against the sacrifices he makes to reach the location and perform the activity, sacrifices in time, money and physical and mental effort, together constituting the so-called generalised costs to him of travelling and performing the activity.

Three aspects should be stressed. Firstly, the values attributed to the items composing the benefits and the generalised costs are subjective: they will vary from individual to individual, but also for one individual through time. The recognition that objectively measurable factors are evaluated subjectively, is of crucial importance to understanding the decision process; fortunately, researchers have in recent years paid more attention to that point than they used to. Secondly, presumably the would-be traveller makes no distinction between the generalised costs of the activity under consideration and the generalised costs of the corresponding journey to reach the location of activity; more likely, he perceives the generalised costs of the journey as an indivisible part of a total generalised cost. Thirdly, the values of both benefits and generalised costs have to be estimated.

The traveller has to complete the decision process while still at his origin; he cannot experience or observe the actual conditions under which he will travel or perform the activity once he gets to his destination. He can only base the estimated values of the items composing benefits and generalised costs on his expectations regarding those conditions; an expectation of conditions to be found in a near or far future will have a more realistic value and be formulated with more certainty if information about past values and trends of these conditions is available. The more elaborate and recent this information, the more the decision maker will feel that he can picture future conditions accurately and the more he is likely to arrive at the proper choice; the same is true when a decision has to be made on the next activity to be performed and on the mode of transport to be used if the activity is to be performed elsewhere. In the context of this chapter, the question arises how advanced telecommunication and tele-information techniques will affect the demand for transportation services, given the above described decision mechanism.

Sources of information available to the would-be traveller

Would-be travellers have always had two fundamentally different sources from which to draw information about a destination, the activity or activities that could be performed there, and the characteristics of the journey necessary to reach it. These sources are:

1 His own experience, gathered during previous visits to the location, and
2 Information provided by third parties.

In general, a person will think his own experience the most comprehensive and most reliable source of information when it comes to making a decision what activity to perform next and where to perform it; however, there is a limit to the number of activities a person can undertake in his lifetime, especially outdoor activities which require spending part of the time on travelling. Therefore, the number of places and activities of which a person possesses knowledge from experience at any moment of his life form only a fraction of the total number of things he could have done anywhere and at any point of time.

Routine journeys

The activities and places a person gets to know from his own experience is limited still further because he needs to make frequent journeys to a limited number of activity points: journeys to school, to work, shopping trips to buy daily consumer goods, visits to church, physician, townhall, chemist, local bank, visits to relatives, friends, clubs, both for social and leisure time purposes, etc.; such routine journeys take up an average of seven in ten of all personal journeys in an urban area (Vidaković, 1970). Fresh information provided by third parties on the activities concerned or on the journeys to their location will hardly affect the frequency of the visits or the corresponding mode of travel, and thus not make much impact on the traffic volumes they produce. In addition, most people are quite conservative in their habits: once they have established a routine, they are rarely inclined to change it.

Outside information has more chance of being heeded when an activity is to be performed for the first time: starting a new job, moving to a new housing area; it will be accepted more easily, however, from (new) colleagues, neighbours and friends than from more impersonal commercial or public sources. The implication seems to be that the role of new telecommunication and tele-information techniques will be minor, and their effect on routine activities and the related pattern of mobility only marginal.

Most routine journeys take place on working days and are short in distance and time, their nature (shopping for daily necessities, visiting relatives, clubs, friends, etc.) do not allow for high generalised costs. The share of these more or less routine journeys in total travel mileage is therefore much less than 70 per cent; its share in the total mileage of personal journeys is hard to tell from the literature.

Non-routine journeys

From what has been written above, about 30 per cent of all personal journeys appears to be of a non-routine nature. They are to be found among all categories of trip purposes, except perhaps work. Non-routine journeys can be defined as journeys to places of activity, the would-be traveller having no personal experience either of the activity or of the trip to be made to reach the place of activity; most of them will come under the headings business, shopping (for durable consumer goods) and leisure, in particular weekend and holiday activities. Some journeys from more social motives might also be non-routine.

Non-routine journeys have in common an unknown as well as relatively remote activity location, outside the traveller's normal range. Leisure time journeys are special in that the traveller often has no prefixed ideas about what specific leisure time activity to undertake; indeed, he is not concerned about it as long as he has the feeling that the time available to him will be well spent.

Before deciding on a non-routine activity and the corresponding journey to its location, the would-be traveller will want as much up-to-date information about the activity, its location and surroundings, and the journey to that place to enable him to make a proper choice from the possibilities available to him. At present he depends mainly on oral information provided by travellers who have made the journey, and on oral and written information provided by interested commercial entities, such as travel agencies, tourist clubs, public transport companies, shipping and airline companies, etc. Gathering the information often requires the traveller to start substantial and well planned action quite a long time before the event. And even then, the information which took such a long time gathering often appears to be outdated or insufficiently detailed to serve the traveller's purpose.

This is where the expected development of telecommunication and tele-information could really play an important role. If from the traveller's point of view the location and activity are practically predetermined (business, sports events, etc.), he will require in particular information about the journey to the location of activity, enabling him to make a subjective estimate of the generalised cost of the modes of transport he could use. The author ventures to express the expectation that the increased availability of tele-information in particular would stimulate the patronage of the commercial modes of transport (bus, train, ship, air). Nowadays most motorists think that planning a journey by (their own) car is less complicated and involves less risk of non-compliance than planning a journey by commercial transport, especially at distances between 100 and 300 km. More accurate and detailed information about travelling by competing modes, geared to the individual needs of the would-be traveller, will induce more individuals to travel by another mode than their own car. Whether such an expected change in modal choice will be marginal or substantial, seems hard to predict. A wide variance is most likely, but the application of tele-information in this field of travel is certainly worth exploring.

A similar effect on the modal choice may be expected for non-routine journeys to a less determined (type of) activity and (type of) location. The would-be traveller would in that case want to know the range of locations where certain types of activity could be performed successfully, such as shopping for certain durable consumer goods, or a certain leisure time activity. Tele-information can enlarge the geographical scope of activity locations which can be brought to the traveller's attention at any desired moment. The effect could be an increase in the average length of trips within the relevant purpose categories, with possibly a more than marginal effect on the mileage spent in these categories. The commercial success of hypermarkets, furniture stores and amusement parks could be interpreted as pointers in that direction. Most of these non-routine journeys will be made during weekends and in vacation periods. Therefore, their expected increase, particularly that in mileage, will hardly affect workday traffic volumes, but will almost certainly add to the difficulties already encountered on so many long-distance routes, especially major highways, during weekends and holiday periods with fair weather.

Summary and conclusions

The expected advance in telecommunication and tele-information techniques will result eventually in an integrated system of telecommunication, data banks, and computer installations. Such an integrated system will enable subscribers to communicate with any other subscriber or to draw the information he wants from data banks, if desired processed by computers connected with the system. The availability of such integrated telecommunication and tele-information systems to the public will presumably have an effect on the demand for transport services:

1 By increasing the efficiency of the various modes of transport, in particular in meeting the needs of the individual would-be traveller, regarding the services offered as well as information about them;
2 By replacing travel for oral communication with another person or persons and for certain types of work;
3 By providing, at less effort from the traveller, more up-to-date and more detailed information about activities he could undertake, their locations and the journeys there.

As to the first point, better service and better information about the service to be provided by the transport system will result in decreased generalised costs of travel as perceived by the would-be traveller, both by mode of transport and with respect to the transport system as a whole. The result should be a shift of the modal split in favour of the commercially operated modes (bus, train, ship, air, etc.) and an increased overall travel volume, but even a rough quantitative estimate of the two phenomena has not yet been made.

As to the second point, substitution for physical travel is not possible if the transport or handling of even the smallest article is involved, or if human emotions inspired by other persons, objects, or the surroundings at the location of activity play a part. Substitution of telecommunication and tele-information for travel can therefore be expected only for journeys in the purpose categories of business, private business, and non-manual work, as well as for a small portion of journeys for a social purpose. Studies indicate that between 10 and 20 per cent of present-day journeys for business, private business and work could be replaced. Such a decrease in journeys for business and private business would have a marginal effect on the total volume of workday traffic, but a 10 to 20 per cent decrease of the number of work journeys would cause a substantial decrease in peak-hour traffic, since more than 75 per cent of work journeys are made in peak hours. In these periods, between 40 and 60 per cent of all journeys are for work purposes: home-to-work in the morning, work-to-home in the late afternoon. That possibility to reduce peak-hour traffic and thus alleviate the problems of transport planning and control especially in and around urban areas, seems worth pursuing.

Finally, more up-to-date, more detailed, and more easily gathered information will presumably affect only the travel habits related to non-routine activities and journeys. For routine activities, the would-be traveller tends to feel he is adequately informed and needs no further information. Many people may well discard information about new conditions in activity or travel, because they are content with their established routine. Routine activities and journeys are found among all trip purposes, and are particularly evident in journeys undertaken for private business, work, school, shopping for daily consumer goods, and social activities. They represent about 70 per cent of all personal journeys on a workday. The introduction of advanced telecommunication and tele-information techniques will hardly affect the volume of demand for transport services or the traffic produced by any mode of transport in connection with these activities; increased use of these techniques will rather be complementary to the journey volume by conventional means.

More up-to-date, more detailed and more easily gathered information will have a perceptible effect on the volume of non-routine journeys, that is, on journeys which the traveller undertakes without previous direct experience of the activity to be performed or its location, the surroundings, and the journey itself. Being better informed of possible activities and the corresponding journeys outside his normal range, he will perceive the generalised costs of travel as lower. The overall result will be on the average longer and more frequent non-routine journeys, in particular journeys undertaken at weekends and in vacation periods, to shop for durable consumer goods and pursue leisure purposes. An increase in traffic volume, particularly on through-routes, is to be expected for all modes of transport; in further studies the phenomenon should be roughly quantified.

References

Commissie Bevordering Openbaar Vervoer Westen des Lands (COVW) (Committee on the Promotion of Public Transport in Western Netherlands) (1972), *Rapport* (Report), Ministry of Traffic and Public Works, The Hague, p.54.

ECMT (1983), Transport and Telecommunications, *Round Table 59*, Economic Research Centre, Paris.

Klaassen, L.H., Verster, A.C.P. and Wagenaar, Sj. (1983), *Ruimtelijke Interactie* (Spatial Interaction), Netherlands Economic Institute, Rotterdam, pp.I.54–I.64.

Vidaković, V. (1970), *Kenmerken van de stedelijke verkeersstructuur* (Characteristics of the urban traffic structure), PhD Thesis, Technical University of Delft, p.159.

Volmuller, J. (1981), *Technische Verkeerskunde, Voortrekker in de Civiele Techniek* (Technological traffic science, vanguard of civil technology), Delft University Press, Delft, pp.7–11.

Index

'Acid rain', 19
Adoption and implementation, 40–1
Agglomeration and regional multipliers, 127
Analysis of core periphery growth, 241 5
Art and Leisure, 83
Assumptions and symbols, 46 –8
Australian urban dynamics, 210–1

Behaviour
  institutional political developments, 154
  technological change, 154
Behavioural hypothesis, 68
Bifurcation theory, 126
Business environment and regional structure, 159–60

Central planner, role of, 123
Ceteris paribus clause, 150
'Change of relations', 125
Cobb–Douglas-type function, 177
Communication
  need or demand, 29
  transmission and diffusion of scientific knowledge, 39–40
Competition, 159
'Consumption versus accumulation', 126
Cross-section research, 12
'Cultural crisis', 19

Data and testing, 114–20
Delta Project, 18
Demand factor, 29
'Dependence', 126
Differentiation, 125
Developed countries
  black sector, 22
Durban–Watson test, 12

East–West co-operation, 19
Economics
Aspects to be integrated due to recent development, 20–3
stagflation, 21
Complications: geographical and historical elements, 18–19
Delta Project, 18
Contribution with a space aspect, 14
Defining space units, 15–16
Distribution of centres across an area, 17
Distribution of industries across areas, 16–17
Hierarchy of areas, 16
Transportation costs, 16
Transportation network, 16
Effect of element of space, 13–14
Connections, 13
Dimensions, 13
Hierarchies of spaces, 14
Simplifying assumptions, 14
Variables, 13
New aspects since (1970), 19–20
Pilot project for East–West Co-operation, 19
Social and Cultural Planning Office, 19
Space-orientated research, 12–13
integration, 13
Education, 83
Effect of change
in factor endowment, 51–3
in taste, 54
Employment, 84, 188
full employment, 78–80
European Community (EEC), 20
Regional Development Fund, 295
Evaluation of natural tendencies, 129
Evolutionary economics, 155
Exclusiveness programme, 139
Export industries, 45–61

Factors, 34, 36, 39, 40
F L E U R-dynamics, 91–8
'Functional Urban Core (FUC)', 188
'Functional Urban Region (FUR)', 188

Game theory, 63–75
Geographical 'handicap', 18
Government organisations, 155
policy making, 155
Government services, other, 83

Health, 83
Hierarchies of spaces, 14

Income distribution, 80–2
residual effect, 81–2
structural effect, 81
Industries
distribution of, across areas, 16–17
Influence of societal developments, 271–3
Institution defined, 156
Institutional hypotheses, 68–73
Institutional approach, 155
'institutional ecology', 155
Interregional general equilibrium, 48–51
for specific functions, 55–7
Innovation defined, 29
Invention, 36–8
communication, 35–6, 39–40
defined, 28, 29
need and demand for, 34–5

Investment
political effects, 142–6
timing to maximise spatial diffusion, 111

Japanese urban systems
defined, 189–90

Land, 135
Land prices, negotiators' behaviour and game theory, 63–75
Dynamic negotiation between seller and buyer, 68–73
Behavioural hypotheses, 68
Institutional hypotheses, 68–73
n-player games, 73–4
Leisure time
behaviour, 275–7
gained, 142
Levelling programme, 139
'Life-cycle' concept, 156–9
Locational boundary, 135
Location quotients
export industries and shift-share analysis, 45–61
Assumptions and symbols, 46
Effect of change in factor endowment, 51–3
in taste, 54
Interregional general equilibrium, 48–51
for specific function, 55–7
Shift-share analysis, 58–60
Location theory, 109–162
Location decisions and regional structure, 149–62
Business environment and regional structure, 159–60
Choice of variables, 150–3
Decision making and institutional aspects, 154
Location and life-cycle of products, 156–9

Location theory, cont.
Political bodies in the allocation of produced locational qualities, 133–48
Allocation of produced locations, 137–41
Political iso-utility curve, 139
Political effects of public investments, 142–6
Problem, 133–4
Production of locations, 134–7
Self organisation, 123–32
New spatial order, 126–9
Objectives, evaluation of natural tendencies and planning solutions, 129–30
Spatial self-organisation theory, 124–9
Steering spatial development of the country, 131–2
Timing of investment to maximise spatial diffusion, 111–21

Mathematical formulations, 29
Markov chains, 126
Methodological individualism, 151–3
Model of cyclical urban development, 177–84

Natural resources, spatial structure, 149
Needs and demands, 29
Negotiators' behaviour, 63–75
New Industrial Cities (NIC), 199
New spatial order, 126–9
N-player games, 73–4

'Objective, structural' conditions, 151

Observed regional shares, 95
Operationalising urban sub-systems and processes, 174–6

Pareto-optimality, 131, 146
Pearson rank-order correlations, 114
Phase transitions, 126
Planning solutions, 129–30
Players' strategies, 65–8
Political and administration process, 171
Political effects of public investments, 142–6
Political iso-utility curve, 139, 141
Pollution, 19
Population, 171
  classified growth rates, 201
Production, 134–7
  characteristics of production function for locations, 136–7
  factors of, 135–6

Quality measures of spatial order, 130
Quality of life: harmed, 19

Radical structuralism, 153
Rank-Size Rule, 141
Regional development, 25–108
  Consistent model for regional-sectoral dynamics, 91–107
    FLEUR-dynamics, 91–8
  Regional impact of welfare state policies in the EEC, 77–90
    Access to social services, 82–5
    Income distribution, 80–2
  Regional research and development revisited, 27–9
    Mathematical formulations, 29–33
Regional development, cont.
    Verbal formulation, 34–42
  Research methodology, 11–24
    Aspects to be integrated, 20–3
Regional-sectoral dynamics, 91–107
Regional variations in urban change, 199–204
'Reprivatisation, versus socialisation', 22

Samuelson-type accelerator-multiplier model, 177
Satisfaction, 85–8
Self-organisation theory, 124–6
Shift share analysis, 58–60
Simplifying assumptions, 14
Snowbelt and Sunbelt compared, 159
Space, 12
Spatial interactions, 128
Spatial planning, 129
Stagflation, 20, 22
Static minimax solution, 67–8
Stochastic process, 154
Structuralism, 151
  radical, 153

Tele-information, 309–21
Third World, 20
Time-series research, 12
Tourism and transportation, 265–319
  Recreation and regional development, 265–76
    Influence of societal development, 271–3
    Leisure time behaviour, 275–7
    Need for vertical coordination, 274

Tourism and transportation, cont.
Tele-information, demand for transport services and vehicle traffic, 309–21
Effect of telecommunication and tele-information on conventional journeys, 315–19
Ideal system, 310
Substituting telecommunication and tele-information for transport services, 311–5
Tourism and regional economic development, 281–298
Advantages of tourism, 290–1
Conditions for regional development, 294–5
Disadvantages and costs, 293–4
Tourism as a strategic activity, 282–89
Transportation facilities and dispersion, 299–307
Factors causing dispersion of people and activities, 300–1
Influence of changes, 305–6
Passenger and goods transport, 299–301
Traffic and transport and location, 301–4
Traffic and transport and conditions essential for location, 304–5
Urban Trends, 163–263
Process of Urban Development, 165–86
Dynamic model of urban development, 172–77
general assumptions, 172–4
Production factors, 174–5
Quality factors, 175
Model of cyclical urban development, 177–8
Economic process, 177–8
Effects of allocation in space, 181–2
Empirical evidence, 182
Political and administrative process, 179–80
Social and cultural process, 178–9
Process of urban development, 168–72
Economic process, 168–9
Political and administrative process, 171–2
Social and Cultural process, 170
Urban system, 166–8
Recent trends in urban development in Japan, 187–211
Change in urban system, 195–99
Change within urban areas, 204–7
patterns of change, 204
Japanese system defined, 189–90
Regional variations in urban change, 199–204

Urban Trends, Process of Urban Development, Recent trends in urban development in Japan, cont.
- Urban change on national level, 190–5
- Urban dynamics in Australia, 211–63
  - Analysis of core periphery growth, 241–5
  - Analysis of study results, 218–25
  - Australian urban growth dynamics, 211–18
    - *Outline of study process*, 214–6
  - Industry-workforce analysis, 226–32
  - Summary and policy implications, 249–61
  - Urban growth dynamics, 232–41
  - Urban Municipalities, 245–9

Verbal formulation, 34–6
Vienna model, empirical results, 146–7
Voivoideships, 131

Welfare, 83
Welfare state policies, 77–90